I0187536

Persophilia

HAMID DABASHI

Persophilia

PERSIAN CULTURE ON THE
GLOBAL SCENE

Harvard University Press

Cambridge, Massachusetts, and London, England
2015

Copyright © 2015 by the President and Fellows of Harvard College
All rights reserved

Second printing

Library of Congress Cataloging-in-Publication Data

Dabashi, Hamid, 1951–
    Persophilia : Persian culture on the global scene / Hamid Dabashi.
        pages cm
        ISBN 978-0-674-50469-1 (hardcover)
    1. Iran—Civilization. 2. Iran—Foreign public opinion. 3. Iran—
Relations—Europe. 4. Europe—Relations—Iran. 5. East and West.
6. Orientalism—Europe—History. 7. Europe—Intellectual life. 8. Social
movements—Europe—History. 9. Transnationalism—History.
10. Postcolonialism—History. I. Title.
    DS266.D24 2015
    955—dc23   2015000709

For

Teresa and Mahmoud Omidsalar

Contents

Persia is the greatest Empire in the World, if you consider it according to the Geographical Description given by the Persians.

—Sir John Chardin (1643–1713)

Introduction

"LUXURY, SENSUALITY, LICENTIOUSNESS on the one hand, Scholasticism and literature on the other, have made the Persian effeminate." This was the opinion of Sir John Chardin (1643–1713), a Huguenot jeweler who wrote a detailed account of his extensive travels in Iran. "The mysticism in which the better spirits of Persia loved to lose themselves was a higher thing, after all, than his keen worldliness." This was the view of Edward Byles Cowell (1826–1903), a keen popularizer of Persian poetry in the Europe of his time. These worldly-wise Europeans were not alone in their penchant for things Persian. G. W. F. Hegel contemplated the nature of mysticism in Persian poetry, while Immanuel Kant, Friedrich Nietzsche, Matthew Arnold, Johann Wolfgang von Goethe, Alfred, Lord Tennyson (poet laureate of the United Kingdom during Queen Victoria's reign), Edward FitzGerald, Ralph Waldo Emerson, Henry David Thoreau, Walt Whitman, Henry Wadsworth Longfellow and later American thinkers and literati wandered around the Persian neighborhood of their imaginations with fruitful results. The list goes on and on, and in fact reads like a who's who of the nineteenth- and twentieth-century giants of European and American literary and intellectual movements who categorically shaped the contemporary contours of their cultures and civilization. Ferdowsi, Nezami, Rumi, Sa'di, Khayyám, Hafez, and numerous other Persian poets and prose stylists were known and admired by these leading European and American poets and philosophers, who used their works in creative or critical ways to make their own marks and shape their own ideas in varied and enduring directions.[1]

Where do these comments and attitudes come from, what do they mean, and why would the most celebrated icons of European and American social and intellectual movements be so particular about things Persian? Even more significant, what were the consequences of this European fascination with things Persian or Persians themselves, for the emerging postcolonial nation-states we would soon recognize as Iran, Tajikistan, or Afghanistan?

Beginning with the seventeenth century there was a sudden and dramatic increase in European interest in Persian language and literature, religion and culture, history, geography, and archeology—in both real and imaginative ways. Why was this the case? Today, we have two classical answers to that question. Whereas Raymond Schwab (1884–1956), in *The Oriental Renaissance* (1950),[2] considered such attentions to Persian, Indian, or any other "Oriental" matter as integral to the European romantic longing for originality, Edward Said (1935–2003), in his *Orientalism* (1978),[3] paid almost exclusive attention to European imperialism as the modus operandi of knowledge production about the Orient in general. These two perspectives in effect complement and corroborate each other: while in one we are witness to the internal dynamics of this attention to the Orient, in the other we understand its more global condition and consequences. Thus the two points of view do not negate each other but in fact result in a more sculpted vision of what we understand as "Orientalism."[4]

Critical as these two texts are to our understanding of "Orientalism," disregarded by both Schwab and Said—and thus my paramount concern in this book—is the far more critical structural transformation of the European (and by extension global) bourgeois public sphere, as Jürgen Habermas—in his *The Structural Transformation of the Public Sphere: An Inquiry into a Category of Bourgeois Society* (1962)—has termed the category of bourgeois society in this period as the principal site of knowledge production about the Orient.[5] My objective here is to trace the origin and disposition of Persophilia in its immediate European context and to focus on its bourgeois public sphere as it spread and became transnational in the course of history and by virtue of the European empires. That global scene both posits and animates a transnational public sphere beyond its European pedigree, with far-reaching political consequences. Iran and its environs are among the particularly receptive atmospheres alert to this globalized scene.

This critical *social* space between the *cultural* concerns of Schwab and the *political* preoccupation of Said recasts the whole notion of Orientalism in a new light. While Schwab considers the Oriental Renaissance a second renaissance that was integral to the nineteenth-century European romanticism that ended the classical age the way the classical Renaissance had ended the medieval age, Said, following Foucault, had read Orientalism as integral to the European imperial mode of knowledge production conducive to its global domination. So while Schwab was concerned with the European *cultural* fascination with the Orient as a source of its romantic inspirations, and Said with the *political* consequences of that cultural accouterment of European imperialism—and thus both effectively with European cultural and imperial history—they both left untapped the *societal* formation of the European bourgeoisies, the emergence and transformation of the bourgeois public sphere, and a fortiori its global repercussions in the making of other public spaces possible in both form and content. The principal proposition that I will put forward in this study is that the content of that public space was contrarian to its form—and thus the tension and the paradox in the political culture enabled by and upon that self-transformative bourgeois sphere.

Because both Schwab and Said were Eurocentric in their perspectives on Orientalism, they both left untapped as subjects the paradoxical bourgeois space on the colonial site that enabled dissent and the anticolonial resistance to the colonial extension of that European bourgeois space.[6] For them Orientalism was primarily a European phenomenon[—one looked at it in the context of European intellectual history and the other in the context of European imperialism]. But combining both their insights leads to the fuller recognition that, through the fact of imperialism, the *social* context of that Orientalism did not stay put in Europe but traveled to the Orient, as it were—and that traveling had critical social consequences. This insight requires a far more *sociological* analysis, entailing an interpretation of economic, political, and cultural history that comes to terms with the inner tensions of this defining moment of European colonial modernity and its global repercussions. It also radically and diametrically shifts the angle of vision from the European to the colonial scene, where the European mode of knowledge production about the Orient began to act as a catalyst on the colonial home front.

On this front a mere documentation of its European vintage or a critique of Orientalist representation is no longer sufficient (though necessary), for here we need to think of the *societal* consequences of those acts of representation on the colonial sites, a task beyond the interests of both literary criticism (Said) and cultural and intellectual history (Schwab). This would also limit the range of Habermas's own theorization of the European bourgeois public sphere; for the public space of the colonial site, though an extension and reflection of its European prototype, ipso facto included subaltern classes that were far more active in the bourgeois public space for a number of reasons, most notably a weak local bourgeoisie, contingent urbanization, an impoverished peasantry, and the radically politicized urban poor.

In this book I wish to focus on the consequences for Iranians of this European (and therefore global) interest, in the form of a potent case study that inquires what happened when people on the colonial side of the imperial divide saw themselves in these European mirrors? My paramount concern is with the structural formation of the *transnational public sphere* as a *discursive space* in Iran—that is, as a prototypical example of a nation-state that emerged from its own dynastic and revolutionary histories in the throes of European colonialism—and with the genealogy of its production, the modes and manners of its organic disposition and diversity. My most important proposition in this book is that, definitive to this structural formation of the public sphere in Iran as a postcolonial nation are the facts that this space was never exclusive to the bourgeoisie, and that it always included subaltern classes. Here on the colonial site the relations of power and production (in the general framework of global capitalism) were naked and exposed; thus the fetishization of commodity and the alienation of classes and their false consciousness (as the foregrounding of the structural formation of the European bourgeoisie) had either not taken shape or had a very fragile and disposable character. To consider "the public sphere" in this larger, more inclusive sense we need to understand Habermas's notion of "Bürgerliche Öffentlichkeit" more as "civic public sphere" or "citizenship public space" rather than as an exclusively or characteristically "bourgeois public sphere." In other words, my concern here is with the active formation of a public sphere on the colonial site where both the local bourgeoisie and its antithesis were concurrently construed.

I thus wish to consider European imperialism not just as a mode of knowledge production about the Orient (Said), but as a medium, the vehicle, the navigational route, of the dissemination of knowledge that was provided by the European bourgeois society (Schwab) about the "Orient" and thereby contributed to the creation of the public space—in both form and content. So, yes, there is a corroborating relationship between (European) culture and (European) imperialism, as Edward Said demonstrated persuasively in his *Culture and Imperialism* (1994).[7] But far more critical for the global condition we have witnessed over the last two hundred years in the postcolonial world is the relationship between European imperialism and non-European cultures—not just the bourgeois culture of accommodation, but the multiple and varied cultures of resistance which that imperialism had entailed. The site of that resistance was not some amorphous gathering of revolutionary thinkers. It was the creative formation of a bourgeois public space that paradoxically both extended its European prototype in form and content and forcefully contradicted it, thus revealing its own paradoxical disposition. As Habermas has noted, the literary and political self-consciousness of the bourgeois class entailed a structural contradiction that crafted the liberal public spheres yet limited them to only one specific class. This paradox was even more acute on the colonial site, in which the public space, though actively appropriated in Europe as a means of sustaining that hegemony, always remained deeply contrarian.

ORIENTALISM

"Before the eighteenth century was out," according to George Jellinek, author of *History through the Opera Glass* (1994), a total of no less than one hundred operas were composed about Alexander the Great (356–323 BC)—so profoundly had his quest for world domination, which included his conquest of Persia and India toward the tail end of the Achaemenid Empire (550–330 BC), fascinated the emerging European bourgeoisie and aristocracy and inspired the imperial conquests they enjoyed around the globe. The list of composers attracted to Alexander's global conquests is hardly run-of-the-mill, including such musical luminaries as Leonardo Leo (1727), Leonardo Vinci (1730), George Frideric Handel (1731), Nikolaus Hasse (1731), Christoph Wilibald Gluck (1745), and Nicolà Piccinni (1758 and 1774).[8] The fact of such operatic representations and their evident or arguable relations to European imperial conquests cannot stop at the mere observation of a mimetic correspondence between the one and the other; more historically significant are the causes and consequences of such attractions—on both the European and the non-European sites. In other words, the question is not just why such an overwhelming attraction to a "European" world conqueror—but what were the historical roots and geographical consequences of such an attraction.

In *Orientalism* (1978), the groundbreaking text that set an entire postcolonial discourse in motion, Edward Said was chiefly concerned with a sustained mode of knowledge production that he proposed to have been coterminous with European imperialism and as a result had facilitated the active formation of a kind of "East" that at one and the same time constituted a world and manufactured it in a manner conducive to imperial domination. In my *Post-Orientalism: Knowledge and Power in Time of Terror* (2009), I took Said's insight and historicized it in both premodern and postcolonial directions, seeking to navigate modes of knowledge production that I called "disposable" and were produced in the domain of an amorphous operation of capital and a corresponding globalized empire that it necessitated.[9] Whereas Said's pioneering work had investigated the narrative manifestations of a colonial relation of power, I had sought to chart the sociological disposition of its unfolding history.

While Edward Said had taken his clue of the relation between power and knowledge from Michel Foucault and localized it in colonial knowledge about "the East," my reading of Orientalism as a mode of knowledge production was entirely pre-Foucauldian and rooted in a sociology of knowledge that went back to Karl Mannheim, Max Scheler, George Herbert Mead, and ultimately Karl Marx. While the pitfall of Edward Said's take on Orientalism was an inadvertent essentialism, I had sought to de-essentialize that mode of knowledge production and concentrate on the varied manners of relationship between knowledge and power as a case of sociology of knowledge in multiple historical contexts. Both history and sociology figured far more emphatically in my reading of Orientalism than the trope of *representation* as it chiefly defined Edward Said's unpacking of Orientalism. In this book I in effect continue with that preference of sociology and history as the necessary mode of reading Orientalism, without in any way discounting the significance of a critical take on the power of representation by and in Said, which I take for granted.

Equally pre-Foucauldian was the work of Raymond Schwab (1884–1956) in *The Oriental Renaissance* (1950), in which he had looked at the European reception of the Oriental literatures and cultures as in fact integral to European intellectual history of the eighteenth and nineteenth centuries. Schwab had successfully bypassed the artificial aspects of European Orientalism and reached for much wider and deeper sets of influences that exposure to non-European literatures and cultures had fostered in the formation of the European literary and artistic imaginary. If exposure to Chinese sources had been influential in the formation of European rationalism, Indian texts had heavily influenced European romanticism. From Herder and Goethe down to Wagner, Nietzsche, and Tolstoy were the immediate and enduring purveyors of this exposure to Indian and other Oriental sources, and both their immediate and their distant echoes were evident and audible in European romanticism. This influence extended from high European culture and reached deeply into secret societies like Freemasonry. At times deeply learned, at others vacuous and impressionistic, the influences that Schwab documents point to the manner in which exposure to Oriental literature had caused vast influences in the formation of European romanticism. Schwab had used the term "Renaissance" advisedly, for he wished to emphasize the groundbreaking significance of exposure to the Orient, and thus Orientalism, placing it on par with the European Renaissance and thus suggesting a second renaissance in the self-realization of the European bourgeois culture.

From Schwab I then take a step forward and, following Habermas, in fact suggest that this exposure to Orientalism, and thus the Oriental Renaissance (and in fact the whole project of European Enlightenment modernity), were instrumental in the formation of the bourgeois public sphere of the eighteenth and nineteenth centuries. Both Said's insights and those of Schwab in fact corroborate each other but leave unattended the site of their identical knowledge production—namely the emerging European bourgeoisie and the public sphere they had crafted and occupied. Even more important for my purpose in this book, that public space was in effect mobile (given the globality of the underlying capital that had occasioned it) and extended from the heart of European societies into the farthest teaches of the colonial world—with the unanticipated consequence of

European Orientalism having a paradoxically enabling effect by virtue of becoming the vehicle for the expansion of that bourgeois public space far beyond Europe, and soon contrapuntally set against European imperial interests. This particular effect of Orientalism has categorically escaped both Said's and Schwab's attention, as in fact the *colonial* site of that public sphere has remained equally dormant in Habermas's notion of the *European* bourgeois public sphere.

PANNING TO "THE EAST"

Europeans of the eighteenth and the nineteenth century were fascinated by the ruling figures of the Persian Empire. "Cyrus the Great," observes George Jellinek, "is gratefully remembered in operatic history largely due to Pietro Metastasio, the most successful librettist of the eighteenth century, whose *Siroe* was set to music by Vinci (1726), Handel (1728), Hasse (1733), and Piccinni (1759). (Ten other operas about Siroe/Cyrus were written to non-Metastasian texts.)"[10] This recognition and celebration of the great emperors of the Achaemenid Empire, and the European Orientalist scholarship that underlined it, were not only critical in the formation of the European bourgeois self-consciousness, projecting the ideology of their own imperial domination to ancient historical figures from Alexander to Cyrus and Darius, but even more important, were instrumental in the recognition of that pre-Islamic history in the making of the postcolonial Iranian nation-state. Persian travelers, diplomats, journalists, and students soon discovered this European penchant for pre-Islamic Iranian history and became the bearers of that fascination back to their own homeland. It is this reflection of the European bourgeois consciousness and the transnational public sphere it helped craft and occupy all the way back to the site of the colonial consciousness that interests me most in this study.

The limitation of both Schwab's and Said's studies of Orientalism is the fact that ultimately they concentrate, though from two different angles, solely and exclusively on Europe and the European texts and context of these Oriental preoccupations. Whereas Schwab navigates the measures and manners in which exposure to Oriental heritage influenced European cultural developments, Said proposes it as the modus operandi of a colonial mode of knowledge production that enabled Europe to dominate the lands and cul-

tures it conquered. Abandoned in both their projects is the fate of these Orientalized sites themselves—or what happens to Persian, Indian, Arabic, or
Chinese literary and artistic traditions (and the emerging public spaces that
start hosting them) once they have been translated into a European context.
The combined, but perhaps unintended, consequence of both Schwab's and
Said's views is the setting up of "the West" as the point of primary reference
in the world, abandoning alternative worlds that existed long prior and then
adjacent to this "West." Tracing the genealogy of the non-European public
sphere in contrapuntal reaction to the European citation of their colonial
conquests remains a critical task for the next generation of scholars on
Orientalism.

Both Schwab's and Said's works thus become the varied texts on European
intellectual and imperial history, and ipso facto (intentionally or paradoxically) Orientalized the cultures and climes that this "West" had conquered
and alienated from their own multiple and varied historical trajectories.
But the cultures thus Orientalized had thrived and continued to thrive in a
history and veracity long before and long after their exposure to "Western"
imperial adventures. "The West" did with these cultures whatever it was that
it did—Orientalizing, exoticizing, and above all cannibalizing them. But
what about these emerging public spaces themselves? What happened to
them *after* they had been exposed to "the West?"

The task this question generates is consequential not only for the literary
and cultural traditions of the "non-West" (thus branded). It also proposes
alternative modes of historiography that do not give unconditional and perhaps unintended primacy to "the Western" narrative, thus in fact essential-
izing an amorphous ideological proposition from which world history—and
the histories of colonially camouflaged worlds—are thereafter narrated. My
purpose in this book is to unearth one such world—the Persian world—that
was enabled by virtue of those fateful colonial encounters, but in terms contrary to those colonial interests (in part because the bourgeois public sphere
in which these Orientalist gestures were performed was itself self-contradictory
and paradoxical). By and through their Eurocentricism, Schwab and Said
in effect cross-authenticated "the West" as the center of universe and categorically disregarded the flip side of their own argument, a blind spot that
later, in his *Culture and Imperialism,* Said at least partially tried to correct.

What happens if we consider the flip side of their argument? We shall
witness the enabling of the emerging public spheres on which people of the

world on the receiving end of European imperialism begin to rediscover their own worlds in fresh, unprecedented, and provocative ways. It is no accident that the Persian literary and poetic works of the last two hundred years have been almost entirely initiated by expatriate writers and poets deeply versed in European languages and cultures. The founding fathers of contemporary Persian prose and poetry, from Mohammad Ali Jamalzadeh (1892–1997) to Sadegh Hedayat (1903–1951), Nima Yushij (1896–1960), and Bozorg Alavi (1904–1997), to pathbreaking scholars like Hossein Kazem-zadeh Iranshahr (1883–1961), Mohammad Qazvini (1877–1949), Seyyed Hassan Taqizadeh (1878–1970), and Mojtaba Minovi (1903–1976), and so on, were all either educated in Europe or else deeply influenced by their exposures to European cultures, and particularly by the attention Persian literature and culture received in these contexts. Their literary and scholarly sensibilities were in fact cultivated outside Iran, while being exposed to the European public sphere in which what Schwab had considered an "Oriental Renaissance" had already adopted their "Oriental heritage." It was in Germany and through Goethe that Muhammad Iqbal (1877–1938) discovered Hafez and turned to him and other Persian poets for inspiration. It was in Paris that Sadegh Hedayat became definitive of Persian literary prose. The same is true about Mohammad Ali Jamalzadeh and a host of other poets and writers in Germany. It was in Istanbul that a whole host of Iranian intellectuals after the early nineteenth century were exposed to European literary traditions and began to translate them into Persian. Even those figures like Nima Yushij who did not travel to Europe were deeply exposed to French roman-ticism, an exposure that had lasting influences on his poetry. The circularity of these events—Persian literati finding themselves (both figuratively and physically) in the European public sphere and extending that space into their own homeland—is the common leitmotif of my arguments in this book.

Here, as a result, my concern is rooted neither in Said's critique of Ori-entalism nor in Schwab's celebration of it as a source of a second Renais-sance for Europe—though both these groundbreaking studies have had lasting influences on our reading of Orientalism as a mode of knowledge production. My concern is far less with the *causes* and far more with the *con-sequences* of the European, and later American, fascination with the Persian literary and cultural heritage. As is the case with any other kind of adapta-tion, at varied moments in their turn to other cultures Europeans and Amer-icans had their own peculiar interests and interpretations of the cultures they observed. There is nothing unusual about that. Nor is it strange that European imperialism fabricated a mode of knowledge about the Orient that was conducive to its desire and design to rule over them; this is in the nature of knowledge and power in any context.

In this study, rather, I take Edward Said's *political* contention and connect it to Schwab's *cultural* history to prepare the groundwork in a different—decidedly *societal*—direction. Here my concern is not with how Persian literary heritage, poetry in particular, was coopted into the European imagination by way of a knowledge production conducive to colonial domination, nor indeed am I particularly interested in the manners in which these encounters with the Persian Orient enriched European intellectual history. I am interested in something entirely different—and in fact lies in the opposite direction. I am interested in Persian cultural heritage and what happens to it when, in the course of the eighteenth and nineteenth centuries and under the influence of European imperial encroachment, it finally exited the Persianate court and emerged to form a bona fide *public space* that it would eventually call *Vatan*/Homeland. In the formation of that public space I detect the paradoxical machinery of modern history, when postcolonial nation-states were formed on a contrapuntal register to bring the contradictory forces of global capitalism to the fore.

In *The World of Persian Literary Humanism* (2012),[11] I have already argued that when Persian literary imagination exited its habitual habitat in the Persianate royal courts, from the Mughals in India, the Safavids in Iran, and the Ottomans in Asia Minor, it was habitually drawn to the new centers of imperial power in Europe; but (and there's the rub) it was not welcomed in those courts, for those courts had their own languages and literatures at the service of their imperial domination, as in fact Edward Said demonstrates in his other magisterial work, *Culture and Imperialism* (1994).[12] Instead, Persian literary traditions, along with the even wider spectrum of Persian cultural heritage, were Orientalized and cast into vastly popular social and intellectual movements like the Enlightenment, romanticism, or transcendentalism. Thus Persian culture entered a *public space* that forced it to evolve in unprecedented dimensions and return to Iran and its environs with renewed and robust force to help Persian literati posit a *public space*. On the home front, Persian poets and literati who had ventured from their courtly habitat had now entered a wide spectrum of non-courtly space (the emerging public sphere), which they called *Vatan*/Homeland. In the formation of that public space (*Vatan*), I contend that the European, and later American, reception of Persian culture in general, and its poetic and literary traditions in particular, had a critical and catalytic effect. In this book, as a result, my attention to the European reception of Persian culture and literature is directed toward the more sculpted and worldly composition of that Iranian public sphere.

In my *Post-Orientalism*,[13] I have already historicized Orientalism and drawn distinctions between the Orientalism of the Greeks, or the Orientalism of the Europeans when facing the threat of the Ottomans, and the Orientalism of European colonialism when conquering the Ottomans and the Mughals. I have already made the argument that Orientalism is not a reality sui generis, and that as a mode of knowledge production at the height of European colonialism ultimately it yields to Area Studies during the Cold War and leads to the production of disposable knowledge without any solid or enduring epistemology. One can offer additional or even alternative variations on the theme of European Orientalism. In a historical context, we might make a distinction among the Orientalisms (in plural) that were evident in the biblical, classical, and medieval periods, and continue with the Orientalism that emerged in Spain during and in the immediate aftermath of Muslim Spain (711–1492) and then move forward to the Orientalism that originated in the Vatican during its appeal to the Mongol Empire (1206–1368) to convert to Christianity, as opposed to the Orientalism of the Crusaders period (1095–1272), before we come to the period of the East India Company (1600–1872) and the formation of colonially instigated Orientalism. All these are different forms and modes of Orientalism with multiple and varied manners in the relationship between power and knowledge that they energized and entailed. My concern in this book is with only the last episode, with only a preparatory reference to the period before it, for it is in this latter period that the Persian literary imagination left its usual habitat in the Persianate courts and transmigrated to new centers of imperial power in Europe. Before that historic development, Persian culture had been perfectly happy and thriving as the lingua franca of multiple empires that gloried in its literary and other cultural achievements.

What happened to Persian literature and culture when it found a vast and foreign domain in which it began to flower in alien languages and cultures? In the European and subsequently American contexts Persian literature moved out of its historical habitat in Persianate courts, came to Europe, but was not admitted to its royal courts. It was instead ushered into the emerging bourgeois *public sphere* of various European intellectual movements. In order to thrive in the new global environment dominated by European empires, Persian literature had to learn to breathe in different languages, cultures, and climes. Persian literature was thus subjected to a set of multiple shocks— being out of its own royal courts, not being admitted to a new court, being forced into a public sphere entirely unknown to itself, and also finding itself rendered into alien and even inhospitable languages. The experience was shocking, destabilizing, yet also invigorating, provocative, self-regenerative. As Persian poets and literati inside the postcolonial nation-state began to fathom a public space in which to rearticulate themselves, the European reception of Persian cultural heritage to their bourgeois public space provided a critical momentum to the configuration of its new worldliness.

It is in that context that I wish to explore the significance of the European and American adaptations of Persian literary, poetic, and cultural traditions and the impact it has had on expanding that public sphere. Like all other Oriental literatures, Persian poetry was first encountered and rendered into European languages by Orientalist scholars and amateurs. It then started to have a direct effect on popular European culture in time for Persian travelers, traders, diplomats, and scholars to come over to Europe and discover these European renditions of their own literary icons. I am thus primarily interested in the *territorial expansion* of the Persian cultural imagination when it traveled away from its natural habitat, entered a European domain, and began to breathe in a different language and culture. As the Persian language started to live a vicarious life in the English, French, German, or Spanish languages, it encountered some of the most world-historic events in the European and North American contexts. Colonialism, Orientalism, romanticism, transcendentalism—all had a historic rendezvous with Persian culture precisely at the moment of European imperial expansionism.

PERSOPHILIA

Late in January 2013, *BBC History Magazine* had a strange but provocative piece that it titled "Why did men stop wearing high heels?" "For generations," the article began, "they have signified femininity and glamour—but a pair of high heels was once an essential accessory for men." It turns out that "the high heel was worn for centuries throughout the near east as a form of riding footwear"—this according to Elizabeth Semmelhack of the Bata Shoe Museum in Toronto. As to how they found their way to Europe, according to Semmelhack, "At the end of the 16th Century, Persia's Shah Abbas I had the largest cavalry in the world. He was keen to forge links with rulers in Western Europe to help him defeat his great enemy, the Ottoman Empire. So in 1599, Abbas sent the first Persian diplomatic mission to Europe— it called on the courts of Russia, Germany and Spain. A wave of interest in all things Persian passed through Western Europe. Persian style shoes were enthusiastically adopted by aristocrats, who sought to give their appearance a virile, masculine edge that, it suddenly seemed, only heeled shoes could supply."[14]

This initially aristocratic and subsequently popular interest in "all things Persian" was not limited to the high heels of the Safavid cavalry, extending far and wide into more varied forms. Persian poetry and painting, literature and mysticism, art and architecture, archeology and philosophy, ancient and medieval history, religion and rituals, flora and fauna, clothing and cuisine, wine and spices—the list is almost endless. But how is this Persophilia, as I would term the phenomenon, different from or similar to Orientalism?

To answer that question, we may first make a distinction among the Arab, Ottoman, Persian, and Indian, or Chinese Orients, so far as Europe creatively manufactured them. The Arab Orient (very much the subject of Said's concern and examination) was by and large part of the Ottoman Empire at the moment of its encounter with European imperialism; whereas the Ottoman, Persian, Chinese, or Indian Orients (very much the subject of Schwab's interests) were massive imperial projects that dealt with Europe from a position of power and pride—in effect picking up from where the Seljuqid and Mongol empires, and before it the Abbasid empires, had left off. In this perspective, the European encounter with the Ottoman, Persian, and Mughal empires was a form of Orientalism of rivalry, not one of domination. The European Ottoman Orientalism was an Orientalism of fear and rivalry (Mozart's opera *The Abduction from the Seraglio,* 1782), which is to be distinguished from the earlier Christian Orientalism of fear and loathing (Dante's *Divine Comedy,* 1308–1321), while their Arab Orientalism was one of domination and denigration, yielding to fertile romanticism about dunes, sands, nomads, their harems, and odalisques, as perhaps is best seen in the Orientalist paintings of North Africa and Arabia (Léon Cogniet, Jean-Léon Gérôme,

Jean-Auguste-Dominique Ingres, Eugène Delacroix). These are decidedly not the defining leitmotifs of the Chinese, Persian, or Indian Orientalisms, which served as different modes of fantasies, as best evident in George Frideric Handel, *Serse* (1738; set in Persia), Léo Delibes's *Lakmé* (1883; set in India), or Giacomo Puccini's *Turandot* (1926; set in China).

There was one more very specific aspect to Persophilia that distinguished its features from other kinds of Orientalism. As Enlightenment-era Europeans[15] began to rediscover their ancient history, from Athens to Jerusalem, everywhere they turned there was something called "Persia," and it was not limited to that profound anxiety-provoking drama embedded in Aeschylus's tragedy *The Persians* (472 BC). For the Greeks, the Persians were their grand imperial nemesis, as they were later for the Romans; and when Europeans turned to their Bible, the selfsame Persia was there in their holiest of texts— in Ezra, in Esther, and many other places. These features made the Persophilia of the eighteenth and nineteenth centuries something of a self-discovery for Europeans, from the remotest corners of ancient history to the newest pages of Hegel's philosophy of history, in which he thought that by the time the historical *Geist* had come to Persians, Europeans would immediately see and recognize themselves. This was not the feature of the Orient at large. There were no "Arabs" for the ancient Greeks; and the Indians were far too distant, while the Egyptians were far too close and amiable. The Persians were the grandest of all imperial threats to the Greeks and the liberators of the Jews from bondage; and as Europeans began to rediscover their Athens and Jerusalem anew, so did they, willy-nilly, also discover that entity the Greeks and the Hebrews called "the Persians."

The specific features of Persophilia, as I propose it here, were thus marked by the European attraction to an imperial heritage that eventually found its way into their bourgeois public space, and from there traveled back to Iran itself to expand and exacerbate the nascent formation of the postcolonial (globalized) public sphere. As the example of the high heels (or the innumerable operas about Cyrus, Darius, or Xerxes) clearly shows, the initial aristocratic attraction to "all things Persian" eventually filtered down to the bourgeois public space. In the case of the Persian literary and poetic heritage, the same is true, and the reception of the European literary public space was from the vantage point of attraction to the European literary, social, and intellectual movements—which movements (from the Enlightenment and romanticism to the Oriental Renaissance)—would in turn expand and enrich the European bourgeois public sphere all the way to the colonial and post-colonial extension of their economic logic and ideological rhetoric.

In European imperial contexts—as in any other imperial context—the Persian literary imagination found a new lease on life in foreign lands and on unfamiliar grounds. The only significant difference was that this time around it was not allowed to enter into the ruling dynastic courts of European empires—for it was not a pair of shoes to wear or a luxurious garment to sport and was thus perforce kept outside. The language of these empires was not Persian, as had been the case with the previous empires, where Persian literary imagination had thrived. So in terms of its location Persophilia was integral to European Orientalism at large—but that is not where its most critical aspects rest. My study of Persophilia parts ways from other studies of Orientalism when I locate it in the European bourgeois public sphere and from there trace it back to Persia, where the representation comes to meet the represented, and where the encounter generates the dialectic of a massive national consciousness, the formation of a thriving public sphere, in *form* similar to its European counterparts, yet in *content* far more radically disposed. This contrapuntal encounter between the representation and the represented, between the European public sphere and its colonial reflections, I consider and suggest to be the engine of postcolonial history.

My argument here is that the European reception of Persian literature and culture was not just as the accouterment of power for their colonialism (Said), or as part of an "Oriental Renaissance" that benefited European culture (Schwab). The experience was also the opening of a critical space, what Habermas has theorized as the European bourgeois public sphere, then expanding beyond that European location into what we can now consider a postcolonial (global) public sphere, one for Persian (or other colonized) poets and literati, thinkers and revolutionaries, to have and behold and occupy. So while Persophilia was part of Orientalism as the modus operandi of colonial knowledge production, it was also paradoxically the condition of emancipation for Persian poets and literati as new "public intellectuals" from the historical tyranny of their entrapment in the royal court. By virtue of no longer being a language of domination, Persian now emerged as a language of resistance; while in its European renditions and translations it found a vicarious life in a new democratic public space. When it rises again in Iran, South Asia, or Central Asia, the new Persian carries within itself the marks both of its sojourn in European contexts and as the site of contestation with

European imperialism in its historic home and habitat though now on a public space of its own making, and no longer contingent on the vagaries of dynastic battlefields.

In short, in the course of the eighteenth and nineteenth centuries, Persian literary imagination forever escaped the confinements of the royal court and entered an open-ended public space, and in this transition European Persophilia had an extended and paradoxical role to play. Toward the end of *The World of Persian Literary Humanism* I documented the internal dynamics of the formation of that critical public space, and now in this book I wish to terrace its external factors—and thereby frame the formation of one particular postcolonial public sphere (and upon it the postcolonial subject) that in its encounter with European imperialism marks a much wider spectrum of theoretical implications.

DECENTERING "THE WEST"

As early as 1654, when Cavalli, and later Bononcini in 1694 and then Handel in 1738, composed their respective operas on Xerxes/Serse, the figure of the Persian emperor was squarely located in the baroque operas as a benevolent lover—as perhaps immortalized in the exquisitely beautiful "Ombra mai fu" aria, originally sung by a castrato but now mostly by a mezzo-soprano, contralto, or countertenor.[16] These early operas on Xerxes take us all the way back to the formation of European baroque music, long before the rise of European romanticism and American transcendentalism, in which we witness a deep and pervasive interest and even fascination with Persian poets of the later periods. European and American bourgeois society was expanding and maturing in multiple and varied forms, and in that expansive maturity Persophilia had a significant place. Why were Nietzsche, Goethe, or Emerson interested in aspects of Persian prose and poetry, religion and culture? Why did Nietzsche name his prophet after the Persian prophet Zarathustra and not Abraham or Buddha or Muhammad? Persian poetic, literary, and cultural tropes traveled from their historic habitat and found a home in these groundbreaking European events, thus going through the growing pain of being given a new spin, a new take, unbeknownst to themselves. These Persian tropes and artifacts now began to speak English, French, or German, and in those inflections discovered something new and strange about themselves.

Xerxes singing Italian in a baroque opera was something far more than just a soiree entertainment for the European aristocracy or bourgeoisie. Something far worldlier was at stake and in the making: the rebirth of a nation—through its historic tropes and metaphors—on a global stage.

The model of the circulation of ideas between East and West of the colonial divide (thus dispensing with the binary) that I suggest is very much the opposite of what is presumed and implicated in Edward Said's *Orientalism,* or even in Raymond Schwab's *Oriental Renaissance;* they assume a unidirectional flow of ideological domination. "The West" either manufactures (Said) or adopts (Schwab) Oriental ideas for its own uses and benefits. Here, in contrast, I offer a *circulation* of ideas, from the colonial fringes of empire to its European centers and then back to where they came from—a circulation that in fact follows the road map of the circulation of capital, labor, raw materials, and markets, a circulation that places both East and West in an identical world economic system. Said and Schwab's presumed model assigns a fixed colonial position to the colonized nations; mine incorporates them into the larger frame of global economy, and of the *world system,* as perhaps best theorized by Immanuel Wallerstein.[17]

The logic of my argument is similarly predicated on the circulation of ideas based on the changing centers of imperial power and not on any assumption about the innate or essential bifurcation between East and West—two colonial constructs that have subsequently assumed fetishized reality predicated on the fetishized commodities the globalized capitalist system procures. After the biblical, classical, and medieval periods, the renewed interest in things Persian (and by extension Oriental) was in the context of the emerging European empires and their colonial (economic) interests. Europeans became increasingly interested in Oriental matters by virtue of the globalized empires they now commanded, and the feeling was reciprocated by the Persianate literati (among others), who had now physically exited their historic habitat at the royal courts and vicariously entered the new public space of European capitals, for they had no access to European courts. By virtue of the French Revolution of 1789 and the European revolutions of 1848, much of the attention to Persian and other Orientalized literatures was now conducted in this public sphere, bourgeois in its disposition and thus heavily influenced by the commercial and colonial interests that had defined the Victorian era in particular—though the origin of the development is much earlier. It is in that public space that this interest developed and it is from that public sphere that it traveled back to Iran and its environs and defined the formation of the public space they now called *Vatan/ Homeland*.

What as a result we are witnessing in and around Persophilia is knowledge production in a new imperial context, not too different from other imperial contexts except for the bourgeois revolution it had experienced and the formation of the public sphere as the location par excellence of the European bourgeoisie. Because of the capitalist revolution that had set a succession of colonial conquests in motion, these new empires were global and globalizing; not that other empires had been any less global, but the engine of their locomotion was territorial conquest, not the extension of an economic machinery with the goal of expansionism beyond any territorial limitation. The production of knowledge at the presumed hearts of these empires was predicated on the ideological formation of a "center" and a contingent periphery for it, giving its self-consciousness a superior and abiding global credence and legitimacy at the expense of glossing over and wiping out the other maps and worldly consciousnesses of the countries it conquered militarily and economically incorporated. Critical studies of this Orientalism (Said), as indeed laudatory studies of its consequences (Schwab), in fact exacerbate the fetishization of this fictive center and thus paradoxically contribute to the self-alienation of the "Rest" of the world that it effectively isolates and makes a stranger to itself.

My objective is to reverse that alienating direction and to overcome that ideological bifurcation between "the West and the Rest" by positing a circulatory episteme of knowledge production in which the presumed center and its fictive periphery, manufactured in order for that center to rule that periphery better, are in fact made integral to each other and operate on porous borders. This project will enable us to retrieve and reassert the worldly consciousness of those worlds that "the West" has overridden and erased from our imaginative geography. It is not accidental that a retrograde and belated panegyrist historian of "the West" calls his book *Civilization: The West and the Rest*.[18] He is bemoaning the loss of a world that never was but was made ideologically paramount by virtue of a binary fiction that enabled him to write voluminously with the same logic that silenced the history of others. My project in this book is precisely the reversal of that imperial silencing of the world.

Predicated on a material reading of the historical reciprocity between capital and labor, between the capital and the colonial, between the ideology that calls itself "the West" and the world that it dismisses as "the Rest," I wish to explore a mode of knowledge production that in fact replicates that circularity and defies the dominant ideology that has thus divided the world so as to conquer and control it better. Persophilia is thus a unit of operation, a nodal point through which I wish to read a renewed—postbiblical, postclassical, postmedieval—interest in matters and manners deemed "Persian" in the Western European (and subsequently North American) contexts in which this circularity begins to take shape and momentum. In this reading, I see the world, not on the receiving end of "the Western" manufacturing of "the East," but in a circulatory transfusion of ideas, replicating the transmutation of labor and capital on a dialectical interface between the capital and the colonial, and then between the colonial and the postcolonial. The insights of the defining moment of my generation of postcolonial thinkers, Edward Said's *Orientalism,* was predicated on a blindness, which I wish to overcome and see through.

Europeans and Americans were never in complete control of what it was they were thinking and producing about the Orient (or about Persia); so far as the *intentio auctoris* (intention of the author) was concerned, yes, but not so far as the *intentio lectoris* (intention of the reader) was concerned (Umberto Eco's hermeneutical terms).[19] Both Said and Schwab concentrated, in two different ways, on the *intentio auctoris* and left the *intentio lectoris* open and even inconsequential, for they were both primarily Europeanists. In contrast, I am far more interested in the consequences of Orientalism and Persophilia than in its causes—to which both Schwab and Said have already attended in two different but ultimately complementary ways.

In the European public space where Persophilia was taking place and world-historic events and movements such as the Enlightenment, romanticism, and transcendentalism were launched, Persian poets and literati had a vicarious life at the center of vastly global and self-globalizing empires. But the very power that enabled Persophilia and fed it into European social and intellectual movements attracted real-life Iranians and other neighboring scholars and intellectuals to Western European and North American countries and climes, and it was from there that they returned home to resonate that echo in resistance or accommodation and thus massively to contribute to the formation of a public space that they now called *Vatan*/Homeland. On this theoretical ground, now I will have to make specific sojourns as to how

Persophilia became a singularly significant episteme not just of knowledge but also of social action production.

In the course of contemporary Iranian history, the fascination with the illusion of "the West," whether celebrated by prominent thinkers like Seyyed Hassan Taqizadeh (1878–1970) or else diagnosed as a disease by others like Jalal Al-e Ahmad (1923–1969), in fact consisted of the public affects of Persophilia returned. Iranians became fascinated with "the West" because they were captivated by their own mirror image—their distant and imagined locations—as produced and envisioned in "the West," in effect falling in love with that image of themselves manufactured by Persophilia in Europe, and with what that image promised or threatened. Whether good or bad, positive or negative, admiring or denigrating—that image was coming to Iranians from a location of power. And whether to emulate it or to reject it, adopt it or denounce it, they were drawn to that image by force of the colonial relation of power that had enabled it. The fascination or fixation with "the West" was a reflection of the emerging identity crisis on the widening spectrum of the European public sphere—a recognition that was at once exhilarating and deeply anxiety-provoking. "The West" thus became a measure of truth not merely by the imperial power of the hegemony that had constituted it but equally by the power of the colonial imagination that was actively partaking in it. In the dialectic of that encounter, the nature and disposition of the public sphere were being defined on the colonial site.

Taqizadeh thought Iranians should all be westernized, while Al-e Ahmad thought exactly the opposite—that they should be de-westernized, for he considered westernization a disease. But what both Taqizadeh and Al-e Ahmad shared was a full, simultaneously exhilarating and anxiety-provoking recognition that the dialectics of the two public spaces in Europe and its colonial extensions was ushering Iran into a new era—one that Taqizadeh thought Iranians should wholeheartedly embrace and with which Al-e Ahmad thought they should critically engage. But despite these differences, the fact is that Al-e Ahmad was too deeply affected by the progressive forces of the "West," while Taqizadeh was more deeply rooted in his own pre-Western heritage than he was perhaps willing to see and recognize. These two facts do not show Al-e Ahmad and Taqizadeh as contradicting their own positions, but reveal the sociopsychological paradigm through which the making of Iranian public space was being paradoxically conceived and dialectically sculpted. These two towering public intellectuals of their time had come to two opposite conclusions in precisely the public sphere that had not just embraced but in fact had occasioned and enabled them. They were exponentially expanding the public space that had been made possible by the fateful encounter between European empires and their colonial outposts—between the two parts of the imaginative geography of power that had made "the West" and "the Rest" possible—an encounter that was far more evident and consequential in the bourgeois public sphere of Europe and its colonial extensions than on the battlefields of their military encounters from the Perso-Russian wars of the early nineteenth century to the CIA-sponsored coup of 1953.

Al-e Ahmad's famous text *Gharbzadegi/West Strickenness* (1962) is thus a case of public psychosis in which Iranians catch themselves trapped and engaged inside a syndrome not of their own making.[20] In *Gharbzadegi*, Iranians cathect and decathect with the psychosis of Persophilia. But both cathecting and decathecting with "the West" is the result of this collective psychosis occasioned by the encounter with Persophilia in "the West." From social uprisings to literary and artistic movements, all are launched from within this psychosis of Persophilia, with its reversed projection naming itself "Gharbzadegi." All of them are signs of entrapment/engagement inside a singular world—"the West"—hegemonically manufactured, that calls itself in a manner that wipes out all its preceding or alternative mappings and topographies yet, paradoxically, enables the dialectical formation of a public sphere that rises to oppose it.

Chronologically, and in the manner of imperial power, first we have Persophilia emerging in Europe as a mode of imperial bourgeois knowledge production in and about the world that it is conquering. Nothing unusual there—all empires, Persianate empires from the Samanids down to the Mughals included—have produced knowledge about the lands they have conquered in a way that sustains those empires in power. Then travelers, diplomats, merchants, intellectual dissidents in exile, visiting scholars, journalists, and so on encounter, become entranced by Persophilia and the place it promises (or threatens) them in the world to come, and take that image and that promise/threat back to their homeland. This is the moment when "westernization" is branded "modernization" by modernizers from Reza Shah to Taqizadeh, and the European project of capitalist (Enlightenment) modernity is thereby uncritically celebrated without the slightest attention to the intermediary function of colonialism—and the modernization project is embraced as the epitome of reason, success, progress, glory, and civility. But soon the antithesis of this thesis emerges, and in the towering figure of Jalal Al-e Ahmad we notice the exponential expansion of the public space, not just by offering an opposing perspective, but by that perspective colliding with the other and sculpting a richly potent public sphere now innate to the postcolonial nation-state and to the subject formation it entails.

LIBERATING A WORLD

Studies of romantic Orientalism have now solidly established that "Persian poetry in translation was available to Byron—notably a number of translations of Hafiz before 1807, and Stephen Weston's *Specimens of Persian Poetry* (1805) which seems to have been widely known."[21] The romantic appropriation of Hafez into European literary movements such as those represented by Lord Byron (1788–1824) liberated and released Persian poetry with a paradoxical gesture that at one and the same time distorted and twisted it to its own benefit. This paradoxical twist was a necessary epistemic act of violence that gave new birth to Persian literary humanism in its own natural habitat—the emerging Iranian public sphere. The route that this literary humanism traversed—from the Persian royal courts, to European bourgeois public spheres, back to the emerging Iranian public sphere—precisely marks the birth canal of postcolonial literary imagination.

When the Europeans (or later the Americans) began using the word "Persian" by way of designating their encounter with the cultural material of their Persophilia, they were in fact *ethnicizing* a vast cosmopolitan culture at a moment when the subject of their interest had gone through varied stages of transmutation in the vast and diversified domains of multiple empires.[22] European and American scholars, let alone their literati, were entirely innocent of these internal dynamics and glossed over them, designating all Iranians as "Persians" and "Persian" as a marker of ethnicity. It is precisely this "Persian" as the marker of Persophilia that came to Iran and emerged in the ethnic nationalism that to this day is a source of dissent and separatist tendencies in the country. As a nation-state descended from multiple successions of multiethnic empires, Iran is by definition not limited to Persians, nor is "Persian" any longer a marker of ethnicity.

The word "Iran" or "*Vatan*/Homeland" emerged in and as the locus classicus of the public domain, primarily by the incoming "public intellectuals" who, as a class of literati, had left the royal court and had nowhere else to go, as their ancestors had customarily left a defeated dynasty and joined its triumphant successors. Encounter with Western European and North American social and intellectual movements was instrumental in both positing and expanding that public domain. But on an ideological level, the term "Persian" returned to Iran as a marker of ethnicity categorically applied to a multiethnic public space with an abiding sense of "the nation." At two levels, the term "Persian" as used by Europeans at the height of their Persophilia is distorting: (1) it designates an ethnicity some fourteen hundred years after the term had gone through systematic transmutation from *ethnos* to *logos* to *ethos* to *chaos;* and (2) it posits an ethnic nationalism at the expense of a multiethnic nation-state built in a public space that it had composed from the remnants of multiple empires. It is that epistemic violence that I in fact argue has paradoxically occasioned, exacerbated, and enriched the postcolonial nation-state.

In the phenomenon of Persophilia as a specific case of Orientalism we encounter the key template of historical consciousness in which contemporary Iranians (like all other postcolonial nations) negotiate a normative place for themselves in world history. An Iranian may never have seen a European opera or read a European work of fiction in which a Persian character is personified. But the historical encounter between Iran and Europe and the rise of Persophilia created an imaginative domain in the European bourgeois public sphere in which Iran as a nation-state now had to place and represent itself. Whether celebrated or rejected, that image became definitive to a world-historic consciousness in which Iran as a modern nation-state was born. Every major social and intellectual movement in Iran from the early nineteenth to the late twentieth century is in one way or another a dialectical engagement with this European Persophilia. The earliest Iranian travelers to Europe, people like Naqd Ali Beg (in 1626) or Mirza Saleh Shirazi (in 1815) encountered it and brought its echoes and reflections back to their homeland as the template of reconfiguring their emerging nation-state.

Upon the initial formations of this emerging public space during the nineteenth century, from the Constitutional Revolution (1906–1911) to the Islamic revolution (1977–1979), every major social and intellectual movement in Iran may be considered the playing out of a domestic echo of this Iranian attempt to locate its country vis-à-vis the idea of "the West" in confirmation or negation: from the democratic aspirations of the Constitutional Revolution, to the "modernization" projects during the Reza Shah monarchy, to the rise of the Iranian communist (Tudeh) Party and its incorporation into the Soviet empire, to Mosaddeq's anticolonial nationalism, all the way to such groundbreaking intellectual movements as those initiated by Nima Yushij in poetry, by Sadegh Hedayat in fiction, all the way to Abbas Kiarostami in cinema.

THE STRUCTURAL TRANSFORMATION OF THE PUBLIC SPHERE

Let me recap the central argument of my book before we get lost in the thickets of a more detailed examination of Persophilia. What Said's *Orientalism* enabled was a critical encounter with the European creation of a geographical domain of imperial domination. But what this very insight ignored was the fact that this mode of imperial knowledge production coincided historically with the formation of the European (soon to be globalized via the machinery of colonialism) bourgeois public sphere and its structural transformations. Said took "the West" for granted, though he dismantled its mode of knowledge production and self-mythologizing proclivities. The phenomenon of Persophilia is an indication that the imperial ground had just shifted and so Persian poets and literati found a new public sphere in which the very figure of a "public intellectual" now made social sense, and that the European bourgeois revolution had actually emancipated these literati from their courtly confinements and let them loose into the newly emerging public sphere. This paradoxical liberation fit into the very logic of colonial modernity that helped craft a public domain (and a public reason) and at the same time enabled the agents of its own contradictions.

The seeds of that paradox were planted in the phenomenon I call "Persophilia" in this book, and the sites of its cultivation were all over the European intellectual history of the eighteenth and nineteenth centuries and in the most momentous occasions of its Enlightenment self-consciousness. "For the general reader," notes C. J. Betts in his assessment of Montesquieu's *Persian Letters* (1721), "Montesquieu will be better known as a political theorist than as the author of *Persian Letters;* it could scarcely be otherwise, with a man whose analysis of the English constitution produced a famous theory of 'the separation of powers' which had a deep influence on the constitution of, for instance, the United States."[23] Betts proceeds to criticize the fact that *Persian Letters* "has too often been treated as merely a forerunner of the political treatise, *Of the Spirits of Laws* (1748)" and how the critics have only paid attention to the passages in *Persian Letters* that anticipate the more famous treatise and disregard the rest. The question for us, then, is why would arguably the most prominent political theorist of the Enlightenment period, the very father of European and subsequently American constitutionalism, write a book like *Persian Letters?* And, even more important, what would be the impact of this recognition when Iranians themselves eventually began to get wind of such texts and similar representations that lay at the heart of European modernity? Throughout the nineteenth century Montesquieu and other leading Enlightenment thinkers heavily influenced leading Iranian public intellectuals. Mirza Saleh Shirazi was one of the first Iranian students who traveled to Europe in 1815, and he wrote an immensely influential travelogue, from which we see that he was intimately familiar with the ideas of Rousseau, Montesquieu, Voltaire, and Diderot. Mirza Saleh was among the first Iranian public intellectuals: he brought back with him a printing machine and with it published the first Iranian newspaper. He is among the most direct links between the effervescent European bourgeois public sphere and the emerging Iranian public reason and discourse.[24]

Betts considers *Persian Letters* as "perhaps the finest French work (the other contender is La Bruyère's *Characters* . . . of a great period of satire, the period which extends, in France, from Molière to Voltaire, and includes in England such figures as Dryden, Pope and Swift. The nearest English equivalent is Addison and Steele's *Spectator*."[25] A book of this significance obviously had placed the trope of "the Persian" right at the heart of French and by extension European Persophilia. As for the lead characters of *Persian Letters,* "Montesquieu's Persian pair are spectators of the French scene, detached but not indifferent, with their own set of 'Persian' values, which turn out—despite a rather obvious split between Usbek's principles and his practice—to be those of a rationalist critic of established institutions, a liberal, or at any rate a believer in liberty and justice, and a utilitarian."[26] The example of *Persian Letters* is a clear indication that the nature of Persophilia in this period is not tangential, haphazard, or frivolous to the cause of European liberalism, but in fact central to the key political and philosophical preoccupations of the Enlightenment, definitive to the European bourgeois public space and beyond.

Persian culture began to exit the Persianate royal courts at the height of European imperialism. European imperialism was coterminous with the rise of the European bourgeois public sphere, which at once sustained and harbored the seeds of its own contradictions. Persian cultural referents and artifacts began to be reimagined and thus reinvigorated in an emerging public sphere that was made paradoxically possible precisely by that fateful encounter between Persian culture and European imperialism. The European bourgeois public sphere was thereby extended and expanded in all its paradoxical force onto the colonial extensions it had made possible at once to sustain and to oppose it.

That Montesquieu would call his book *Persian Letters* and opt to launch his criticism of European institutions and articulate liberty via two fictitious "Persian" characters was no accident. The world at large was witness to a major historic shift. The rise of Persophilia in Europe coincided with the defeat of Muslim dynasties in which Persian language and literary culture had their home, so that Hafez, Sa'di, and Ferdowsi suddenly ceased to sing in the luxurious courts of mighty empires and the triumphant dynasties of the Mughals, the Safavids, or even the Ottomans, and began to murmur in English, French, or German in the European bourgeois public sphere—all the way from Montesquieu's political theories to Hegel's philosophy of history to Nietzsche's iconoclastic countermetaphysics. As Orientalist scholarship emerged and manuscripts accumulated in European libraries and museums, Iranian scholars like Mohammad Qazvini, and after him Mojtaba Minovi, went to Europe and revolutionized scholarship, thus reinventing scholarly literary studies and enriching the emerging Iranian public space by introducing scholarship in the reading of history for the public in what Habermas called the "literary public sphere."

Persians and Persian culture, from ancient to contemporary times, were now depicted in Europe—in operas and political treatises, creative imagination and critical thinking alike—which in turn informed the contemporary European bourgeois culture and enriched its public spheres. From Europe these images began to travel to Iran via diplomats, merchants, scholars, and so on, who now became the figures of "public intellectuals," namely thinkers and activists who by definition had no organic link with the dominant courts and were integral to the formation of the emerging public sphere in their homeland. Iranians thus began to see themselves reflected and represented in the European public sphere—far beyond their own clime, culture, or control. These images and Iranians' reflections upon them posit the simulacrum of an emerging identity on a global scale beyond Iranian territorial control—this dialectic is my primary concern in this book.

European courts and colonial officers might have used aspects of Persophilia by way of knowledge production in their colonial conquests, but at the same time Persian literature was breathing in a different language in a public sphere, with a bourgeois readership unfamiliar to its history. This experience gave Persian literature a vicarious public space on which to rethink itself. Iranian diplomats, merchants, and intellectuals then became the conduits of taking that very public space and expanding it to cultivate a public sphere in their own homeland. Such pioneering periodicals as *Iranshahr, Kaveh,* and others, mostly published in Europe, also began to expand the European bourgeois public space into their homelands. What is important about this active period of Persophilia, as indeed with Orientalism in general, is that it coincides with what Habermas calls "the structural transformation of the public sphere" in European bourgeois society, and that is precisely what is categorically eclipsed in Edward Said's *Orientalism* and *Culture and Imperialism.* Following his reading of Foucault, Said concentrated on power and knowledge, and thus on the imperialist extension of the European bourgeois societies. But in a different reading of Foucault, the attention should be focused on subject formation, and that subject formation is not entirely or merely *discursive,* as Foucault had detailed, but *societal,* as Habermas has described it for European societies. On the colonial edges of European empires subject formation is equally in that public sphere, and our task is historically to unearth and map it.

CHAPTER ONE

Distant Memories of the Biblical and Classical Heritage

HALFWAY THROUGH MARCH 2013, as Iranians and others attentive to the ancient Persian calendar were getting ready for the celebration of Noruz, an equally ancient relic of the Persian past began its historic U.S. tour. "The 2,600-year-old clay cylinder, almost the size of an American football," BBC reported on the occasion, not missing the chance to bring the ancient Persian relic metaphorically closer to an American icon, "was made on the order of the Persian King Cyrus after he captured Babylon in 539 BC. Referred to by some scholars as the 'first bill on human rights,' the cuneiform inscriptions on the cylinder appear to encourage freedom of worship throughout the Persian Empire and to allow deported people to return to their homelands."[1] The BBC report, citing Julian Raby, the director of the Freer and Sackler Galleries, where the piece was to be on display, made note of the fact that "the Cyrus Cylinder is touring American museums at the time when "relations between the US and Iran are not in their healthiest position."

The organizers and curators of this exhibition in the United States were obviously careful to make the significance of the relic clear to their American audience. The BBC wished to assure them that the country they were now targeting for crippling economic sanctions and perhaps even military strikes was far closer to their sacrosanct certainties than they perhaps knew. "It was the first state model based on diversity and tolerance of different cultures and religions," the BBC quoted Neil MacGregor, director of the British Museum, from which the cylinder had come to America. "But the greatest discovery for many people," MacGregor said, is "the importance of Cyrus to those who wrote the constitution of United States"; and then came the punch line: "The story of Persia, Iran, is part of the story of [the] modern United States."

CYRUS AND THOMAS JEFFERSON

It was not only at the formative period of the American republic that the Persians and their most famous monarch were present. Cyrus the Great was also there to liberate the Jews from slavery. "Although the cylinder does not refer to the Jewish people by name," the BBC report adds, "it has been mentioned in the Book of Chronicles and Book of Ezra that Jews were among those liberated by Cyrus and returned to their land to build the second temple. Mr. MacGregor says these acts, which have been interpreted as allowing freedom of worship and repatriating deported people, have earned Cyrus a reputation as a 'liberal and enlightened monarch.'" So the implications, barely to be lost, were equally clear for the Iran–Israel animosity at the time of this tour. The organizers and curators of the exhibition were quite obviously anxious to make the contemporary relevance of the ancient relic known and appreciated by the public at large.

The link between the ancient Persian monarch and the founding figure of the United States was far deeper than merely symbolic. "In addition to the objects borrowed from the British Museum, a copy of *Cyropaedia,* Xenophon's book on Cyrus, is on display at the exhibition in Washington DC," the BBC reported. Why *Cyropaedia?*

> The book, a bilingual Greek and Latin version published in Europe in 1767, is one of the two copies of Cyropaedia belonging to Thomas Jefferson that is currently held at the Library of Congress. A contemporary of Socrates, Xenophon wrote on how Cyrus ruled a diverse society based on tolerance. The book became popular during the Enlightenment among political thinkers in

Europe and America, including those who drafted the US Constitution in 1787. "In the eighteenth century, that model of religious tolerance based on a state with diverse cultures, but no single dominant religion, became a model for the founding fathers," said Mr. Raby.[2]

The relic and the Persian monarch who occasioned it were thus squarely located not just in the immediate vicinity of the American constitution but deep in the heart of the European Enlightenment and, before it, at the height of the Greek classical age of Socrates, Plato, and Aristotle. The BBC further clarified: "The Cyrus Cylinder was unearthed roughly about 100 years after the United States Declaration of Independence was published. People like Thomas Jefferson, who drafted the Declaration of Independence and became the third president of the United States, had to rely on Xenophon's *Cyropaedia* as a reference for the life and leadership of the Persian king." Mr. Raby further added: "The copy of *Cyropaedia* displayed at the Freer and Sackler Galleries is testament to Jefferson's thorough examination of the book. He pointed out a line in the book that had been crossed out by Jefferson, perhaps because he considered it problematic as it did not appear in earlier versions." The occasion of this display was now used not just to trace the origins of the American Constitution but in fact to rethink the entire history of Europe and the United States:

> Jefferson not only studied the book in detail, but also advised his family to read it, according to Massumeh Farhad, Freer and Sackler's chief curator. Ms. Farhad said Jefferson in a letter had asked his grandson to study Cyropaedia. "He wrote, 'when you start learning Greek, the first book you should read is Cyropaedia,'" Ms. Farhad said. Although a source of inspiration for European and American philosophers, the state model created by Cyrus, based on diverse cultures, but no single dominant religion, was only picked up on in the eighteenth-century United States. "No European state managed to build tolerance into the structure of the state," Mr. MacGregor said. "They either have a state religion like Britain or they are against all religions like France, after the revolution."[3]

To sum it up, the BBC quoted Raby, who said: "What's extraordinary about Cyrus is that he appears as a paragon of princely statesmanship in the two pillars of Western cultures, that is, the Greco-Roman tradition and the Bible."

It was not just the BBC. The print media and the Internet were in fact abuzz with the news and analysis of this momentous occasion when the Cyrus Cylinder came to the United States—an occasion for Americans to be reminded how, "in the sixth century BC, Cyrus the Great of Persia conquered the Middle East and a large part of Asia. Upon his entry into Babylon, he freed the many captive peoples found there. His magnanimous gesture liberated the Jewish nation and entitled her people to return to Jerusalem with their Temple treasures and begin rebuilding Solomon's Temple destroyed by Nebuchadnezzar. The Prophet Isaiah referred to Cyrus as 'anointed by the Lord.'"[4] Nor was it just the Jews who benefited from his magnanimity: "Xenophon, a student of Socrates, wrote The Cyropaedia, a biography of Cyrus which extolled his virtues. Alexander the Great and Julius Caesar carried copies with them. America was directly founded under the benevolent monarch model offered by Cyrus' example. Thomas Jefferson read the Cyropaedia frequently. Commentators anointed the declarations on Cyrus's Calendar to 'the first Bill of Rights.'"[5]

That was not the end of it. The influence was far more global: "In addition to the influence of the *Cyropaedia* on the US founding fathers, its core principles resonate with those of the United Nations. The high-minded concepts fathered by Cyrus in Persia thousands of years ago have found expression in the Universal Declaration of Human Rights. Brought to life by John Peters Humphrey and the UN Commission on Human Rights chaired by Eleanor Roosevelt, the Declaration was adopted by the United Nations on December 10, 1948." From the Hebrews and the Greeks down to the European Enlightenment and the American Constitution to the Universal Declaration of Human Rights, all the cornerstones of "Western Civilization" were now cast under the extended shadow of Cyrus the Great and his "first declaration of human rights" or "Bill of Rights." Conclusion: "The current Middle East fiasco should defer us once again to Cyrus the Great for a history lesson. Cyrus' vision of leadership was a forerunner to the UN 1947 resolution for the future of Palestine. Neil MacGregor, Director of the British Museum stated, 'Cyrus set up a model of how you run a great multinational, multifaith, multicultural society. . . . It left a dream of the Middle East as a unit, and a unit where people of different faiths could live together.'"[6]

WHAT'S CYRUS TO HIM OR HE TO XERXES?

Much of these enthusiastic pronouncements must be attributed to the excitement of the moment about witnessing a magnificent archeological relic. Of course, even in the midst of these celebratory voices, there were those, in both the academic world and the press, who challenged this rosy picture. "The UN made a serious mistake," Klaus Gallas told *Spiegel* magazine. "German experts are now clamoring to dismantle the cylinder's claim to fame. Among them is ancient history professor Josef Wiesehöfer, who derided it . . . as 'a propaganda inscription.' 'It has become a very celebrated document,' he said, 'but Cyrus himself ordered it done, trying to make himself appear righteous. The real king was not more or less brutal than other ancient kings of the near east, like Xerxes, but he was cleverer.' "[7]

Although the gist of the celebrations remained fairly representative of the manner in which Cyrus had been represented and imagined before in much of European history, nevertheless it represented a concerted effort to domesticate the Achaemenid emperor to an American audience—the same American audience who only a few years before had come together to make a film called *300* a global phenomenon, when this evident Persophilia had positively degenerated into an Iranophobia. In its literally monstrous Iranophobia, Zack Snyder's *300* (2007), celebrating the Battle of Thermopylae (480 BC), was a veritable force hell-bent on staging the myth of "the West" as the moral and military redemption of the world.[8]

Ever since its original narration by the Greek historian Herodotus, the Battle of Thermopylae had increasingly accrued a symbolic significance far beyond its original import at the time of its occurrence. Not just at Thermopylae, but also at Marathon and Salamis did the Greeks put up heroic resistance to the imperial expansionism of the Achaemenids. Small skirmishes at the farthest frontiers of the Achaemenid Empire at the time they were fought, Thermopylae, Marathon, or Salamis increasingly assumed ahistorical, prophetic, and even divine significance in furthering the myth of "the West" as the presumed center of the universe and the Christian God's gift to humanity. What Zack Snyder had done in *300* had much deeper roots in European self-centering fantasies.

The increasingly ahistorical significance of these battles between the ancient Greeks and the Achaemenid Empire corresponds squarely with the expansion of European imperialism and its concomitant self-designation as "the West" as the generic rubric under which Europeans launched their global conquest. The origin of the glorification of the Greco-Persian wars in modern history goes back to Michel de Montaigne (1533–1592), who first identified the "glorious defeat of King Leonidas and his men at the defile of Thermopylae" as more glorious than "the fairest sister-victories, which the Sun has ever seen." Appalled by the Turkish domination of Greece, Lord Byron (1788–1824) would later join Montaigne in decrying the defeat: "Earth! Render back from out thy breast/a remnant of our Spartan dead! /Of the three hundred grant but three/To make a new Thermopylae!" Reporting these earliest records of reading the Battle of Thermopylae historically, the British historian Tom Holland says "no wonder, then, that the story of the Persian Wars should serve as founding-myth of European civilization; as the archetype of the triumph of freedom over slavery, and of rugged civic virtue over enervated despotism."[9] From Montaigne to Byron down to Holland himself, the imperial myth of "the West" was firmly contingent on the trope of "the Persian." This evident ambivalence toward "the Persian," a love-hate relationship—loving to hate and hating to love—is perhaps the clearest indication of the uncertainty of the sign of "the West" about itself.

The shared sentiments of Montaigne and Byron about Thermopylae were soon to be taken up by grand officers of the British Empire and expanded to other Greco-Persian wars. John Stuart Mill (1806–1873), for example, spoke on behalf of the entire British colonial character when he said that "the battle of Marathon, even as an event in English history, is more important than the battle of Hastings." Giving philosophical momentum to European colonialism, Hegel (1770–1831) had already chimed in that "the interest of the whole world's history hung trembling in the balance." European Orientalist opera was to have a ball with Xerxes and the battles of Thermopylae and Salamis. Francesco Cavalli (1602–1676) in 1654, Giovanni Bononcini (1670–1747) in 1694, and most famously George Frideric Handel (1685–1759) in 1738 had a great deal of fun setting the Achaemenid king to song and dance. Although in Handel's *Serse* the Persian emperor gets to sing one of the most beautiful arias of the opera, "Ombra mai fu," one need only compare it with Aeschylus's *The Persians* (472 BC) to note the vast difference in how the Greeks themselves saw and empathized with their adversaries and how the Europeans of the baroque period staged their "Persians"—at once assigning their imperial conquest to a distant pedigree while assuming the moral high ground in doing so.

The Orientalist opera became integral to the artistic and ideological makeup of the European bourgeoisie. The more European bourgeois historiography became conscious of its own colonial globalization, the more the minor skirmishes between the Achaemenid Empire, the very first globalized empire the world had ever seen, and the tiny Greek city-states on its borders assumed extravagant, ahistorical, and entirely mythic significance. It seems that the more European imperialism modeled itself on what it called "the Persian Empire," the more it claimed the embattled heritage of a tiny archipelago it had appropriated as its point of civilizational origin. The bourgeois public sphere in which this feat was being staged was simultaneously the bedrock of this imperial fantasy and the modus operandi of its expanded globalizing into the farthest corners of its colonial conquests. "Persian Empire" became the imaginative blueprint for European imperialism as it paradoxically also claimed a small archipelago on the margins of that empire, the Greece of Plato and Aristotle, as the origin of its species. The simultaneous celebration of Xenophon's *Cyropaedia* posits precisely the bedrock of that selfsame paradox.

This sense of imperial projection is no matter of mere speculation, for European imperial identification with the Persian Empire was entirely self-conscious. John Stuart Mill's glorification of the Persian Wars was premonitory of its further celebration by other British colonial officers. It is not accidental at all that Lord Curzon (1859–1925), just before he became viceroy of India, visited the ruins of Xerxes's Palace with a certain sense of dual identity. "It might have flattered the British Empire," as Tom Holland puts it, "to imagine itself the heir of Athens; but it owed a certain debt of obligation to the mortal enemy of Athens, too."[10]

Following in the footsteps of European ahistorical historians, Orientalist storytellers, and British colonial officers, Adolf Hitler positively adored the Battle of Thermopylae. "To the Nazis," Tom Holland has pointed out, "as it had been to Montaigne, Thermopylae was easily the most glorious episode in Greek History." This was not all: "The three hundred who defended the pass," Tom Holland reports, "were regarded by Hitler as representative of a true master-race, one bred and raised for war, and so authentically Nordic that even the Spartans' broth, according to one of the Führer's more speculative pronouncements, derived from Schleswig-Holstein."[11]

Thermopylae has indeed made very strange bedfellows of European historians, poets, philosophers, colonial officers, world conquerors, and mass

murderers. Soon after Montaigne, Lord Byron, Hegel, British colonial officers, and Hitler, it was the turn of the British novelist William Golding
(1911–1993), who in the early 1960s wrote his famous essay on the event,
"The Hot Gates" (1965), in which he gleefully declared: "a little of Leonidas
lies in the fact that I can go where I like and write what I like. He contributed to set us free."[12] "Freedom," by now the sacrosanct term of European
capitalist modernity, was thus firmly rooted in the expansive myth of the
early "Western triumphs" over "Oriental despotism." Take Persia and the
Persians away from this binary, and "the West" would lose itself too.

Reporting all these creative adoptions of the Battle of Thermopylae with
a sense of historical duty, Tom Holland himself is not immune to his own
fantasies. "Had the Athenians lost the Battle of Marathon," the British popular historian firmly believes, "and suffered the obliteration of their city, for
instance, then there would have been no Plato—and without Plato, and the
colossal shadow he cast on all subsequent theologies, it is unlikely that there
would have been an Islam to inspire bin Laden."[13] To be able to write a sentence like that with a straight face is a sublime indication of a powerful
historical fantasy that can both sustain and delude itself.

Instead of dismissing these sorts of phantasmagoric narratives as delu-
sional fantasies, we must place them squarely within the imaginative historiography of an imperial phantasm that had historically invented the myth
of "the West" to posit itself as the universal measure of history. As the decade of Thatcher and Reagan dawned on the world, a new lease on life was
given to the Battle of Thermopylae. Throughout the 1980s, and then the
1990s and beyond, there was a resurgence of books on the battle. The British
historian Ernle Bradford wrote his *Thermopylae: The Battle for the West* (1980);
Steven Pressfield his *Gates of Fire: An Epic Novel of the Battle of Thermopylae*
(1998); and Paul Cartledge his *Thermopylae: The Battle That Changed the
World* (2006)—and it is right here that we need to place Frank Miller's pre-
9/11 comic book *300* (1998), with colors by Lynn Varley, on the basis of
which Snyder made his post-9/11, CGI virtuoso, adaptation of *300* (2007).

INVENTING THE PERSIANS

The production of "Persia" as a European trope on the site of the bourgeois
public sphere and in the course of the Enlightenment modernity and be-

yond was not entirely ex nihilo. Persia and the Persians were not unknown terms and sentiments in European history. They were known facts and projected fantasies from their biblical and classical heritages: from Herodotus (c. 484–425 BC) to Ctesias of Cnidus (died c. 374 BC) to Xenophon (c. 430–354 BC), down to the battles of Salamis, Marathon, and Thermopylae, and in plays like Aeschylus's *Persians,* as well as references in the Bible in Ezekiel, 2 Chronicles, Esther, Daniel, and Ezra, among many other places. Herodotus, Ctesias, and Xenophon had given serious, frivolous, and at times imaginative accounts of Cyrus's life and his empire, while in the Bible he appears as a benefactor to and liberator of the Jews from their Babylonian bondage.

Among all the early Greek sources, Xenophon's *Cyropaedia* has had a particularly enduring though multifaceted history. For millennia it was considered a masterpiece of Greek wisdom literature and was closely studied for its political insights, and yet subsequently "much reviled" for its irrelevance, as the distinguished Xenophon scholar Christopher Nadon puts it in his *Xenophon's Prince: Republic and Empire in the Cyropædia.*[14] "Xenophon," he reports, "was among the most widely read and the *Cyropaedia* considered a masterpiece. When the classical learning revived in Europe, his work was among the first carried from Byzantium."[15] Since the recent revival of interest in *Cyropaedia,* scholars now believe that Xenophon's intention was to provide a historical model for leadership. The *Cyropaedia* has been compared to Plato's *Republic,* or even ranked above it.[16] As such, the text is reported to have been a favorite of Alexander the Great and Julius Caesar. It continued its literary life into the production of the mirrors of princes during the medieval and Renaissance periods until it reached Machiavelli, who read it closely and enthusiastically when writing his *Prince.* From Machiavelli to Montaigne, Montesquieu, Rousseau, Francis Bacon, Jonathan Swift, Benjamin Franklin, and Thomas Jefferson, *Cyropaedia* has had quite an illustrious readership.

Another major work of Xenophon is his *Anabasis,* for generations a major Greek classic of foreign adventure, conquest, and return.[17] In this book we read how Xenophon accompanied "Ten Thousand" Greek mercenaries hired by Cyrus the Younger, who was determined to seize the throne from his brother. Cyrus was killed in the battle and the expedition became an unqualified failure. But Xenophon helped by leading these proverbial ten thousand Greek mercenaries through hostile territory back to safety. The book remained a source of inspiration for generations of European conquerors and adventurers, including Alexander the Great. It was also the source of inspiration for Arrian (AD 92–175) when he was writing *Anabasis Alexandri/The Campaigns of Alexander*,[18] and it was a favorite of T. E. Lawrence ("Lawrence of Arabia," 1888–1935) during the 1916 Arab revolt and the writing of *Seven Pillars of Wisdom*.[19] Between *Cyropaedia* and *Anabasis*, Xenophon projected the image of the doyen of Persianists among the Greeks. To be sure, Herodotus was equally fair and balanced in his treatment of Persians, as is attested to by the fact that he was called a "Philobarbaros" by Plutarch in his critical essay *On the Malice of Herodotus* for not having been sufficiently appreciative of Greek chivalry.[20]

In a magnificent study of Greek tragedies, Edith Hall has shown how the Greek self-definition was in fact instrumental in their invention of the term "barbarians," by which they meant primarily the Persians, their most powerful, palpable, and omnipresent nemesis.[21] Hall successfully demonstrates how, through the attribution to them of such character traits as "incest, polygamy, murder, sacrilege, impalement, castration, female power, and despotism," the Greeks were in effect seeking to invent their own virtues in opposition to this constellation of malice. Based on earlier generations of scholarship going back to R. Hecht's *Die Darstellung fremder Nationlitäten drama der Griechen* (1892), Hall provides a detailed examination of the rise of Greek tragedies at a time when the invention of "the barbarians" coincided with their radical reinterpretations of ancient myths from a decidedly ethnocentric vantage point that reveals the historic moment of "the combined Greek efforts against the Persian empire" and "the consolidation of Athenian democracy and Athenian hegemony in the Aegean."[22]

VERITIES OF ORIENTALIST BEHAVIOR

From this classical and also biblical heritage Europeans eventually began to draw freely and match and mix the ideas found there with whatever they could muster or imagine about Persia—ancient and/or contemporary—in some cases to be able to conquer and control them better, and in some others to borrow and expand metaphors for their own political, moral, and intellectual reasons and purposes. These traces of Persophilia were later resuscitated and recycled in the formation of a renewed interest in things Persian. While the biblical and classical heritage of Persophilia was very much limited to learned circles and the European courts, beginning with the eighteenth century it eventually entered the bourgeois public sphere and became integral to the European social and intellectual movements. It is also in this context that Iranians begin to rediscover their own ancient history in relation and juxtaposition to European history—but this time around in a mode of historiography that was directed at emerging public interests rather than destined for court (dynastic) or clerical (mosque-madrasa) uses and abuses. The Achaemenid dynasty and the figure of Cyrus the Great, of course, were of particular interest to the Pahlavi dynasty (1925–1979) and its sense of monarchical legitimacy, but by then from the ancient to the modern history of the land was the domain of a public sphere equally well disposed to dismantling that legitimacy.

Before it reached Iran proper and deeply affected the formation of its public sphere, this European Persophilia had a history that dovetailed with Orientalism, of which one can offer alternative variations. In a historical context we need to make distinctions among the Orientalism that emerged during and in the immediate aftermath of Muslim Spain (711–1492); the Orientalism that originated in the Vatican during its appeal to the Mongol empire to convert to Christianity as opposed to the Orientalism of the Crusade period; and the period of the East India Company and the formation of colonially instigated Orientalism. As I have argued in my *Post-Orientalism,* these are all different kinds of Orientalism, with different points of origin, disposition, and purpose.

The place of Persophilia in the larger context of Orientalism defines the multivariate character of its attraction in various historical circumstances. In the aftermath of the classical and biblical attention accorded Persia, much of the medieval European focus was directed toward Muslims and Islam, either for competitive theological or philosophical and scientific reasons. This, of course, was because of the Christian disposition of this attention, which had seen Islam as a major theological challenge to itself. Theological, philosophical, and scientific interests went almost hand in hand throughout the medieval period. The Tunisian physician Constantine the African (1017–1087) was chiefly responsible for the translation of scientific sources from Arabic into Latin. Franciscan friar Roger Bacon (c. 1214–1294)—the Doctor Mirabilis of scientific inquiry—was inspired by both Aristotle and Alhazen. Even when a philosopher-physician like Avicenna was studied in Europe as a link with Aristotle, his Persian pedigree was of no particular concern: "In the first third of the thirteenth century, Avicenna's works were no longer studied only in connection with writers of Neoplatonic inspiration such as pseudo-Dionysius, St. Augustine, John Duns Scotus, or Erigena; they were also used in the study of Aristotle. Avicenna's own paraphrases of Aristotle met the needs of the first Aristotle interpreters until superseded by Averroes's literal commentaries. Before the Western Christians became acquainted with Averroes, Avicenna's influence on Latin Aristotelianism was very marked."[23]

Whereas Christian Orientalists were engaged in making translations and writing commentary to refute Islam for scholastic reasons, Jewish scholars were far more neutral in the matter and were doing these translations for a critical expansion of their own scholastic and philosophical knowledge. Moses ibn Tibbon (1240–1283) was concerned with works written by both Arabs and Jews on philosophy, mathematics, astronomy, and medicine. Here Muslims, Jews, and Christians were engaged with each other's work either directly for theological reasons or else for philosophical and scientific purposes with any evident, or not so evident, connections to those theological purposes. Gerard of Cremona (c. 1114–1187) was particularly interested in translating scientific books from Arabic into Latin. This generation of translators was eager to transfer sources of scientific and philosophical importance from both Greek and Arabic into Latin—as perhaps is best evident in Gerard's translation of Ptolemy's *Almagest* from Arabic texts found in Toledo, which remained authoritative until the rise of Copernicus. These attractions and the intellectual movement that they indicate ultimately led to the establishment of chairs in European universities in Arabic and Islamic fields. Ramon Llull (c. 1232–1315), a Majorcan philosopher and Franciscan priest, was chiefly responsible for the establishment in 1311 of teaching positions in Hebrew and Arabic, among other languages.

Beyond this crucial moment of Christian rivalry with the threat that Islam had obviously posed to its universal claim to truth, we have travelers like the Jewish Benjamin of Tudela (1130–1173), who journeyed widely throughout Europe and Asia, and after him Marco Polo (1254–1324), whose travelogue became a major rouser of curiosity about the Orient. This period then connects to the First (1095–1099) and the Second (1147–1149) Crusades, which picks up from the earlier Christian preoccupations with Islam and weds it to the new imperial contexts of the Seljuqids. When Giovanni da Montecorvino (1247–1328), a Franciscan missionary who traveled as far as India, or the Flemish Franciscan missionary William of Rubruck (c. 1220–1293), or Giovanni da Pian del Carpine (1182–1252), one of the first Europeans to visit the Mongol Empire, traveled East and wrote their accounts, "Persia" was once again integral to the European imagination.

It was Benjamin of Tudela who began to bring Persia into fuller focus in European attention beyond its biblical and classical pedigree. While his travels to the East, including to Susa in Persia, were circa 1160, evidently his reports were not published until the sixteenth century.[24] Pietro della Valle visited Persepolis, among other ancient cities, in the seventeenth century, "and was the first to send back to Europe copies of cuneiform texts from Persepolis."[25] Carsten Niebuhr visited Persepolis in 1765 and had begun reading these inscriptions by 1788. By 1802, Georg Grotefend, a German schoolteacher, had "established the values of thirteen Old Persian cuneiform signs."[26] Historians of ancient Persia link these early discoveries directly to the next generation of scholarship spearheaded by Henry Rawlinson, a British colonial officer who is famously known for having been instrumental in deciphering the cuneiform inscription at Behistun, near the city of Kermanshah in Iran. This period of British imperial interest in Iran may be traced back to Sir Thomas Herbert (1606–1682), an English traveler who visited Shah Abbas. But Rawlinson's career is of an entirely different caliber.

Major General Sir Henry Creswicke Rawlinson, 1st Baronet GCB (1810–1895), was a British East India Company army officer turned Orientalist. He was a major strategist of British imperialism in Central and South Asia during the height of its rivalries with the Russian Empire. He personified a perfect specimen of the British colonialist Orientalists, both determined to rule the world and also to understand what it was they were ruling by reading and reciting a corresponding history for their past that determined their present. Here it is noteworthy that, in his *British Orientalists* (1943), A. J. Arberry makes a very crucial point about the origin of the current use of the word "Orientalist." He notes: "it was during the educational controversy in India which was settled by Macaulay's celebrated *Minutes of 1834,* the orientalists were those who advocated Indian learning and literature, while their adversaries, who desired English to be the basis of education in India, were called Anglicists."[27] This early conception of an Orientalist in fact points to a mode of knowledge production about the conquered lands that dovetailed with the imperial incorporations of those lands into the bosom of their new imperial designation. While the Anglicists were calling for an imposition from the top down as to how colonized people were to see themselves—look Indian on the outside, as Macaulay saw it, but think British from the inside— the Orientalists were after something even more sinister—namely, they wanted them to look and think like Indians, Persians, or Arabs, but do so in a manner, recall their own history in a mode, compatible with their desired imperial disposition. So Indians would think Indian thoughts, or Persians Persian thoughts (whatever they might be), but the new epistemic foregrounding of those thoughts were now historically determined to produce subjects of the British Empire.

There are of course all sorts of holes in this desired imperial design. Here is one of them: Rawlinson has left behind a pretty heroic legacy for himself for having hung perilously from a mountain rock in order to read the inscription of Darius. As one historian of ancient Persia has put it: "It was the daring of the Englishman Henry Rawlinson, which was responsible for the complete decipherment of cuneiform. At the total disregard of life and limb he copied the trilingual inscription (Old Persian, Elamite, Akkadian) of Darius at Behistun (Bisitun) between 1837 and 1843. . . . Over a century later George Cameron rechecked Rawlinson's copies in a somewhat less precarious manner—by means of a boatswain's chair and a painter's scaffold."[28]

But the truth is a bit less of a testament to British imperial heroism. Yes indeed, Rawlinson did venture into perilous heights to read the Darius inscription; but at a critical point where he did not dare trail,

> the resourceful Rawlinson was stymied by a looming overhang, and so he resorted to a classic imperial move: he delegated the job to a native. No local tribesman would agree to risk his life for the sake of scholarship, but "a wild Kurdish boy, who had come from a distance, volunteered to make the attempt, and I promised him a considerable reward if he succeeded." . . . the boy squeezed himself up a cleft alongside the overhang, then he inched across the cliff "by hanging on with his toes and fingers to the slight inequalities on the bare face of the precipice, and in this he succeeded, passing over a distance of twenty feet of almost smooth perpendicular rock in a manner which to a looker-on appeared quite miraculous." Once in position, the boy made a paper pressing of the desired passage.[29]

That nameless, faceless, fearless, "wild Kurdish boy" was the link between British imperialist Orientalism and the arduous history of his homeland.

David Damrosch, who uncovered this bit of quite unsavory Orientalist history entirely by serendipity, gives a detailed account of the discovery of the epic of Gilgamesh, which was almost simultaneous with that of Cyrus's Cylinder—a discovery that is coterminous with the attempt of leading British adventurers and Orientalist colonial officers like Rawlinson, who was instrumental in cracking open the mystery of the cuneiform.[30] But what also emerges from Damrosch's study is the interest the British, and by extension the European, public had cultivated about these discoveries. The *London Daily Telegraph* and other newspapers closely followed the excavation that British archeologists, Orientalists, adventurers, and colonial officers were conducting in search of lost biblical sources and ancient empires alike.[31]

Canon George Rawlinson (1812–1902), the younger brother of Sir Henry, soon emerges as one of the greatest Orientalist historians of his age, whose seminal works—including *Five Great Monarchies of the Ancient Eastern World* (1862–1867), *The Sixth Great Oriental Monarchy* (1873), and *The Seventh Great Oriental Monarchy* (1875)—paved the way for subsequent excavations and scholarship.[32] When A. T. Olmstead published his *History of the Persian Empire* in 1948, he lamented the fact that for eighty years no other work of scholarship on the Persian Empire had surpassed Rawlinson's work.[33] A generation before Olmstead, the pioneering American archeologist James Henry Breasted (1865–1935) began commissioning prolonged projects of excavations on ancient Near Eastern sites for the Oriental Institute of the University of Chicago that, in collaboration with other scholars like Ernst Herzfeld and Erich F. Schmidt, eventually resulted in findings that Olmstead considers "spectacular beyond the wildest hopes." These new discoveries eventually led to new assessments of the relation between the Greeks and the Persians—so that a new generation of scholars could now come to terms with the far more integral relationship with the ancient nemesis: "The dawn of a Hellenistic age is sensed in the increasingly deeper penetration of the Greek mercenaries and merchants, by the utilization of Greek physicians, athletes, sculptors, and cooks, by visits of Greek philosophers, literary men, and scientists."[34]

As British (and later American) Orientalists discover these tablets, eventually decipher them, and begin to piece together *Gilgamesh,* read Cyrus's Cylinder, and other relics, in effect they are also demythologizing their own history. They stumble upon epics and empires that complicate their own history as they also complicate other people's histories—and all of these are reflected on the pages of the newspapers in London and other European capitals in which these discoveries are actively and enthusiastically publicized. Through the mechanism of imperialist propagation around the colonial world, these discoveries begin to travel and penetrate other national and transnational public spheres that are now informed by subversive and transformative discoveries.

From these literary and historical discoveries eventually emerged the discipline of "comparative literature" and ideas such as "world literature," which in turn, and not so paradoxically, covered other people's worlds and literatures. *Gilgamesh* and Cyrus's Cylinder were in fact discovered at almost the same time judging from the evidence of the tablets that were produced not too far from each other in 620 BC and 530 BC, respectively. The two discoveries were, then, the subjects of not only vigorous Orientalist scholarship but also of intense public interest, as is evident in the newspaper reports of the discoveries, particularly because of the flood story in *Gilgamesh,* which echoes the biblical story of Noah's flood. Thus, as Europe began nervously to exit the Bible and enter history in its bourgeois public spheres, so did the history of the Mesopotamian empires, and along with them the rest of global history. So by the time Hegel was writing his *Philosophy of History* (1837), his conception of history was informed by centuries after Herodotus and Xenophon and decades before the discoveries of new epics and empires.

THE PRE- AND POST-WESTPHALIAN WORLDS

The transnational disposition of these ancient discoveries and their eventual propagation across the colonial world immediately raise the question of their non-European extensions and the nature of the public sphere they thus actively implicate. Nancy Fraser has made an exceedingly critical extension of Habermas's notion of public sphere. In her "Transnationalizing the Public Sphere: On the Legitimacy and Efficacy of Public Opinion in a Post-Westphalian World" (2007), she has sought to investigate the decoupling of the notion of "public sphere" from the original conceptualization of the idea within the confines of the nation-state.[35] This argument has serious implications for my contentions in this book, where I am tracing the influence and (intended and unintended) consequences of European public sphere far beyond its national boundaries in one European nation-state or another and well into its colonial sites. Fraser's interests are neither contemporaneous with the rise of European public spheres nor particularly attentive (except in passing) to the colonial extension of that space; but nevertheless she raises some very crucial points that facilitate my arguments in this book.

Fraser rightly states, "at least since its 1962 adumbration by Jürgen Habermas, public sphere theory has been implicitly informed by a Westphalian political imaginary: it has tacitly assumed the frame of a bounded political community with its own territorial state."[36] She then extends her critique of the presumption of the sovereignty of nation-states that lies at the conceptual root of Habermas's theory to include even those who have taken legitimate issue with the limitations of his theory: "the same is true for nearly every subsequent egalitarian critique of public sphere theory, including those of feminists, multiculturalists and antiracists." Her own concern with transnational disposition of the public sphere, however, is informed only by more recent developments: "Only very recently, in fact, have the theory's Westphalian underpinnings been problematized. Only recently, thanks to post-Cold-War geopolitical instabilities, on the one hand, and the increased salience of transnational phenomena associated with 'globalization' on the other, has it become possible—and necessary—to rethink public sphere theory in a transnational frame."[37] That may be so, but my contention is actually at the very root of the time of the Peace of Westphalia in 1648 and Habermas's theorization of the public sphere at the height of European bourgeois ascendancy in the eighteenth and nineteenth centuries, wherein the colonial extensions of those public spheres were of critical consequence. Fraser's concern, however, is rightly placed with the potentially emancipatory disposition of the notion of public sphere:

> Yet these same phenomena force us to face the hard question: is the concept of the public sphere so thoroughly Westphalian in its deep conceptual structure as to be unsalvageable as a critical tool for theorizing the present? Or can the concept be reconstructed to suit a post-Westphalian frame? In the latter case, the task would not simply be to conceptualize transnational public spheres as actually existing institutions. It would rather be to reformulate the critical theory of the public sphere in a way that can illuminate the emancipatory possibilities of the present constellation.[38]

My concern here is not to "theorize the present," for I believe that long before the so-called post-Westphalian world the actual Westphalian world itself was anything but limited to the nation-state, and that the already globalized circulation of capital, labor, raw material, and market had far-reaching extensions for European imperialism and had paved the way for the European bourgeois public sphere to have colonial consequences.

What is critical in Fraser's essay is the first of her three objectives—namely, her explicating "the implicit Westphalian presuppositions of Habermas' public sphere theory" and showing how "these have persisted in its major feminist, anti-racist and multicultural critiques." The other two objectives—that is, identifying "several distinct facets of transnationality that problematize both traditional public sphere theory and its critical counter-theorizations," and proposing "some strategies whereby public sphere theorists might begin to respond to these challenges," thereby repoliticizing "public sphere theory, which is currently in danger of being depoliticized"—are all noteworthy but entirely presentist, for in effect she takes it for granted that at the time of Westphalia, or perhaps even at the time of Habermas's theorization, Westphalian thinking was valid, but not anymore. My contention is that neither at the time of the Peace of Westphalia in 1648 nor a fortiori at the time of Habermas's theorization in 1962 was the unit of nation-state a valid conceptual cornerstone of the idea of public sphere, if we have a more organic conception of the colonial extensions of capitalist modernity in mind.

Because of these critical limitations, although her ambition was to open up Habermas's theory to what she calls a "Post-Westphalian world," much of Fraser's discussion remains still very Eurocentric, until she cites a critical constellation of studies that mark the crucial point that "publicity has been transnational at least since the origins of the interstate system in the 17th century." It is here that she notices, by "citing Enlightenment visions of the international 'republic of letters' and cross-national movements such as abolitionism and socialism, not to mention world religions and modern imperialism, this camp [of the scholars she cites] contends that the Westphalian frame has always been ideological, obscuring the inherently unbounded character of public spheres," conceding "that metropolitan democracy arose in tandem with colonial subjection, which galvanized transnational flows of public opinion."[39] This last point is very germane to my thinking in this book, for it is right here that the production of public sphere in Europe, in both literary and institutional forms, begins to implicate the larger trans-national public spheres across the colonial and postcolonial world.

What Fraser's insightful essay disregards, for it is not in the purview of her immediate concerns, is the simultaneous impact of the European bourgeois public sphere on the colonial site in an extended and organic manner through various mechanisms of transference, from the presence of the colonial officers on that site to the diplomats, merchants, or students who traveled to Europe. Fraser and her colleagues are all concerned with Westphalia versus post-Westphalia dichotomy. I am concerned with the colonial shadow of Westphalia, what the European bourgeois public sphere both enabled and overshadowed.

THE FLOATING CYLINDER

The European discovery of ancient Persia, eventually framed within Hegel's philosophy of history, in effect ushered Iran into colonially mitigated modern history. For centuries an imperial imaginary that had based itself on the Muslim conquest of the Sassanid Empire had been the framing trope of the history of Persians, their kings and dynasties. Effectively combining myths, legends, and histories from time immemorial down to the Sassanids and then the Muslim invasion, and from there on to Islamic history, generations of Iranians had seen and placed themselves within successive imperial settings. The European discovery of ancient Persian history, from the Elamites down to the Achaemenids, systematized a teleological history for Iranians that constructed a different façade to their historic self-consciousness, which included but was no longer limited to their "Islamic" history.

The effect of European historiography, revelatory and iconoclastic to Europeans themselves as to others, was that, through it, Persia ultimately entered Hegel's philosophy of history almost at the same time that Iranians had begun the process of their postcolonial nation building. No longer in possession of any imperial history except in their past, they were deeply engaged in manufacturing a postcolonial national history, effectively imagined and mapped out by the public intellectuals (scholars, diplomats, journalists, artists, literati, etc.) who were emerging upon their public space. The project was not entirely under the spell of the European bourgeois historiography or its adaptation of the Hegelian philosophy of history, for soon, under the influence of Soviet Orientalism, the concepts of "*Khalq*/Masses" and their "*Qiyams*/Revolts" were crafted and introduced into Iranian historiography. So, as Europeans were consolidating their historical periodization of ancient, medieval, and modern, Iranians found "Persia" (and with it "Persophilia") right at the heart of the European imaginary, now exercising a not entirely unchallenged hegemonic power in modes and manners of knowledge production. That mode of knowledge production was dialogical; for as the Hegelian philosophy of history placed Persia on the teleological linearity of the unfolding historical *Geist,* at once integral and yet alien to it, Soviet Orientalism narrated a revolutionary history that emphasized the urban poor and the impoverished peasantry as the engines of history. The two themes then came together to inform and animate the literary and historical imagination of the place of "Persia" in the modernity of their postcolonial history.

From the depiction of Persia and the Persians in the Bible, down to the classical age of the Greeks and the Romans, and subsequently through the medieval and Renaissance periods, these varied and colorful pictures eventually came together in the bourgeois public sphere of the eighteenth and nineteenth centuries for a whole new gestation. As is best evident in the paradoxical celebration of Greco-Persian wars from Marathon to Thermopylae, the image of the Persian Empire was adapted for the self-projection of European imperialism—so that the Achaemenids were in fact assimilated into the Romans as the world-historic model of imperialism. Persophilia thus provided a template for imperial domination and the structural expansion of the bourgeois public sphere—from which location they then traveled to Iran and resuscitated its imperial age and narratively posited it decidedly against the Islamic period, despite the fact that the transition from the pre-Islamic to the Islamic period was far more integrated and organic. That drastic bifurcation becomes definitive to the Qajars, but more so in the Pahlavi period. Through European Orientalism, and Persophilia in particular, the "Ancient History/*Tarikh-e Bastan*" decidedly enters Iranian historiography to bifurcate it and through that bifurcation to exacerbate and agitate that space by doing an epistemic violence to it by projecting a false opposition between being an Iranian and being a Muslim; yet precisely through that epistemic violence it inevitably both enabled and enriched the public reason it set in motion.

When we look at the Cyrus Cylinder today,[40] we are witness to multiple levels of varied and divergent signification of what it meant to be a "Persian" in the European classical age, in the time of the Hebrew Bible, during the European Enlightenment, in the eras of American constitutionalism, British imperialism, American imperialism, and ultimately when Persophilia finally came to meet its darker side in Iranophobia. The sojourn of the Cyrus Cylinder in the United States during a particularly tense relationship between the two countries brought together the history of that artifact and what it has represented. A relic of the Persian Empire had now come to the beleaguered heart of the American empire at a time when a succession of social movements in the Arab and Muslim worlds had come to meet equally critical social uprisings in the United States and Europe, and deep into Brazil and the rest of Latin America. Discovered in 1879 by Hormuzd Rassam (1826–1910), an Iraqi archeologist as well as a native Assyrian and Christian Assyriologist, British diplomat, and traveler, the artifact became a floating signifier of meaning and meandering. The late shah of Iran Mohammad Reza Shah Pahlavi tried to bank on the Cyrus Cylinder to extend the myth of his own legitimate ties to ancient history—a feat he tried to authenticate via the celebration of the 2500 Persian monarchy. The icon remained so powerful that, even in the aftermath of the Islamic revolution in Iran, the Islamic republic was very particular to keep its claim on the object.[41] Spun around the Cylinder was the misty swirl of facts and fantasies enabling public spaces upon which private interests and political subjection kept reproducing and confounding each other.

CHAPTER TWO

Montesquieu, the Bourgeois Public Sphere, and the Rise of Persian Liberal Nationalism

THROUGHOUT THE EIGHTEENTH and nineteenth centuries, leading European philosophers, literati, artists, composers, and scholars emerged in their bourgeois public spheres to create the figure of "public intellectual" and thus to lead social and intellectual movements that, in the form of the Enlightenment modernity, would radically redefine European social and moral history. These movements eventually had normative and structural repercussions for the formation of counterpart public spheres on varied colonial sites, including but obviously not limited to Iran. These towering figures were pursuing their own critical projects, moved by the transformative spirit of their age, as they formed an intellectual trajectory domestic to their own European domains—and yet they had a spatial designation for things they considered "Persian," and that very space—real or imaginative—later became the conduit for the structural transformation of their and other bourgeois public spheres, not just in their own European homelands, but, by the force of the imperial machinery that embraced and defined them, all around the world. Montesquieu's *Persian Letters* (1721) was one such critical text—integral to the European Orientalist Renaissance—which would later coincide with the height of Napoleon's interest in Iran in the early Qajars period.

Despite much deeper and more ancient roots, the modern origin of the European interest in things Oriental as the framing of their own issues, concerns, and predilections goes back at least to the eighteenth century— namely, precisely when Montesquieu (1689–1755) was writing his *Persian Letters.* "During the eighteenth century the oriental fairytale became the popular frame work for contemporary fiction," reports Sarah Searight in her study of *The British in the Middle East* (1969).[1] She further adds that "the difference between eighteenth-century pseudo-oriental and nineteenth century oriental romances . . . was that the former concentrated on the moral content of the tale to the detriment of the oriental background; later writers used all the available orientalia to produce as authentic a tale as possible regardless of the moral, except for the convention of the triumph of good over evil."[2] Though the line between the "pseudo-oriental" and the "oriental" might not be as clear-cut as Sarah Searight suggests, still, it is in this context that Edward Pococke (junior) translated Ibn Tufayl's (c. 1105– 1185) *Hay ibn Yaghdhan* into Latin, from which it eventually found its way into English, which in turn is believed to have reached Daniel Defoe when he was writing his *Robinson Crusoe* (1719), just two years before Montesquieu's *Persian Letters.*

European Orientalism progressed apace from Arabic, Indian, Chinese, Japanese, and Persian into French, English, or German and other languages, and included the eventual incorporation of *Arabian Nights* into European fantasies as the epitome of the genre. It is in this context that Sarah Searight then reports: "France set the fashion for adapting the oriental tale to satire on contemporary society; Voltaire wrote *Zadig* and Montesquieu *Lettres Persanes.*"[3] This model did not remain limited to the French, for Montesquieu's *Persian Letters* "was imitated by Lord Lyttelton in *Persian Letters,* in 1735, in which the Persian Selim in London writes letters to his friend Mirza in Isfahan, satirizing English society and politics."[4] The trope of non-Europeans visiting Europe and writing critical letters back home to their compatriots continued with Oliver Goldsmith (c. 1730–1774) publishing *The Citizen of the World* (1760–1761), in which we find a Chinese traveler in England, Lien Chi Altangi, commenting critically on British society. Our reading of Montesquieu's *Persian Letters* must be located in the social, literary, and cultural context of this particular episode in European intellectual history as it grows in the fertile soil of the effervescent bourgeois public sphere. Yes, there is a common element of Orientalism to all these constellations of texts, but that is not the whole story, or even the most important part of it. What is far more, or at least equally, critical is the place of these tropes in the social and intellectual movements, with far-reaching consequences in the European and soon transnational public spheres—a fact left theoretically neglected by both Schwab and Said, as well as all their admirers and detractors.

There were, of course, many real-life Persians who visited Europe either from Iran or from India and wrote extensive travelogues of their visits—these texts were later instrumental in opening up the public sphere in their own country and cultivating the figure of the public intellectual.[5] The point here is the manner in which European Persophilia created a vicarious public sphere for things Persian in a European domain, and for European purposes at once social, political, intellectual, and literary. The colonial extensions of that sphere were then instrumental in facilitating the subsequent generations of Iranian public intellectuals reimagining themselves and their homeland in the larger, global public sphere.

THE *PERSIAN LETTERS* IN FRENCH

Montesquieu initially published his *Persian Letters* in Holland in 1721 and under a pseudonym. The book became an instant success. Scholars of Montesquieu credit this and his subsequent volume, *The Spirit of the Laws* (1748), for having had a lasting influence on the French Revolution and all subsequent constitutional revolutions in Europe, and particularly across the sea in the writing of the American constitution. Though Montesquieu wrote his most famous treatise *The Spirit of the Laws* a few years later, the significance of the former has now been thoroughly reconsidered and much appreciated. And although one might consider *Persian Letters* more as a frivolous and jovial precursor of *The Spirit of the Laws,* it nevertheless announces the kinds of political thinking that would later result in the famous separation of power into the legislative, executive, and judiciary branches of government that became a hallmark of liberal democracies. After the publication of these two seminal books, Montesquieu spent the rest of his life writing on the decline of the Roman Empire and searching widely and variedly the causes of tyranny in Europe. Montesquieu, Voltaire, and Rousseau were the three instrumental thinkers of the French Revolution who collectively constitute the moral and philosophical imagination of European political modernity.

The narrative trope of *Persian Letters* is in the genre of the epistolary novel and focuses on two Persian aristocrats, Usbek and Rica, who are traveling through Europe and write back to their compatriots in Isfahan about the strange behavior of the French. As one scholar of Montesquieu summarizes the character of these two Persians: "Rica, the younger of the two principal writers, is good-humored, sarcastic, and represents the lighter side of Montesquieu's nature. His lively intellect makes him a keen observer; his youth and health enable him to go everywhere, see everybody, and experience everything. . . . Usbek is older, graver, given to meditation and reflection. Although from his earliest youth a courtier, he has remained uncorrupted. As he could not flatter, his sincerity made him enemies, and brought upon him the jealousy of the ministers."[6]

The epistolary novel had become quite popular at the time of Montesquieu, as evident in such prominent samples of the genre as Samuel Richardson's *Pamela, or Virtue Rewarded* (1740), Jean-Jacques Rousseau's *Julie, ou la nouvelle Héloïse* (1761), Laclos's *Les Liaisons dangereuses* (1782), Goethe's *Die Leiden des jungen Werthers* (1774), or Hölderlin's *Hyperion* (1797). The instant success of Montesquieu's *Persian Letters* and his having opted to write it in this particular type of narrative might be attributed to the popularity of the genre at the time of its publication. The popularity of such genres among the reading public cannot be ignored in any assessment of their Orientalism, for that popularity points to what Habermas calls a "literary public sphere" and "the interiorization of an audience-oriented subjectivity," as David Randall calls it,[7] and not merely the colonial and imperial implications of those genres.

The two Persian travelers keep writing letters to their harem back in Isfahan, and as they receive news of the intrigues in their own inner quarters they also expostulate on the strange behaviors of the French, giving Montesquieu ample opportunity to use the exotic setting of the Oriental harem as the backdrop for the equally outlandish behavior of European monarchs and the pope. Though on the surface all these harem references amount to supercilious Orientalist clichés that Montesquieu obviously used to give his narrative something of an exotic authenticity for his European audience, paramount in his book is his satirical tone, in which, as one of his

English translators and commentators C. J. Betts puts it, everything is seen "through the mock-innocent but unforgiving eyes of the two Persians."[8]

There is of course an alternative way of reading Montesquieu's harem references. He goes through a whole gamut of French society and its institutions of power, from religious to political to cultural to academic, and pokes fun at them, criticizes their vanity, their consistently missing the point just about everything. Betts rightly informs us that, because of Montesquieu's reputation as a political philosopher we may have a tendency to read his *Persian Letters* more in the spirit of *The Spirit of the Laws*—in both of which he detects a common fear of despotism. This despotism is feared in France but purportedly practiced in the Persia of Montesquieu's imagination, but it is precisely the selfsame fear that will later inform his trademark theory of the separation of power. He does present Persia as the model of fearful despotism and tyranny. But in effect he is also using this "Persia" as the simulacrum of France and by extension Europe, for because of the censorial policies that governed the book trade under Louis XIV (1638–1715) his criticism of the monarch throughout *Persian Letters* is quite mute and circumspect. So Montesquieu's Persia is in effect France—and thus his Persian harem the European aristocratic courts. In letter 37, for example, we read Usbek writing to Ibben, at Smyrna: "The king of France is old; we have not one instance in our history, of a monarch who reigned so long. He is said to possess to a very great degree the art of making himself obeyed; he governs with the same spirit, his family, his court, and his kingdom; he hath often been heard to say, that of all the governments in the world, that of the Turks, or of our august Sultan, pleased him best; so highly does he esteem the politics of the East!"[9]

The curious balance between the two Persians' preoccupation with their European observations, punctuated by their repeated letters back home about their harem intrigues, has thus rightly led John Davidson to believe that the Persian harem is in fact a metaphor for the French aristocracy: "The story of the revolt of Usbek's harem, though belonging to a style long out of fashion, is skillfully told, and will be found to interest the most prudish reader in spite of some disgust. The forsaken wives, the long-winded pedantic eunuchs, are all French, of course, French people of the Regency; and Usbek himself is as jealous as a petit-maître. As for the story of Anais, and the sexual love of brother and sister in 'Apheridon and Astarte,' all that need be said of them is that they are characteristic of the mood of the Regency."[10]

So as we rush to detect Montesquieu's Orientalism we may also wish to pause to see how the use of a foreign frame of reference in his Persophilia also allows him to make the familiar in Europe foreign. It is possible that Montesquieu meant his *Persian Letters* as a test of his audience to see how they would respond to these sorts of critical ideas when they were presented frivolously in foreign garbs before he developed them, decades later, in the more serious and theoretical tone of his *The Spirit of the Laws*.

Two prominent French travelers have been identified as the primary sources of Montesquieu's knowledge of his contemporary Persia: "From the travels of Chardin and Tavernier, Montesquieu derived his knowledge of Persia. To Chardin he is particularly indebted, not only for the background, but for his theory of despotism and his theory of climates."[11] John Chardin (1643–1713) was a French jeweler and traveler whose travelogue of Persia is one of the earliest modern European sources of information about the country. Jean-Baptiste Tavernier (1605–1689) was a French diamond merchant and traveler famous for his travelogue about the East. We also know of two other French travelers, two diplomats, Lalain and Laboulaye, whom in 1665 during the reign of Louis XIV his Intendant of Finances, Jean-Baptiste Colbert, had dispatched to Isfahan as leaders of a delegation to cultivate commercial relations with the Safavids.[12] It is also possible that Montesquieu may have known of certain Persian travelers and diplomats in France and Europe at this time.[13] But what is certain is that the team of two Persians visiting France has definite historical antecedents of two Frenchmen visiting Persia—which fact makes the allegorical self-reflection of the narrative trope of *Persian Letters* even more poignant.

What Montesquieu thought of his *Persian Letters* in the light of posterity we may never know—but we may have a clue: "He found his daughter one day with the 'Persian Letters' in her hand. 'Let it alone, my child,' he said. 'It is a work of my youth unsuited to yours.'"[14]

AKHONDZADEH AND A TRANSNATIONAL PUBLIC SPHERE

In his own immediate context, Montesquieu's *Persian Letters* contributed significantly and was in fact integral to the rise of European Enlightenment, but later he and his intellectual legacy were instrumental in the emergence of Francophone liberalism among the Iranian public intellectuals that during

the Constitutional period (late nineteenth and early twentieth centuries) culminated in the moral and imaginative disposition of poets like Iraj Mirza,
Mirzadeh Eshqi, Aref Qazvini, Ali Akbar Dehkhoda, and ultimately to the
interest of Nima Yushij in French romanticism and the rise of modernist Persian poetry.

Closer to Montesquieu's own time, Mirza Fath Ali Akhondzadeh (1812–
1878), a leading Iranian dramatist, literary critic, essayist, and above all
public intellectual, was deeply affected by Montesquieu's writing, and his
own *Maktubat-e Kamal al-Dowleh/Correspondences of Kamal al-Dowleh* is believed to have been written most noticeably under the influence of French
Enlightenment thinkers—not just Montesquieu but also Voltaire and Rousseau. Akhondzadeh and his contemporary Jalal al-Din Mirza (1827–1872)
became instrumental in the rise of Iranian liberal nationalism, promoting
the necessary simplification of Persian prose and articulating a kind of nationalist historiography that went all the way back to pre-Islamic Iran and
became virulently anti-Arab by way of an emotive demarcation of Iranian
territorial and cultural nationalism.

Born and raised in Azerbaijan, Akhondzadeh emerged as one of the most
prominent public intellectuals of the Constitutional period in Iran. He was
educated in the region and received thorough exposure to progressive Russian thought in Tbilisi, where he mastered Russian (among other languages).
But he was also profoundly influenced by French and English liberalism and
became widely involved in the rise of Iranian liberal nationalism. Montesquieu's *The Spirit of the Laws* (1748) and Rousseau's *Social Contract* (1762)
had a strong impact on his thinking. He specifically mentions John Stuart
Mill as the source of his thought.

In his *Maktubat-e Kamal al-Dowleh* Akhondzadeh's criticism of despotism shows the direct influence of his reading of Montesquieu and others.
His use of such terms as "despotism," "civilization," "liberal," and "parlia-
ment" in their original French and simply transliterated into Persian is a clear
indication of the entry of these concepts into Persian prose directly under
the influence of Montesquieu and other French Enlightenment thinkers.

It is impossible to exaggerate the significance of Akhondzadeh in the production of the public sphere and as a central and towering figure within it
in the decades leading up to the Constitutional Revolution of 1906–1911.
He is famous for having tried to change the Persian alphabet in a manner
that would facilitate a more public form of literacy. He was a fierce advocate

of public education. His nationalism was in fact an extension of his notion of "nation" as the public sphere. His fascination with ancient Iranian history was a typical bourgeois intellectual's attempt to generate a long genealogy for that public sphere. His anti-Arabism must also be understood in the light of his position against the clerical class and its exclusive claim on the public sphere as an extension of the mosque. He was a rationalist through and through, highly critical of his contemporary Islamist thinkers. He was adamant to separate politics from religion, just like Montesquieu, and was a pioneer in advocating for women's rights and their participation in public affairs. He was also a pioneer dramatist and literary critic, promoting these fields as the domain of the active production of new forms of public knowledge as distinct from those generated both at the court and at the mosque.

According to Fereydun Adamiyat, the leading scholar of nineteenth-century intellectual history in Iran, the intellectual career of Akhondzadeh can be divided into three distinct phases: the first when he was writing socially conscious plays and fiction; the second when he was campaigning to change the Persian alphabet; and the third when he finally turned to critical political writings.[15] Akhondzadeh is recognized as the pioneering champion of nationalism as a political ideology in the Qajar and Ottoman territories. *Maktubat-e Kamal al-Dowleh/Correspondences of Kamal al-Dowleh* is the most mature and widely celebrated work of this latter period, in which he launched his critical thinking against the two institutions of monarchic despotism and clerical legalism; in between the two he wished to carve out a new public sphere ruled by reason and unencumbered by religious or political despotism and absolutism.

Maktubat-e Kamal al-Dowleh (1863) is written in the form of four letters, which Akhondzadeh attributes to a fictitious Indian prince writing from Tabriz to his Iranian friend Jalal al-Dowleh in Egypt—thus in effect crossing over the Indian, Ottoman, and the Arab worlds in embracing radically reformist ideas. Three of these letters are written by Kamal al-Dowleh, the Indian prince, a fictive son of Aurangzeb, and the fourth letter is the response that Jalal al-Dowleh writes to him from Egypt. The three letters of Kamal al-Dowleh are in praise of liberal democracy, while Jalal al-Dowleh's response is critical of his friend. Akhondzadeh thus attributed the liberal ideas to an Indian prince and the defense of the status quo to an Iranian—and "the West" is nowhere in sight. Did Akhondzadeh write this book in the epistolary mode under the influence of Montesquieu's *Persian Letters?* Probably not, but there is an uncanny similarity between his two authors' exchanges in *Maktubat* and those of the author of *Persian Letters* and most definitely of the more famous *The Spirit of the Laws.*

Discussing the full dimensions of Akhondzadeh's liberal nationalism, Adamiyat provides an extended analysis of the roots of nationalism in this period and seeks to distinguish its origin from its European vintage, tracing the roots of the word "*mellat*/nation" or "*vatan*/homeland" to 1848 when they were used by the reformist prime minister Amir Kabir; but he gets lost in the midst of trying to generate a premodern Iranian origin for it as opposed to the extension of a European conception, whereas it is most obvious from Akhondzadeh's writings that at this point the conception of *vatan* is clearly carved somewhere between the two institutions of monarchy and clergy—namely, that which we would later consider the "public sphere." Akhondzadeh's criticism of Islam and admiration for Zoroaster and Zoroastrianism are precisely a reimagining of a prolonged "national" history dismembered from its Islamic period. This flawed reading of both Akhondzadeh and his liberal nationalism has underlined his loudly racialized overtones and underread his far more serious constitution of a public sphere between the incompetent monarchy that ruled Iran and the Shi'i clericalism that competed with it.

In a protracted way, and particularly through Akhondzadeh's influence, what Montesquieu had started in his *Persian Letters* (1721) and subsequently brought to completion in *The Spirit of the Laws* (1748) became the threshold of an enduring impact on the colonial and postcolonial history of nation building in Iran. One might even reverse the order of his historic significance and suggest that it was with his *Persian Letters* that Montesquieu became a prominent public intellectual and prepared his European and subsequently his American audiences for his globally celebrated *The Spirit of the Laws,* which became the founding document of the French republic, other European liberal democracies, and the drafting of the Constitution of the United States.

Montesquieu was doing in France and Europe in the middle of the eighteenth century what Akhondzadeh and his contemporaries were doing in the middle of the nineteenth century in Iran and central Asia—namely, carving a space in between monarchic despotism and clerical absolutism and calling it *Vatan*/Homeland, nation, people, and so on. What that designation projects is nothing more than the public sphere with a politically powerful and publicly appealing term. It is in this context that Akhondzadeh's going back to ancient Iranian history is for the same reason: his anti-Arabism is his anticlericalism; and his advocacy of women's rights is to bring and include them in and thus enlarge the public sphere.

Montesquieu's passing Persophilia is the link between social and intellectual movements in Europe and similar developments in Iran and environs, both as extended expressions of the rise and consolidation of transnational public spheres. While Said's conception of Orientalism is politically potent, as he indeed meant it to be, we also need to think socially. In a critical passage in *Orientalism* Said observes: "The Orient that appears in Orientalism, then, is a system of representations framed by a whole set of forces that brought the Orient into Western learning, Western consciousness, and later, Western empire. If this definition of Orientalism seems more political than not, that is simply because I think Orientalism was itself a product of certain political forces and activities."[16] Indeed it was—but it was also a cultural (Schwab) and social phenomenon, and it was the critical component of social and intellectual movements that had far-reaching and even unintended consequences beyond its political parameters.

THE PARAPHRASED PERSIANS

Soon after the publication of Edward Said's *Orientalism* (1978), a number of books appeared with the word "Occidentalism" in their title and with a decidedly anti-Saidian position in their arguments—among them James G. Carrier, ed., *Occidentalism: Images of the West* (1995); Mohamad Tavakoli-Targhi's *Refashioning Iran: Orientalism, Occidentalism and Historiography* (2001); and Ian Buruma and Avishai Margalit's *Occidentalism: The West in the Eyes of Its Enemies* (2005). The most theoretically serious among these books (and pertinent to my concerns here) was Tavakoli-Targhi's *Refashioning Iran.*[17] But almost a decade before the publication of this book, M. R. Ghanoonparvar had published another important book, *In a Persian Mirror: Images of the West and Westerners in Iranian Fiction* (1993) that had addressed similar issues, though with a theoretical position not patently anti-Saidian.

Ghanoonparvar's *In a Persian Mirror* is a groundbreaking work in which he gives an exhaustive review of Persian literature in the nineteenth and twentieth centuries that deals with the image of "the West" among Iranians.[18] His book exposes the sort of critical perspectives on "the West" that have existed in the Iran of the last two centuries. Ghanoonparvar's reading is rightly directed toward the dialectic of *self* and the *other* that this fabrication of "the West" entails. But what his study exposes more than anything else is the literary manifestation of a larger colonial context in which Iranians, like most other colonized people, have found themselves on the receiving end of an apparently omnipotent "Western" power. Ghanoonparvar's project is not to give any anti-Saidian argument but to demonstrate how the proposition "the West" had in fact created a binary of *self* and *other* in the formation of social personae, a perfectly solid and reasonable argument.

Almost a decade later, Mohamed Tavakoli-Targhi published an equally important book, *Refashioning Iran: Orientalism, Occidentalism and Historiography* (2001), in which he "challenges the conventional national histories of Iran, which often depict modernity as an historical epoch inaugurated by 'Westernizing' and state-centralizing reforms." He further explains: "By viewing modernity as a global process that engendered various strategies of self-fashioning, this study seeks to break away from the dehistoricizing implications of 'Westernization' theories that are predicated upon the temporal assumption of non-contemporaneity of European and non-European societies."[19] Rightly criticizing what he calls "self-Orientalizing rhetorical arguments," Tavakoli-Targhi took upon himself the worthy task of seeking "an alternative understanding of modernity."

While the notion of "multiple modernities," articulated theoretically perhaps best by S. N. Eisenstadt,[20] is perfectly plausible and has had a wide range of literature, Tavakoli-Targhi's assumption of the existence of an institutional ability to return the European gaze is historically inaccurate and theoretically flawed. He is partially correct that, at a certain stage, Orientalism "was not a discourse of domination, but a reciprocal relation between European and Indian scholars"[21]—and as I have already argued in my *Post-Orientalism,* the very phenomenon of Orientalism is much in need of historicization. Tavakoli-Targhi, too, believes, "the challenge of postcolonial historiography is to re-historicize the processes that have been concealed and ossified by the Eurocentric accounts of modernity."[22] But it is precisely this task of historicization at which he fails. As I have demonstrated in *Post-Orientalism,* the phenomenon that both Said and Schwab theorized in a specific period of European cultural and imperial history has had a much longer and deeper history, both prior to that imperial phase and in the aftermath of its transmutation into area studies and think tanks.[23]

The assumption of Persianate "Eurology," or that Iranians or Indians are gazing back at European women (Tavakoli-Targhi's favorite example) is equally flawed because it (just like his notion of Occidentalism) conflates, confuses, and thus glosses over the declining moments of the Mughal empire (1526–1857) and levels it with the rising moments of the European imperialism. There are sexual fantasies about all other cultures produced at the heart of all empires—including the Arab and Persianate empires. Joseph Massad's groundbreaking *Desiring Arabs* discusses in detail all sorts of sexual fantasies about "the Persians" in the dominant Arab cultures from medieval to modern times.[24] All empires produce both knowledge and fantasy about the world like the Mughals, the Safavids, and the Ottomans about Europe, and, before them all the way back to the earliest formations of Muslim empires, as is perhaps best evident in Alberuni's *India,* a formidable project of knowledge production about India from the vantage point of a conquering Muslim army. The question is the declining power of these empires in producing hegemonic knowledge coinciding with the rising power of European imperial cultures and their abilities to produce self-universalizing knowledge—this is the central theoretical point (and historical fact) that Tavakoli-Targhi categorically misses.

Even more flawed is Tavakoli-Targhi's notion of "homeless texts" of Persianate modernity. As I have extensively demonstrated in *The World of Persian Literary Humanism* (2012), central to defining the literary and historical narrative of the last fourteen hundred years is the imperial context in which they were produced—and there should not be an iota of doubt that the Persian texts produced in India during the Mughal empire are Indian: they belong to the Indian literary and cultural production as another Indian language. So they are not "homeless." They are perfectly at home in India. Tavakoli-Targhi's assumptions are in effect the victims of his own criticism of ahistorical nationalism, which he sets out to criticize and dismantle but ironically ends up corroborating and authenticating.

The critique of Eurocentric modernity is a perfectly fine and worthy project, but it in effect takes "the West" and its narrative tautology for granted. However it tries to place it in its global context in effect—and paradoxically—it ends up cross-authenticating it, whereas the point is precisely the opposite, to deauthenticate the myth of the "West" and historicize the colonial condition that had generated and sustained it, thus seeing it as the sign of one among many successive empires or imperial adventures not too different from any other. Opting for Foucault's "heterotopia," as Tavakoli-Targhi says he does, rather than "utopia," is all good and well, but the more such heterotopias are imagined in terms domestic to that utopia, the more paradoxically he ends up reauthenticating the very Eurocentrism he wants to displace.

The central question of Montesquieu's *Persian Letters,* contrary to what Tavakoli-Targhi says on another similar occasion, is not "How can one be Persian?"[25] This is an entirely false, superficial, and flawed characterization of the book, a clear indication that one did not actually read it but is regurgitating worn-out clichés. The Iranian traveler Mohammad Riza Bayk (d. 1717), who visited France in 1715–1716, may or may not have been known to Montesquieu when he was writing his book. But that is an entirely irrelevant question, for it misreads the location of *Persian Letters* in the context of Montesquieu's own work and in the general contour of European Persophilia (or, for that matter, Sinophilia or Indophilia)[26] and what its function was, not merely on the political (Edward Said) or cultural (Raymond Schwab) level, but, far more important, on the *social* and *intellectual* planes.

Where exactly in *Persian Letters* does the phrase "How can one be Persian?" occur? It is the very last sentence of letter number 30, written by Rica to Ibben at Smyrna. It is a satirical missive composed expressly to expose the pedantic provincialism of Parisians and the oddity of seeing a Persian among them.[27] The first sentence that in fact precedes this one and is equally, indeed even more important is "Il faut avouer qu'il a l'air bien persan. Chose admirable! /You have got to admit, he does really look Persian. Admirable!"—meaning that he corresponded to the caricatural image of the Persian the Parisians had constructed in their minds—and in fact Rica reports that there were portraits of him everywhere in Paris in order for people to get a better look at him.[28] So the question "How can one be Persian?" is completely lost if it is not read in the context of this earlier statement just a few sentences earlier in the very same letter, according to which not only being a Persian is not a mystery but in fact is a known caricature.

Tired of this unwanted attention, Rica decides to change his Persian attire and hand himself over to a proper Parisian tailor, which helps him become inconspicuous. It is in this context that he now manages to appear at parties without immediately being recognized as a Persian, and thus when he is introduced as a Persian, people are startled and wonder, "How can one be Persian?"—or, more precisely: "Ah! Ah! monsieur est Persan? C'est une chose bien extraordinaire! Comment peut-on *être* Persan?/ "Oh! Oh! Is he Persian? What a most extraordinary thing! How can one be Persian?" This phrase has now accrued a whole history of rather ridiculous overemphasis and metaphysical significance that is entirely alien to the context of the letter and the story in which it appears. Rica has dispensed with all his Persian appearances and assumed a European disguise, and thus the question underlines the point of the letter from the very beginning—namely, the astonishing provincialism of the French rather than the oddity of the Persian.

Ghanoonparvar's book is a critical study of the cultivation of certain literary tropes in modern Persian literature and as such provides a reliable panorama of how Iranians saw what they called "the West" and eventually cultivated an angle of vision toward it. Tavakoli-Targhi, however, has a larger theoretical claim that is fundamentally flawed at its very inception, for he navigates the Oriental gaze backward at the European by way of a narrative reciprocity almost entirely oblivious to the colonial relation of power that had already slanted the direction of that gazing. This ahistorical perspective is theoretically lopsided because it ignores the relation of power in production of knowledge—and that insight (the relation between knowledge and power) predates Edward Said by decades and goes back not just to Michel Foucault but in fact to Karl Marx and Max Sheller.[29] Shorn of that historical context, any attempt at altering historiography is itself ahistorical.

Tavakoli-Targhi takes the scattered textual evidence as a sign of the narrative ability to gaze, to manufacture, and to represent, which it is not. The colonial, by virtue of being the colonial, lacks, in the general economy of representation, that power to represent, or for that representation to be actively commodified in the general market economy of power. I take that relation of power to represent for granted, trace the source of that power on the global stage by virtue of its imperial abilities to navigate the transnational operation of capital, labor, and market (facts about which Tavakoli-Targhi is entirely silent), and then go to the colonial site to retake that representation to its logical conclusions in manufacturing a public sphere. Tavakoli-Targhi launches his project effectively against Said's, whereas the far more critical task at hand is to do an archeology of the public sphere that made the colonial and postcolonial public reason possible, a project categorically ignored by both Said and all his detractors. Be that as it may, both

Ghanoonparvar and Tavakoli-Targhi have drawn the necessary attention toward the colonial site and its centrality in redirecting the perspective of our historical assessments of the condition of coloniality.

THE FALL AND RISE OF CULTURAL HEGEMONIES

There is no reading or writing of any national history without placing it in the regional and global geography of power. The postcolonial production of the nation-state was always already predicated on a colonial cartography of domination and resistance. The task at hand today is a careful reading of the layered genealogy of the public sphere upon which the postcolonial subject has become historically agential, and not the prolongation of false binaries by manufacturing "alternative modernities" that keep reproducing the European colonial modernity.

Montesquieu wrote his *Persian Letters* (1721) at a critical moment in world history: as the European empires rose, Persianate empires declined in Iran, India, and central Asia, beginning to lose cultural hegemony, for the dominant languages emerging in the new global configuration of power were the European languages, which Iranians, and by extension the Persianate world, did not know. Thus, in a very strange way, they found themselves back in the seventh century, when their world was run by yet another imperial language, Arabic, which they did not know and had to learn—except now they did not even try to master the new languages, for now the capitals of European empires were no longer contiguous to their land. These empires were amorphous, centered in a fictive imaginary they called "the West" and far removed from the imagined geographies of "the East" they had fabricated and to which now the Persians and other Orientals were relegated. Iranians thus continued to produce in their own defeated language, which was no longer the lingua franca of any empire as it had been through successive empires and for more than a millennium, but the language of an aggressively colonized condition. Meanwhile the European imperial languages—French and English in particular—began to be interested in Iranians, but not just to rule them with state functionaries as in India or Egypt or Algeria but also interpret them to the newly formed educated public, upon the emerging public spheres and on a decidedly public sphere for the bourgeois class. Montesquieu's *Persian Letters* was so vastly popular that it went through ten editions in the first year of its publication, and "booksellers were pulling authors by sleeve . . . pleading with them to do a version *Persian Letters* for their firm."[30] The swelling of that European bourgeois public sphere would eventually expand to include the colonial world and its postcolonial consequences.

Persian literature entered the European bourgeois public sphere vicariously through European languages, so that before Iranians had come to Europe as travelers, merchants, students, or diplomats, their literature and poetry had preceded them—such as through Goethe's reading of Hafez, or FitzGerald's reading of Khayyám, or Matthew Arnold's reading of Ferdowsi, or Montesquieu's going after the portrayal of the social malaise of his country through the fictive narrative of two Persian travelers. That entry into the European public domain eventually facilitated the departure of Persian literature and literati from their historic home at the Persianate courts and ushered them into the public domain, which they now began actively calling "*Vatan*/Homeland."

From the inaugural work of Edward Said we have learned that the colonial state apparatus and its intellectual accouterment did have an Orientalist project to facilitate its domination of the colonized territories. But at the same time the bourgeois public sphere which that very condition of coloniality had equally occasioned was the fertile ground of innovative social and intellectual movements in Europe—from the Enlightenment to romanticism and transcendentalism. These movements were critical in pulling the Persian literary imagination out of the royal courts and absorbing it into their public sphere, wedding it to the most transformative social and intellectual movements at the heart of European bourgeois revolutions. This, in turn, liberated Persian literary culture from its royal habitat at the court—so that what did not happen in the sixteenth century during the Safavids, or happened only to a limited degree in the nineteenth century domestically, now happened in Europe *vicariously* in European languages and then, through Persian travelers, students, diplomats, and so on, eventually went back to Iran. Persophilia, in the sense that I am theorizing it here, was indeed a liberating and emancipatory force entirely opposite to the colonially mitigated Orientalism that was narratively delimiting and distorting.

Iranians traveled, translated, and wrote critically on everything from the domestic to the foreign, and Istanbul was a vital site of these transformative moments. In my *Iran: A People Interrupted* (2007), *Shi'ism* (2010), and

The World of Persian Literary Humanism (2012), I have extensively detailed these transformative developments. The point here is to trace the formation of European Persophilia and its extended colonial shadow in the formation of the public sphere and the genealogy of the postcolonial subject to both domestic and foreign factors. In those books, I have already navigated the internal, regional, and imperial contexts immediate to Iran. Here I am concerned with the new imperial settings and their colonial consequences—all geared toward the formation of an inter-imperilistic subject formation that is no longer limited to European modernity, colonial modernity, alternative or multiple modernities, but in fact has no alternative modernity at all, but, as I have argued toward the end of *The World of Persian Literary Humanism,* an alternative theory *to* modernity, not *of* modernity.

My search for an alternative theory *to* modernity (which for the non-European world is a colonial modernity, and thus a contradiction in terms) is predicated on my sustained investigation into the historical formation of the postcolonial subjects and the public spheres in which they are developed around the world. Neither the thrust of sheer colonial power nor the ideological manners of resisting that power, nor, a fortiori, the dialectical result of that fateful encounter do I consider sufficient in charting the historical agency of that postcolonial subject or the texture of the public sphere upon which it was formed. That subject has been, first and foremost, formed upon the layered trajectories of the public sphere, which has been shaped by social and intellectual movements upstream from those political forces and subterranean to any cultural transformation. Before and after any discursive formation of the disciplinary powers of the social sciences or the humanities, biological or economic sciences, it is this public sphere that frames and conditions the historical agency of that subject. Even, or perhaps particularly, the constitution of gender and sexuality is in effect a by-product of the social relation that frames the public posturing of power and expands it into what it calls and considers "private." So the conception of "the public sphere" with which I go about mapping the formation of the postcolonial subject is not at the expense of "the private" but in fact coterminous and integral to it.

CHAPTER THREE

Sir William Jones, Orientalist Philology, and Persian Linguistic Nationalism

IN THE EIGHTEENTH CENTURY, Persian suddenly became a European language—and before long there were those in Iran who thought it should actually be written in the Latin alphabet! The invention of Persian as a European language happened in Europe, in the formidable discipline of philology, and thereby Persians could feel at home in Europe when speaking their ancestral mother tongue. If European empires had alienated Persian-speaking literati from their own imperial language because it was no longer the language of the new empires, philology gave it back to them as a European language, and thus made it integral to the new imperial map of the world. Sir William Jones, who is definitive to this stage of Orientalist philology, had a special place in it for Persian, which proposition gave rise to Persian linguistic nationalism, which in turn corroborated the positing of Persian into a Europeanized conception of itself as opposed to "the Semitic languages," so that Persian effectively became a European language, and those who spoke it an extension of "the West!"

This philological Europeanization of Persian happened at a time of wide and pervasive Persophilia in Europe, when major and minor literary and philosophical figures all had a Persian ingredient to the alchemy of their intellectual happiness. Although the Greek and Roman literatures were the primary sources for the European Renaissance and Enlightenment, the period of the Crusades had already marked a turn to the Muslim cultures for inspiration. Travel accounts like those of Chardin and Tavernier and the literary output of writers like Pierre Corneille, Racine, Voltaire, Madeleine de Scudéry, and Montesquieu reveal the public and literary domain of these interests. Persian poets like Sa'di, Hafez, Omar Khayyám, Attar, Nezami, Ferdowsi, Jami, Manuchehri, Naser Khosrow, Anvari, Baba Taher, and many others were translated into European languages; and as Sainte-Beuve praised Ferdowsi, Goethe and Nietzsche admired Hafez, and Joseph-Ernest Renan celebrated Sa'di, Montesquieu wrote his *Persian Letters* (1721), Goethe, *West-östlicher Divan* (1814–1819), Thomas Moore, *Lalla-Rookh* (1817), Matthew Arnold, *Sohrab and Rustum* (1853), and Edward FitzGerald, *The Rubáiyát of Omar Khayyám* (1859)—all of which soon became staples of literary learning for the bourgeois public at large. In the literary public sphere of the European bourgeoisie, Persian language and literature now had a thriving, vicarious life.

THE ORIGIN OF PERSIAN LINGUISTIC NATIONALISM

"FitzGerald rarely moved beyond the borders of his native Suffolk," historians of British Orientalism report, "and the mind that called back to life the spirit of a Persian dead these many centuries was the mind of an Englishman whom Rossetti, Swinburne and Meredith were delighted to call friend."[1] The distinguished British Orientalist A. J. Arberry then proceeds to complete this piece of recollection by reporting that, without Sir William Jones, Edward FitzGerald might never have come to know and translate Omar Khayyám, and without that translation the world would never have known "the philosopher-poet that will last as long as the English tongue will remain."[2] That is no mean praise for FitzGerald, or for Omar Khayyám, or, above all, for the place of the Persian language in English. But who was this Jones, and why was he so significant for FitzGerald and beyond?

Sir William Jones (1746–1794), a prominent Anglo-Welsh philologist who is considered the founding father of European Orientalism, was the champion of Persophilia par excellence, known in fact as "Jones the Persian," having Persianized his own name and calling himself "Youns Oksfordi." Jones is reported to have had a "prodigious memory," as is evidenced by his once having written down the entirety of Shakespeare's *The Tempest* by heart. Although its origin is much older, Jones is usually considered chiefly responsible for theorizing the idea of "Indo-European languages"—linking Greek, Latin, Persian, and Sanskrit to a common root. His philological speculations about the Indo-European languages generated an elective affinity between Indo-Persian and Indo-European worlds. In 1784, he established the Asiatic Society in Bengal, thereby crafting an imaginative geography—from India to Europe—that embraced Iran in a larger frame of cultural references.[3] His translation of the classics of Persian poetry into English became very popular, and by comparing Iranian and Greek poets he assimilated them for the two respective cultures. By writing a Persian grammar he made the Persian language widely popular in Europe.

The speculative incorporation of Persian into a presumed Indo-European family of languages created a compelling frame of symbolic references to locate the emerging Iranian public sphere in the increasingly globalized circulation of capital, labor, and market, and had far-reaching social and intellectual implications for Iran and its neighbors. The origin of the idea of "Indo-European languages," which in various formulations includes German, Persian, Sanskrit, and many others, and for which some (mostly German) scholars in fact prefer the term "Indo-Germanic," is deeply rooted in the history of European philology and is much older than Jones's ideas.[4] By the end of the sixteenth century, Thomas Stephens (c. 1549–1619), a Jesuit priest visiting India, had already suggested similarities between Sanskrit, Greek, and Latin. Filippo Sassetti, an Italian traveler who flourished in the second half of the sixteenth century and who traveled to India in the 1580s, had also suggested similar family resemblances between the Italian and Indian languages. By 1647, Marcus Zuerius van Boxhorn (1612–1653), a Dutch scholar, had proposed the existence of a primitive common language to which belonged Dutch, Greek, Latin, Persian, and German. Johann Elichmann (c. 1601–1639) had similar ideas, as did Leibniz (1646–1716).[5] It was against this background that in 1786 William Jones proposed:

> The Sanscrit language, whatever be its antiquity, is of a wonderful structure, more perfect than the Greek, more copious than the Latin, and more exquisitely refined than either, yet bearing to both of them a stronger affinity, both in the roots of verbs, and in the forms of grammar, than could possibly have

been produced by accident, so strong, indeed, that no philologer could examine them all three without believing them to have sprung from some common source, which perhaps no longer exists. There is a similar reason, though not quite so forcible, for supposing that both the Gothick and the Celtick, though blended with a very different idiom, had the same origin with the Sanscrit, and the Old Persian might be added to the same family, if this were the place for discussing any question concerning the antiquities of Persia.[6]

The more troubling aspects of the philological adventure into Indo-European nomenclature are explored diligently by Maurice Olender in *The Languages of Paradise: Race, Religion, and Philology in the Nineteenth Century* (1992). In this book Olender demonstrates the fascination that scholars had with finding one common language from which all the others had emerged. Olender argues that these scholars were driven by a determination to demonstrate how European languages were providentially determined to be distinct from the biblical languages and thus far better positioned to universalize the Bible's European vintage. Their invention of the binary of "Aryan" and "Semitic" was instrumental in facilitating their research into philological domains, yet with catastrophic implications in the racialization of the pair. Soon, what began as a philological proposition assumed anthropological and blatantly racial overtones, in which the presumed and speculated characteristics of these languages were also attributed to the people who spoke them. As "Semitic" people (mainly Jews and Arabs) became passive and static (just as their language was characterized), "Aryan" people (mainly Europeans, but also by extension Indians and Persians) became the agile engines of history.

Olender digs deep into the philological theories of such doyens of the field as Johann Gottfried Herder (1744–1803), Joseph-Ernest Renan (1823–1892), Friedrich Max Mueller (1823–1900), Adolphe Pictet (1799–1875), Rudolf Friedrich Grau (1835–1893), and many others who used the "Aryan/Semite" bifurcation of language families, understanding them in increasingly racialized terms in order to show the theological, and even mythological, underpinnings of European philological theories. He demonstrates how, as Sanskrit and Hebrew competed for the position of mother of all other languages, Christianity turned out to have a profound impact on the rise of modern philology. It is in this context that Herder considered Hebrew "an impoverished yet beautiful and pure country girl,"[7] whereas Renan went on to emphasize the contrast between Aryan and Semitic languages, considering the "Aryan superior to the Semitic,"[8] and Max Mueller upped the ante by maintaining: "The Semitic languages are poorer than those of the Aryan family. . . . Aryan words are very different. The root, swamped by prefixes, suffixes and derivatives is less easy to discern, to the point where the substantive sense of the word is blurred; words cease to be appellations. Aryan words are probably freer than Semitic words. They have greater charm, and their seductive richness no doubt encourages the creative imagination."[9]

These racialized theories of language and the binary division into "Semitic" and "Aryan" languages continued to wreak havoc on Europe, but the induction of Persian into this European family of languages suddenly gave it a new lease on life in the new global order of power and hegemony. When Persian literati left their Persianate courts, they entered into the formative period of their social self-awareness, and it was precisely in the European public sphere that they now discovered their language was in fact European!

STRUCTURAL TRANSMUTATIONS OF THE BOURGEOIS PUBLIC SPHERE

Persian cultural production—from prose and poetry to painting and music—eventually exited the royal court from the early nineteenth century, roughly from the time that Abbas Mirza Qajar (1789–1833) dispatched a group of Iranian students to England to study in 1815. The chief humanist among this group, Mirza Saleh Shirazi, is famous for having brought back with him from London a printing machine with which he published the very first newspaper in Iran. He was instrumental in simplifying Persian prose in writing for this paper, and this was subsequently definitively important to the translation movement from French and English that ushered in a whole new vista on global history. These momentous developments coincided with the rise of Persophilia in Europe that opened a space for Persian culture in the European social and intellectual movements—from the Enlightenment to the various romanticisms to transcendentalism.

These movements were launched and performed in the European (and subsequently American) bourgeois public spheres and then, through the conduit of European imperialism, were extended into the colonial world at large. The result was not the "westernization" of the world or its "modernization," as Eurocentric historiography has had it. The result was the dialectical formation of a transnational public sphere into which European social and intellectual movements entered and intensified the antecolonial constitution of the public spheres, which were by definition more radical and open-ended in their symbolic and institutional implications. The formation of the postcolonial subject on these inherently transnational public spheres I propose as the self-propelling force of a history habitually hidden under the label "the West."

The nativist Europeanization of the domain of these social and intellectual movements has given Europeans a false sense of civilizational identity that they have sealed and concealed under the rubric of "the West," while the very same term has alienated the colonial world from the structural formation of its own public spheres and postcolonial subject formation. A flawed consequence of Edward Said's reading of Orientalism has been the fetishization of "the West" and the alienation of the colonial world from the terms of its constant global worldliness, and thus Said has been read precisely in the opposite direction of his own decidedly cosmopolitan worldliness. My investigation into the dialectical relationship between postcolonial Persian cultural formations and European imperialism is meant to unravel that false identity of "the West," as well as its concurrent self-alienation from "the East."

The philological Europeanization of the Persian language meant the introduction of Persian prose into a new phase in its long history, when the etymological roots of the language began to be assimilated westward and its historical linkage with Arabic decoupled. This new theorization of the Persian language coincides with its active simplification by successive generations of merchants, diplomats, and students, all of them now emerging to form the nascent class of public intellectuals. In the making of that category, the introduction of the printing press and publications of the first newspapers had pivotal roles to play. The production of a public literary sphere was the logical consequence of all these seminal developments. The Persian language was no longer the prerogative of the court-affiliated literati or the exclusive claim of the clerical class and their juridical preoccupations. It was, literally, in the public domain. The active hostility of the clerical class to the opening of public schools and public education was only one indication of this shifting ground in the social makeup of the national consciousness. Usually the establishment of the Dar al-Fonun College by the legendary reformist prime minister Amir Kabir in 1851 is considered a landmark event in this respect. But the educational reforms of Haji Mirza Hassan Tabrizi, known as Roshdiyeh (1851–1944), are far more critical for public education. Roshdiyeh was instrumental in establishing the very first public schools and reforming the education system, initially in Tabriz and subsequently in Tehran. It is, however, crucial to remember that while Amir Kabir emerged from the royal court, Roshdiyeh was born to the clerical class, and yet their revolutionary reforms in public education were precisely against their own class interests, a clear indication of the rise of a class of public intellectuals who were now morally and imaginatively rooted in the public sphere. All of these developments were liberating Iranians from the tutelage of the clerical class and the royal court and inaugurating a public sphere within which its future would be redefined.

Soon would follow a translation movement from European sources into this simplified prose, in which Persian travelers would also write their travelogues, journalists their newspaper columns, essayists their treatises on liberty, poets their lyrical panegyrics for the cause of freedom, and public intellectuals their fiery speeches. As the structural transformation of the European bourgeois public spheres was being globalized through its imperial machinery, at least since Mirza Saleh Shirazi's journey to Europe in 1815 forward, we witness the preparation of Persian prose for the public sphere, a process that culminated in the provocative and purposeful prose of the Constitutional period (1906–1911). The philological Europeanization of the Persian language incorporated it into the European public sphere and paradoxically enabled it to partake in groundbreaking social and intellectual movements from the French Revolution of 1789 to the Russian Revolution of 1917, from the Enlightenment to romanticism, and thus prepared it for further purposeful rejuvenation on the site of the Persian public sphere, where the logic of that very imperialism that had enabled it will be, paradox upon paradox, radically contested.

LATINIZING THE PERSIAN SCRIPT

This ongoing course of the reconstitution of the Persian language as the cornerstone of postcolonial nationalism finally led to the defining moment of state formation of the Reza Shah period in the early decades of the twentieth century. But before that eventuality still far more radical implications of the incorporation of Persian into the European language family were in the offing. The Eurocentric reconstitution of the Persian language was not limited to the breaking of its historic link to Arabic or its simplification for larger public use but also led to an all-out effort to change its very alphabet from Arabic to Latin, an idea aggressively championed by the same Mirza Fath Ali Akhondzadeh who was the standard-bearer of Iranian liberal nationalism.

The leading scholar of Akhondzadeh, Fereydun Adamiyat, indicates that the idea of reforming or even changing the Persian alphabet was the result of the encounter with "the Western civilization" or, alternatively, with "the ascendency of European civilization."[10] This language, though generic and imprecise, does point to the general sentiment from which the idea of Latinizing the Persian alphabet emerged. In these discussions, to be sure, there is a persistent self-Orientalization in which "the East" in general is presumed to be backward because of the "flawed" and "difficult" alphabets in which its languages are written. But the rhetoric of this self-Orientalization needs to be placed in the context of the driven determination to devise the linguistic and literary wherewithal of the bourgeois public sphere. Literacy at this point was very much limited to the clerical class at the madrasa system and the literati at the royal court. The presumed difficulty of the script was held to be relative to the exclusionary disposition of these two institutions and the emerging democratic will of the nation now articulating the terms of its literary mobilization, which included a radical rethinking of its script in a way that the language could not only be more easily taught but, even more important, confiscated from the ruling classes.

Later advocates of Akhondzadeh like Fereydun Adamiyat are quick to point out that the problems with the Arabic and thus the Persian alphabet have been known to many Muslim thinkers including and as early as Alberuni (973–1048), and they also remind us that even Engels was fascinated with how easy the Persian language would have been "had it not been for the nasty Arabic alphabet."[11] It is also important to remember that Akhondzadeh had written his treatise on changing the alphabet so that it could be used for Arabic and Turkish as well as Persian, and he spent fifteen years promoting the idea. He initially suggested a limited reform of the alphabet, but eventually abandoned that idea altogether and thought that the whole alphabet had to be thrown out, and Persian, Arabic, and Turkish written in the Latin alphabet and from left to right.[12] This in effect amounted to the complete Europeanization of Persian and potentially of other languages in which Islamic culture and civilization had thrived for centuries.

Adamiyat believes that Akhondzadeh was probably under the influence of Peter the Great (1672–1725) when proposing this radical change in the Persian alphabet, for the Russian czar had similar plans for changing the Russian alphabet. But even Adamiyat clearly recognizes the possibility of reading this proposition to change something so definitive to Persian language and culture as an indication of Akhondzadeh's hatred of Arabs and their presumed negative influence on Iranians. However, he then dismisses this sentiment and suggests that Akhondzadeh's interests were far more "rational than emotional."[13] Be that as it may, the blatant racism of Akhondzadeh against Arabs fits entirely within his liberal nationalism, in the context of which he was determined to Latinize the Persian script. This pernicious racist streak also partakes of the selfsame European theorization of the "Aryan" as opposed to "Semitic" languages of which Maurice Olender writes in his *Languages of Paradise,* though while in Europe the prejudice was directed primarily against Hebrew while in Iran it was decidedly against Arabic.

Once Akhondzadeh suggested this idea in his *Alefba-ye Jadid/New Alphabet* (1857), and soon after his contemporary reformist Mirza Malkam Khan (1833–1908) followed suit with his own similar ideas, Ottoman reformists began to pick up on the idea and consider it in the context of their own Tanzimat projects (1839–1876).[14] Adamiyat credits Mehmet Fuad Pasha (1814–1869), an Ottoman statesman who had spent years in European capitals and became a prominent reformer during the Tanzimat period, with the proposal—within the larger frame of reference of the Ottoman empire—to change the Turkish, Persian, and even the Arabic alphabets.

Be that as it may, pursuing the line of anti-Arab racism or blind "westernism," though a perfectly legitimate line of criticism, conceals a far more crucial factor. The fact is that Akhondzadeh wanted to change the alphabet so that "*kaffeh mellat*/the entirety of the nation," as he termed them, could read and write, whether they were "city dwellers or peasant, sedentary or tribal, men or women, just like people in Prussia."[15] His purpose was to prepare the groundwork for public education, and the clerical establishment and its network of preparatory schools (or the madrasa system) stood between his ideas and that project. He wished for people at large to become literate and learn about modern sciences, "and eventually to catch up with the Europeans."[16] Akhondzadeh's anti-Arab racism was integral to his liberal nationalism and primarily aimed against the Muslim clergy, whom he wished to discredit and dismantle as the custodians of the public weal. He clearly saw both the monarchic and the clerical establishment as obstacles to the formation of the public sphere, for the active and involved literacy of which he wanted to change the alphabet so that the language would become a quicker tool for both forming and mobilizing the public, and literacy would be liberated both from the courtly clerks and the clerical class.

Akhondzadeh prescribed mandatory education for everyone and the formation of a committee to begin rewriting old masterpieces in the new alphabet. Despite all his tireless efforts, he ultimately failed in Iran; but in the Ottoman Empire reformists like Munif Pasha (1830–1910), who knew Persian and was very kind to expatriate intellectuals, took him very seriously in their own efforts to change the Turkish alphabet. These reformists invited Akhondzadeh to Istanbul and had Ottoman authorities consider his suggestions, but they ultimately rejected his propositions as impractical. Akhondzadeh returned to Iran and revised his plan in response to the criticism he had received in Istanbul. Later on, Malkam Khan also joined his cause and the debate continued apace in the Ottoman territories until the Young Turks picked it up and, under Mustafa Kemal Atatürk (1881–1938), brought it to fruition. So, in a roundabout way, the European Persophilia had an indirect but critical role to play in the more immediate extension of the European literary public sphere into the post-Ottoman Turkish intellectual scene.

PERSIAN LINGUISTIC NATIONALISM

The European romancing of Persia was integral to vast and pervasive social and intellectual movements, from the American to the French revolutions, from Enlightenment modernity to romanticism. As these European social and intellectual movements unfolded apace, their extended implications for the formative stages of the Iranian (and other postcolonial) public spheres had significant consequences. In this particular case, the incorporation of Persian into the Indo-European domain contributed to the state formation along the lines of linguistic nationalism. The Europeanization of Persian language and literature was subsequently instrumental to the centrality of both in reconstituting Iran from the extended domains of Persian and Islamic empires into a modern nation-state. In the course of this seismic alteration, Persian was transformed from the lingua franca of successive empires from the Mediterranean to central Asia to the Indian subcontinent into the defining moment of Iranian linguistic nationalism. The rise of anticolonial and postcolonial nation-states enabled the centralizing rhetoric of Persian linguistic nationalism and, at one and the same time, disabled other forms of ethnic and linguistic nationalism within the boundaries of the Iranian nation-state, now reconfigured between the Caspian Sea and the Persian Gulf, and between the postcolonial nation formations of Afghanistan and Pakistan on one side and Turkey and Iraq on the other.

Here, Benedict Anderson's notion of nationalism as an "imagined community" assumes a critical significance.[17] Iranian nationalism of the anticolonial and postcolonial periods was always conscious and particular about its precolonial and imperial genealogy. This imperial genealogy was resuscitated in the course of Iranian encounter with European imperialism. The postcolonial construction of Iran as an "imagined community" was in part predicated on the active recollection of that imperial history, as it also assumed a nasty anti-Arab (and occasionally even Islamophobic) disposition by way of discrediting the powerful clerical Shi'i order, and then, above all, via linguistic nationalism that prepared the ground for the rise of the public sphere. For the crafting of a postcolonial nation-state with the widest possible range, the transmutation of Persian from a transnational imperial language to a national tongue was entirely inevitable. But far more important was the formation of a multifaceted public sphere via the centrality of that common language, of which all Iranians, regardless of their ethnicized identity or even separatist disposition, partook.

Akhondzadeh's liberal nationalism later became essential to the rise of the Constitutional Revolution (1906–1911) and its strong anticolonial disposition, targeting both British and Russian imperialism. He was one of the principal architects of the ideological foregrounding of the revolution, and his political ideas were definitive to its aspirations. Though he did not succeed in changing the Persian alphabet, the combined forces of the clerical class and the court preventing any such radical alteration of a vast and pervasive literary and scholastic heritage, his literary criticism, philosophical speculations, theories of historiography, and perhaps particularly his pioneering works in introducing modern drama did succeed in creating a new discourse of public knowledge, set decidedly against the interests and the domain of both the royal court and the clerical class. Akhondzadeh crafted the powerful prose of his writing about vital contemporary issues in a language that was positioned outside both court and Shi'i clerical parlance. His liberal nationalism soon morphed into anticolonial nationalism, and his preoccupation with Iranian ancient history and his adamant anti-Arab sentiments were pointedly targeted at the clerical class with the largest claim over that very emerging public. His advocacy of constitutionalism and the rule of law were pointedly aimed against the juridicalism of the Shi'i clerics and their juridical claims on civic life. He wrote specifically against the applicability of Sharia to the emerging world. Voltaire, Renan, and Hume were chief among the European thinkers he admired and cited; particularly appealing to him was their anticlericalism. He was severely critical of mandatory veiling, and radically and provocatively rethought the early Islamic history and the life of the Prophet as viewed against the specific interests and narratives of the clerical class.

A significant role in the transformation of Persian into a national language was played in the next generation at the critical stage of state formation during the Reza Shah period. Definitive to that project was the towering figure of Mohammad Ali Foroughi Zoka' al-Molk (1877–1942), a distinguished literary and political figure who commanded an exemplary Persian prose and was instrumental in the promotion of the Persian language as a central force in the national culture and polity. In November 1936 Foroughi wrote an extremely important letter to Farhangestan Iran (the Academy of Persian Language), in the establishment of which he had been very involved, in effect drawing the blueprint for its future operation. Farhangestan Iran was established in 1935 for the preservation and "purification" of Persian as the common language of the nation-state under Reza Shah. Foroughi was the chief architect and first head of the Farhangestan, which included such luminaries of the literary establishment as Malek al-Sho'ara Bahar, Ali Akbar Dehkhoda, Sa'id Nafisi, Ali Asghar Hekmet, and Abd al-Azim Gharib.

In his famous *"Payam man beh Farhangestan*/My Message to the Academy" Foroughi gives an outline of his vision of the way the Persian language ought to serve the crucial function of unifying the nation and advancing Iran toward its future. In this letter he speaks of his affection for Persian and his love for Iran, and he avers that Iranian nationhood is entirely contingent on Iranian culture, and Iranian culture is squarely founded on the Persian language. He outlines two sets of problems for the Persian language at that time: first, that it is mixed with too much Arabic; and second, that it lacks proper equivalents of vocabulary that correspond with modern discoveries in the sciences, philosophy, and technology. Far less radical than Akhondzadeh in his position vis-à-vis the Shi'i clerics or his opposition to Arabic in Persian, in this letter Foroughi tries to strike a balance between two extremes: complete purification of Persian and complete immersion in Arabic. He strikes a happy medium on this at the time deeply divisive issue, as he does with the second vexing matter of coining neologisms to deal with modern sciences, philosophy, and technology.[18]

The project of the "nationalization" of the Persian language and literary heritage confronted two sorts of resistances from two opposite directions: (1) the transnational/imperial history of the language; and (2) the subnationalized communities (Kurds, Azaris, Baluchis, etc.) who were disenfranchised by the aggressive nationalization of a postcolonial nation-state that denied or repressed their "national" language. This double bind in turn led to the structural contradictions and thereby to the dialectical reinforcement of the public sphere in the production of Iranian cosmopolitan culture. In the historic development of Iranian *Jahanshahri*/cosmopolitanism, the active integration of Persian culture into European social and intellectual movements meant the reconstitution of the national consciousness to a global worldliness. The internal version of this *Jahanshahri*/cosmopolitanism is what in Persian I have termed *Iranshahri*/Persopolitanism—namely, the collective national consciousness generated by the colonial and anticolonial experiences of the nation-state that implicated all Iranians into generations of shared memories beyond their ethnicized identity politics.[19]

The philological incorporation of Persian into the speculative domain of the Indo-European family of languages, a key component of European Persophilia, shifted the increasingly nationalized language into the larger frame of social and intellectual movements. From the heart of European empires to the farthest reaches of their colonial conquests, the Persian language began both to tease out the hidden and uncharted implications of those movements and, in a fantastic historical twist, oppose and confront the very imperial machinery that had made their globe-trotting adventures possible.

CHAPTER FOUR

Goethe, Hegel, Hafez, and Company

THE CENTRAL PROJECT of both Raymond Schwab's and Edward Said's seminal works revolved around a significant episode in European intellectual history, with Schwab being primarily concerned with its domestic dimensions in Europe (how the Indic Renaissance inspired romanticism), while Said was habitually preoccupied with how "others" (thus "othered") were *represented* in this dominant mode of European knowledge production. But both being Europeanists by profession and scholarly interests, neither of them had any serious interest in what happens when the working of the self-same imperial machinery that was instrumental in the production of such curiosity and knowledge expanded them globally and perforce brought that knowledge (produced on what Habermas has called the European bourgeois public sphere) to any specific country or region in this "Orient" itself. In their respective works, we learn far more about London, Paris, and Berlin than about Delhi, Cairo, Istanbul, or Tehran. Said, in particular, because of his academic and scholarly discipline and the critical thrust of his *Orientalism,* was entirely inattentive to the fact and phenomenon of the European public sphere (as distinct from its royal courts, its Christian missionary projects, or its colonial enterprises), of which aspects of European Orientalism were in fact essential to such groundbreaking social and intellectual movements as the Enlightenment, as well as to the foregrounding of the American and later the French revolutions, as, for example, we clearly see in Montesquieu's *Persian Letters* as a precursor of many of his later political ideas that altered the course of history around the globe. The transnational expansion of that literary public sphere through the mechanism of European imperial machinery and cultural hegemony in turn became the intellectual, moral, and imaginative engine driving colonial and postcolonial change around the globe, but with specific dispensations in every country and clime in Asia, Africa, and Latin America.

It was precisely in that literary public sphere that the Persian language was philologically Europeanized, and this renewed imperial appropriation of the language pushed it to face new historical challenges. The location of the language somewhere between its own imperial history and the subnational resistances to it (by Kurdish, Azari, etc.) was subsequently intensified by its incorporation into the Indo-European family of languages and thereafter in European social and intellectual movements. This entire enterprise opens up a whole new worldliness for Persian language and literature, a new worldly cosmopolitanism that is dialectically conversant with European intellectual history but traversing intersectionally with it to explore new horizons, a kind of cosmopolitanism that is innate to its historical experiences in and out of its Iranian epicenter and no longer even European, let alone "Western." To see how this appositional stand of non-European worldliness (both similar and different) happens, we need to go beyond the mere domain of language and explore the way in which European Persophilia showed itself in the wider domain of the European Enlightenment, something that was best evident in Montesquieu's *Persian Letters* but was by no means limited to it.

EUROPEAN ENLIGHTENMENT AND PERSIAN HUMANISM

The philological transformation of Persian from its historical habitat adjacent to Arabic, Turkish, and Hendi/Urdu into a European language via dangerously racialized theories happened almost simultaneously when Persian literature was finding a very hospitable home in the most spectacular social and intellectual movements of the time. The emplotment of Persian literature in the vicissitudes of the rise of the Enlightenment has long been noticed by specialists in Persian translations. "For all practical purposes," one literary historian reports, "the European discovery of Persian literature came about in the seventeenth century, during the Age of Enlightenment. Serious study of it was launched a century later in the Age of Reason, and its chief exploitation was conducted in the nineteenth century during the Romantic Age."[1] In successive European intellectual movements, paraphrased Persian became central in the critical phases of Europe's redefinition of itself. This world-historic redefinition as a global codification of power was launched with a crucial element of Persophilia central to the changing and rapidly alternating historical consciousness of the age: "Because Sa'di's moral didacticism appealed to the Enlightenment and the Age of Reason, both the choice of selections from his works and the manner in which they were translated reflect the bias of those times. Similarly, Hafez in the Age of Reason could only be perceived as a sort of pseudo-classical lyrist—the 'Persian Anacreon.' In the later Romantic Age, he was permitted to show his consanguinity with mystics."[2] As Europe was pacing and redefining itself, its Persophilia was successively integral to those changes. It was a colorful mirror in which Europeans would see what they wanted to see—not to manufacture any "other," but to re-manufacture themselves, repeatedly.

Persian poets became integral to the changing literary and public sentiments dominant in the European public spheres. The Enlightenment project was delivering Europe from its aristocratic and ecclesiastical orders, and Persian and other non-European poets and thinkers were providing it with ample evidence of a universe that existed beyond its Christian imagination. Persian poets were now integral to a more universal drive to link the Greeks and Romans to a humanistic tradition that offered a view of the world different from that offered by Christian scholasticism. Translations from Persian sources played a pivotal role in helping the European Enlightenment (on behalf of the European bourgeoisie) to feel and think its way from a provincialized scholasticism to a universal humanism more compatible with its transnational disposition in an imperial age. The Enlightenment thinkers were anxious to give the European bourgeoisie a sense of identity independent of the Christian churches and doctrines and their historical affiliation with aristocratic feudalism. In Persian humanism they had detected a formidable literary ally in their fights against both monarchic tyranny and

Christian dogmatism. Persophilia was a primarily bourgeois public affair, though it had its attractions for the aristocracy and the Christian clergy as well, to the degree that they identified with popular trends in the literary public sphere.

It is not accidental that the Enlightenment interest in Persian literature, or any other kind of non-European literatures, preceded its interest in religious texts. We know that "even before André du Ryer made his French translation of the Koran in 1647, he had rendered portions of Sa'di's *Golestan* into the same language (1634). In England, George Sale's influential translation of the Koran (1734) was preceded by Thomas Hyde's study of the Zoroastrian religion and his rendition (in Latin) of poems by Hafez and Omar Khayyam."[3] These Persian poets were giving the European bourgeoisie the moral imagination with which to authenticate their universal claim on humanism. The "great contribution" of the Enlightenment is believed to have been to "cultural history" and to "its glimmer of awareness that even the non-Christian religions were legitimate efforts to regulate ethical life, and that the art of letters was not the exclusive prerogative of either Christian Europe or pagan Greece and Rome."[4] The expansive domain of capital, labor, and market could no longer be contained in the Christian missionary zeal to convert the world to its doctrine of salvation. The world was being delivered differently.

The choice of translation into Latin and Greek or into one of the European national languages is a good index of the presence of the paraphrased Persians in the rise of the European bourgeoisie and the public sphere upon which it thrived and recognized itself. The Latin translation of Sa'di's *Golestan* as *Rosarium* in 1651 by the Dutch Orientalist George Gentius points to the beginning of interest in Persian literature at the Latin end of feudal Europe; while the German translation of the same text, this time in 1654 and as *Der Persianischer Rosenthal* by Adam Olearius, who later added to it Sa'di's *Bustan* as *Der Baumgarten,* from a Dutch version, points to the immediate identification of these translations with linguistic nationalism among the European bourgeoisie. Similarly appealing to the formative period of the European bourgeois palate was the Persian-inspired Voltaire's *Zadig ou la Destinée/Zadig, or The Book of Fate* (1747), while Johann Gottfried Herder (1744–1803) and Joseph Addison (1672–1719) were doing the same with the Persian poetic sources they translated into their respective national languages, German and English. Interest in the Greek and Latin translations of Hafez

and Sa'di remained constant in the eighteenth century. Sir William Jones
and the Polish diplomat Baron Reviczky were chief among other enthusi-
asts of paraphrasing Hafez into Greek and Latin.[5] So, in a sense, this period
of translation of Persian poets into European languages both appropriates
Persian poetic legacy for the whole idea of Europe in Greek and Latin translations and then for individual bourgeois public spheres of one national
language or another.

PARAPHRASED PERSIAN AND BRITISH COLONIALISM

Persian language and literature could hardly be so utterly Europeanized
without serving the cause of European colonialism. The link between European colonial interests and their attraction to Persian literature can neither
be ignored nor exaggerated—if the proposition is kept squarely in the bourgeois public sphere and its commercial and cultural interests. The famous
Pitt's India Act of 1784 came at a crucial point when the leading British Persianist Sir William Jones was threatening to destroy his collection of Persian material. This act brought the commercial activities of the East India
Company under the immediate supervision of the Crown, and with it Persian language and literature suddenly became a matter of imperial interest.
The consequence of this for the promotion of Persian language and culture
by and for the British colonial interest can scarce be overestimated—nor indeed its perhaps unintended consequences for the bourgeois public sphere
ignored. As Yohannan observed:

> The cultivation of the Persian languages, which was the court language of
> India, and of Persian literature, which informed the entire Islamic civiliza-
> tion of that land, now became a patriotic necessity. A flurry of linguistic and
> literary activity ensued, and to Jones's Persian Grammar was added, as working
> tools, a Persian-English dictionary, various handbooks, and numerous transla-
> tions from Persian authors. The purpose of these books was frankly utilitarian,
> but as their content was often literary, the names of Ferdowsi, Sa'di, and Hafez
> soon became household words in England, occasionally preempted as nom[s]
> de plume by poetasters unable to make it on their own.[6]

What this fascinating chapter in British colonialism and European Persophilia points to, more than anything else, is both the practical and the

ideological affinity of the European bourgeoisie for the kinds of attention they now lavishly poured over Persian poets. The height of British colonial interests in India coincided with the rise of Persophilia among British colonial officers and Orientalists as one particularly poignant point when the universalizing ideals of the European Enlightenment were in manifest alliance with the colonial extensions of the very logic of capitalist modernity. The purpose of this attention lavished upon Persian poets by the British might have been to aid and abet in the colonial conquest of India, but the public at large was now putting the extended domain of that interest to civic and literary uses in the context of European Enlightenment and romanticism alike.

One of the most crucial consequences of this colonially constituted attraction of the British to Persian poets is the cross-canonization of a body of literary texts in the dual direction of a universal literary humanism that appealed to the British and other members of the European bourgeoisie, and an active *nationalization* of Persian literature that appealed to the colonially constituted projects of nation building among the Iranian bourgeoisie. What kind of poets and poetry were attractive to the British at this time? They picked and chose Abd al-Rahman Jami, for example, because he lived and wrote in Herat (in contemporary Afghanistan), and from the array of his poetic works it was his didactic poetry they emphasized most. The choice of Attar's *pand-nameh* equally reveals this predilection toward a universalizing didactic literature. Sa'di, too, was paramount in the mind of the British colonial officers, because his work was regarded "as the best means of acquiring a proper understanding of Muslim manners and morals."[7] What the British, and by extension the Europeans, were doing with these texts, however, was not just learning how to rule the Muslims. They were, in effect, creating a universalizing literary humanism for themselves and their newly acquired Indian subjects—and the project was to have an enduring effect on Iranian literary historians of subsequent generations, who took their cues from these British colonial officers in writing their own (now necessarily nationalized) literary histories.

One might argue that while English literature, as Gauri Viswanathan has demonstrated in her *Masks of Conquest*,[8] was used in the ideal typical construction of a colonial humanism in British India, Persian literature was used to narrate a universal humanism conducive to that colonial purpose among the British officers themselves. In this respect, it is crucial to remember that up until 1834 Persian was the official administrative language of British India. Persian language and literature as the defining moment of the Indian subcontinent had achieved its zenith during the reign of the Mughals, the last precolonial, heavily Persian, Muslim dynasty. It was precisely in this language that the British sought a colonially necessitated universal humanism in which the British colonial officers were to be trained. Between Pitt's India Act of 1784 and the Macaulay edict of 1835, which put an official end to the centrality of Persian language and literature in India, British colonialism sought a globalizing ideology of conquest in what they now saw as a Persian literary humanism.[9]

Even after the substitution of English for Persian in 1835, Sa'di continued to be read as the example par excellence of a universal humanism serving British colonial interests, first by training the colonial officers and their subjects in a secular humanism necessitated by the cultural logic of capitalist modernity. Sa'di's *Golestan* was chiefly responsible for the production of a post-Christian political ethics among the European bourgeoisie. The British in India, and later the French coveting their colonial possessions, read Sa'di as a Machiavellian Persian instructing them in far more than just the art of ruling their Muslim subjects.[10] We know that Sa'di "retained this political usefulness well into the twentieth century: during the occupation of Iran by British and Russian troops in World War II, a parable of his was made to serve the purpose of anti-German propaganda by British intelligence."[11] We also know that "Britain's commitments in Asia not only provided a training ground for the linguistic skills required in translation, but also guaranteed a reading audience for what would otherwise have been a rather esoteric foreign literature."[12] But the equally crucial consequence of such translations was the active production of a post-Christian political ethics with which the European bourgeoisie had charged its Enlightenment project. All of this meant the transformation of European Persophilia into a cogent component of its literary public sphere—both in its domestic social and intellectual movements and in its extended global colonial conquests.

It is to the same stage of this project that we owe the active canonization of Persian literary and poetic texts soon to be narrated into the production of a *national* literary history for the Iranian nation-building project. Almost exactly the same texts that were now serving European colonial interests in the Indian subcontinent by helping them define a universalizing literary humanism became the defining elements of the emerging literary historiography of a Persian national literature. It was not until the early 1900s that the prominent British Orientalist E. G. Browne would write his monumental *A Literary History of Persia,* but the nationalizing parameters of his narrative were actively selected for both the British and the Persians right here on the colonial site of India.[13]

What this episode of Persian literature and its cross-canonization in British colonialism reveals—for the construction of a universal humanism and, in Iran, for the production of a national literature—is the metamorphic nature of literary sources serving precisely two *opposite* objectives, yet both contingent on the local requirements of the logic of the capital and the rhetoric of cultures it occasions. The universal literary humanism that was conducive to globalizing British colonial interests in India made use of and thus eventually canonized precisely the same textual sources that were later to be used for the construction of a national literary history in the nascent nation-state of Iran that would rise to oppose those colonial interests. This is perhaps the best, but by no means the only, example of the paradoxical function of Persophilia on the site of the European bourgeois public sphere and its extended logic and rhetoric when that sphere became transnational and crossed the colonial divide.

GOETHE, ROMANTICISM, AND HAFEZ

Farther to the east of England, Persian poetry was having a feat of an entirely different sort in Germany. As British colonial officers were learning Persian to rule India better and in order to partake of a universal literary humanism that was narrated to embrace them and their Indian subjects at the same time, the Germans were in the midst of the Napoleonic Wars (1803–1815). The three hundred or more states that composed "the Germanys" were now completely subject to the French emperor's whim. France had annexed some one hundred small states to the left bank of the Rhine. By 1806, some two hundred small German states, too weak to defend themselves, were swallowed by their more powerful neighbors. The German turn to romanticism occurred in the context of an almost complete political and economic disintegration. The German attention to Persian poetry happened at precisely the intersection between the Frühromantik (Early Romantics) and Hochromantik (High Romantics) early in the nineteenth century.

Joseph von Hammer-Purgstall (1774–1856) translated Hafez into German
in its entirety in 1812–1813. This was at a time when Friedrich Schlegel
(1759–1805), the prominent figure among the early German Romantics, had
just died, but his equally influential brother, August Wilhelm (1767–1845),
was still alive and active. Hammer-Purgstall's *Geschichte der Schönen Redekünste Persiens* appeared in 1818. Friedrich Rueckert (1788–1866) followed
suit and began to compose ghazals of his own in 1819. Goethe (1749–1832),
too, wrote his *West-östlicher Divan* in 1819 under the influence of Hammer-
Purgstall's translation. The impact of introducing Hafez to the German
literary public sphere was not limited to Goethe. Suddenly a whole flock
of German "Hafezes" surfaced. As German literary historian Annemarie
Schimmel noted, "Following Hammer-Purgstall's rather mundane interpretation of Hafez, a considerable number of mediocre German poets of the
nineteenth century adopted his name as a trademark for their drinking
poems and love songs, and especially for their attack against the clergy."[14]
Goethe soon began to identify with Hafez, considering the Shirazi poet his
own "brother." Later German literary historians thrived in recollecting this
family resemblance; and soon, in America, this particular brand of Persophilia would resurface with Ralph Waldo Emerson's thinking himself the
reincarnation of Sa'di.

This was during the heyday of the High Romantics, when Wilhelm Heinrich Wackenroder (1773–1798), Johann Ludwig Tieck (1773–1853), Novalis
(1772–1801), Ludwig Achim von Arnim (1781–1831), Clemens Brentano
(1778–1842), Adelbert von Chamiso (1781–1838), Joseph Freiherr von
Eichendorff (1788–1857), Baron Fouqué (1777–1843), Heinrich Heine
(1797–1856), E. T. A. Hoffmann (1776–1822), and Eduard Friedrich Mörike
(1804–1875) were actively defining the contours of German High Romanticism. It was exactly at this time, as Schimmel put it, that "It took a poet
like Goethe to discover behind the rather unpolished translation by Hammer-
Purgstall the greatness of Hafez, who appeared to him as his 'twin,' nay
rather, to whom even the comparison with himself seemed too daring. It was
thanks to his German echo of Hafez's divan that the name of the poet of
Shiraz became almost a household word in Germany; and his remarks about
the characteristics of Persian poetry . . . are still valid."[15]

As "twins," "brothers," and "reincarnations," European and American
poets and literati from Goethe to Emerson could not have enough of appropriating Persian poets as their own. Goethe's attention to Persian literature

was no trifling curiosity about only one poet whom he made into a household name in his homeland. In his *Noten und Abhandlungen* to his *West-östlicher Divan* he paid sweeping attention to all genres of Persian literature. He noted, for example, what he thought (falsely) to be the absence of dramatic narrative—plays in particular—in Persian literature.[16] The identification of Goethe with Persian poets became so proverbial in his time, and after that in Europe, that he began to be assimilated into the idiomatic hagiography of the iconic figures of Persian literature. Speaking of the amorous relationship between the Persian poet Jalal al-Din Rumi and his object of affection, Shams Tabriz, the French author Maurice Barrés has compared their relationship to those of the friendships of Socrates and Plato, or Goethe and Schiller.[17] This systematic admittance of Persian poets into the European literary and philosophical pantheon was perhaps the most powerful manifestation of European Persophilia during the High Romantic period. And this homoerotic dimension of European Persophilia would remain integral to it for generations to come.

The significance of *West-östlicher Divan* in Goethe's oeuvre is not of an accidental Persophilia. "Hafez had an enormous impact on Goethe in his old age, the direct result of which was 'West-östlicher Divan,' considered by many Germanists to be next in importance to Faust."[18] The significance does not stop there. "Goethe's interest in Hafez, shared and expressed in beautiful poems by Platen and Rueckert, inspired German scholars to undertake important studies on this subject."[19] Goethe's penchant for Persian poetry was contagious. "At about the same time [as Goethe's], the young German Orientalist Friedrich Rueckert published a collection called *Östlicher Rosen* (eastern roses), which contains some verses that incorporate the spirit of Hafez much better than all later versions (including Rueckert's own masterful verse translation of some eighty ghazal)."[20] What we are witnessing here is no trifling Orientalism intended to (mis)represent or dominate anything. This is High German Romanticism being thought, felt, dreamed, and radically transforming the spirit of European intellectual history through an active incorporation of Persian poets into a European habitat.

Goethe's interest was not just in Hafez. Sa'di was equally attractive to the German poet. But why? The eminent German literary historian, the late Annemarie Schimmel, herself perhaps the greatest example of romantic Persophilia of the later period, believed that in Sa'di's *Golestan* Goethe had found a kindred soul, whose serenity in dealing with the Mongol invasion of the thirteenth century was inspirational to the leading German public intellectual of the period. "It was perhaps this serenity of Sa'di which, in a certain way, inspired the German poet Goethe to migrate spiritually to the 'peaceful east' some 650 years later, at a time when Europe was shattered by the Napoleonic wars and, afterward, the war of freedom in Germany. At that point, Persian poetry became Goethe's consolation, and Sa'di's verse was among the sources that inspired him, just as it may have consoled some of the poet's contemporaries hundreds of years earlier."[21]

The path for the translation and reception of Hafez in 1812–1813 and Goethe's publication of his *West-östlicher Divan* in 1819 had been properly paved in the earlier decades in the Sturm und Drang (storm and stress) movement, in which the young Goethe, as well as Schiller, Herde, and Jakob Michael Reinhold Lenz (1751–1792), had actively participated. In these figures, prefiguring Goethe's reception of Hafez, the German Romanticism was now in full swing. What were the social aspects of German Romanticism at this time?

Martin Kitchen described them thus:

> It was a protest movement of young writers, most of them in their twenties, who were in revolt against their stuffily "enlightened" elders. They were self-appointed geniuses and outsiders, most of whom were to end their lives with dramatic suicides or as poverty-stricken pariahs. They rejected the schoolmasterly pedantry of the Enlightenment philosophers and the restrictive norms of behavior dictated by bourgeois conformism. . . . [They] emphasized feelings, sensations, and the power of nature. The young Goethe saw this ideal personified in the proud rebel Prometheus (1773). Goethe produced the archetypal "Storm and Stress" figure in Leiden des Jungen Werther ("The Sufferings of Young Werther"). Soon sensitive young men throughout Germany and beyond dressed in Werther's blue tails and yellow waistcoat, fell unhappily in love and ended their tormented lives with a pistol.[22]

In addition to Prometheus and the Young Werther, there was yet another tragic hero whom Goethe had immortalized, and this one came straight out of Hammer-Purgstall's translation of Hafez. The third romantic hero was none other than the proverbial Moth who out of desperate love flies into the Candle's flame, never to return alive. *Sham'-o-Gol-o-Parvaneh-o-Bolbol* (The Candle, the Rose, the Moth, and the Nightingale) comprised the paramount quartet in Persian lyrical poetry, coming to their tragic destiny in the ghazals of Hafez. The Moth here represented absolute fixation on the truth and reality of one final and true love. The Moth is fixated on the light of the Candle, circles around it in veneration and devotion, and finally throws itself into its fire and dies the sublime death in the Beloved.

The romantic obsession with annihilation had found a perfect source of inspiration in the Persian poetic sources that German poets were now putting at their disposal. They began to read the classics of Persian mysticism in their own new light. From Mansur al-Hallaj's (c. 858–922) and other mystics' writing in Arabic the interest came directly to Persian sources, "where it surfaced again in the poetry of the Shirazian writers, notably Sa'di. It became one of the favorite metaphors for the following generations of Persian poets until it was transformed, on the basis of Sa'di's verse, into one of the greatest German poems, Goethe's *Selige Sehnsucht*."[23] "Goethe's famous poem 'Selige Sehnsucht,' in his West-östlicher Diwan, reflects this very mystery of dying in love and reaching a new, higher life in union. The Goethean Stirb und werde, 'die and become,' translates very well the Prophetic tradition 'die before ye die' (in order to gain new life), which formed one of the cornerstones of Sufism and, of course, of Hallaj's theories."[24] This may all sound perfectly poetic, romantic, and innocent now, but as we shall soon see there was a monstrous abstraction lurking under that innocence that would shortly come out both in Germany and Iran and devour millions of innocent human beings.

HEGEL, HISTORY, AND PERSOPHILIA

If the philological theories of Indo-European languages suddenly turned Persian into a European language with which Goethe could easily start composing his lyrics à la Hafez, it was only natural for Hegel (1770–1831) to turn Persians themselves, not just their language, into Europeans. This is how the spirit moved for Hegel: "The European who goes from Persia to India, observes, therefore, a prodigious contrast. Whereas in the former country he finds himself still somewhat at home, and meets with European dispositions, human virtues and human passions—as soon as he crosses the Indus (i.e., in the latter region), he encounters the most repellent characteristics, pervading every single feature of society. With the Persian Empire we first enter on continuous History. The Persians are the first Historical People."[25]

Something extraordinary happens in Persia for Hegel: "Here in Persia first arises that light which shines itself, and illuminates what is around; for Zoroaster's 'Light' belongs to the World of Consciousness—to Spirit as a relation to something distinct from itself. We see in the Persian World a pure exalted Unity, as the essence which leaves the special existences that inhere in it, free—as the Light, which only manifests what bodies are in themselves—a Unity which governs individuals only to excite them to become powerful for themselves—to develop and assert their individuality."[26]

Persia plays a central role in Hegel's philosophy of history: "The principle of development begins with the history of Persia. This therefore constitutes strictly the beginning of World-History; for the grand interest of Spirit in History, is to attain an unlimited immanence of subjectivity—by an absolute antithesis to attain complete harmony." He constantly favorably compares Persia with India and China, and whereas he dismisses the latter two, Persia for Hegel commences world history, because "In the Persia principle, Unity first elevates itself to the distinction from the merely natural; we have the negation of that unreflecting relation which allowed no exercise of mind to intervene between the mandate and its adoption by the will. In the Persian principle this unity is manifested as Light, which in this case is not simply light as such, the most universal physical element, but at the same time also purity—the Good."[27] In the case of China, "Man is not free there; he possesses no moral element," while in India, "Rights and Duties in India are intimately connected with special classes, and are therefore only peculiarities attaching to man by the arrangement of Nature." But in Persia, "Man sustains a relation to Light—to the Abstract Good—as to something objective, which is acknowledged, reverenced, and evoked to activity by his Will."[28] As Hegel begins to chart the course of history for the European bourgeois public independent of the court and the church Persia is definitive to his philosophy.

Hegel's attraction to Persia and its centrality in his philosophy of history had a larger frame of reference in German Romanticism. The organic link between the German, and by extension European, romanticism and Persian literature has long been detected and documented by literary historians. In this development, Sir William Jones's translations had a pivotal role to play. "Herder's Orientalism," meanwhile, "had been at first largely a humanistic response to a newly discovered chapter of history, but when Jones' translations became available to him, he made adaptations of Persian and Indian works that were to pave the way for the Romantic flowering of the *Orientalische Richtung* in Goethe, Rueckert, Platen, and Bodenstedt."[29] But this was not all, for this phase of German Persophilia had larger claims on German intellectual disposition that included Hegel:

> The interest in Persian poetry evinced by so important a figure in German cultural history as the philosopher Hegel testifies to the new uses to which the foreign literary importations were being put. German philosophy, now given over to organicism, intuitionism, and even mysticism, found an ally in Persian Sufism. Meanwhile German philologists such as Tholuck, von Hammer-Purgstall, Brockhaus, and Rosenzweig-Schwannau were producing texts and translations of Persian literature for the use of not only German but also English and American writers.[30]

Constitutional to German Romanticism was a universal claim to humanism that became paramount in Herder's attempt to work out a universal *history*, Goethe's notion of *Weltliteratur*, and even Hegel's philosophy of history, in all of which Persian history and culture assumed a prominent place. Goethe and Hegel were simultaneously attending to two different aspects of the European project of capitalist modernity as articulated in the bourgeois public sphere. At the very same time that Goethe was assimilating Hafez into the bosom of German Romanticism, his close friend and associate Hegel had an entirely different function for "Oriental" cultures in general. For an accurate understanding of what it was exactly that German Romanticism was doing with its Persophilia it is crucial to remember that Goethe published his *West-östlicher Divan* (1819) three years after Hegel began to teach at the University of Heidelberg and one year into his permanent teaching position at the University of Berlin. Between 1818 and 1831, at the very height of the German (Goethe's in particular) adaptation of Hafez into romanticism, Hegel delivered and gradually polished his famous three lectures on art, religion, and the history of philosophy at the University of Berlin. His categorical dismissal of even the possibility of philosophy in cultures to his east is the indispensable background against which we need to read the active romanticization of Persian poetry in his time.

Why is it, exactly, that Hegel believes that "no philosophic knowledge can be found in the East"?[31] Why is it that he categorically believes "philosophy proper commences in the West"?[32] The answers that Hegel provides to this set of complementary questions goes a long way in explaining to us what exactly Hafez is doing among his newly found German friends. The reason the Orientals are incapable of philosophy is that they are still in an infantile state of fear. Hegel has heard of the famous prophetic statement "fear of the Lord is the beginning of wisdom," and he quotes it in his lecture on the history of philosophy as an ultimate indication that this fear has been constitutional to the absence of real philosophy in the East.[33] "But man must also have overcome fear through the relinquishment of finite ends," Hegel objects, and stipulates, "and the satisfaction that religion affords is confined to what is finite, seeing that the chief means of reconciliation are natural forms which are impersonated and held in reverence."[34]

What Hegel has to achieve here to sustain the confidence of the European bourgeoisie is the assumption that freedom of self-consciousness and self-assertion as the necessary prelude for the mind to be able to "descend into itself"[35] occurred only in its immediate neighborhood, namely in the Greece that he imagines as its historical ancestor. In order to do so, he had to locate a realm, a much larger asylum than Michel Foucault would imagine decades later, in which he could imprison unreason. Here is that "asylum" for Hegel: "In religion we even find self-immersion in the deepest sensuality represented as the service of God, and then there follows in the East a flight to the emptiest abstractions to what is infinite, as also the exaltation attained through the renunciation of everything, and this is specially so amongst the Indians, who torture themselves and enter into the most profound abstraction. . . . This, then, is not the soil of freedom."[36]

What is significant here is Hegel's insistence on characterizing "the East" as precisely the opposite of what he believes has happened in "the West" in order to invent that "West" the way he wishes; and evidently without that "Eastern" model of exactly the opposite of "the West," it would not have a reality sui generis. "The subject in the Orient, Hegel insists, is "negative and perishing," predicated on "a vanishing away of consciousness" the result of which is a "spiritually dead relation [that] thus comes into existence, since the highest point there to be reached is insensibility"; and, as a result:

The conclusion to be derived from this is that no philosophic knowledge can be found here. To philosophy belongs the knowledge of substance, the absolute universal, that whether I think it and develop it or not, confronts me still as for itself objective; and whether this is to me substantial or not, still just in that I think it, it is mine, that in which I possess my distinctive character or am affirmative: thus my thoughts are not mere subjective determinations or opinions, but, as being my thoughts, are also thoughts of what is objective, or are substantial thought. The Eastern form must therefore be excluded from the history of philosophy. . . .[37]

This Hegelian *thinking* of the Eastern out of philosophy is in organic solidarity with the Goethean *feeling* of Hafez into romanticism. The Oriental is to be un-thought by Hegel in order for Goethe to integrate the Persian into romanticism. The dual projects are exclusively German and European, but the consequences of this seesawing between reason and revelation, Enlightenment and romanticism, in the heart of European capitalist modernity will soon of course become entirely global.

One can, of course, amplify this Hegelian un-thinking of the Oriental by reading the location of the Persian in his philosophy of history as the purgatorial state of humanity, or even in Kant's philosophy, of the aesthetics in which the Oriental has no place except one of "grotesquery," except for Persian again being Europeanized by being called "the French of the Orient." Between Hegel and Goethe, the position of the Persian became purgatorial—insofar as being a Muslim he is incapable of thinking and to the degree that he is European. Hegel's characterization of the Oriental as incapable of thinking begins with a prophetic tradition in Islam and continues and extends into a pervasive characterization of Hinduism, sparing the Persian his depiction as the gateway of the European into full historical presence. Goethe's celebration of Hafez's and Hegel's characterization of the Persians as the forerunners of Europeans into history dovetails with Goethe's love for Hafez, so that between the two of them they produce a purgatorial Persian passage for the European (bourgeoisies) to escape the dark age of prehistorical inferno and enter the European paradise. The Persians and the Greeks come together to make the idea of "the European" or "the West" as the code name for its bourgeoisie possible. Here is the central significance of Persophilia for the rise of European Enlightenment as the birth canal of "the

West." This philosophical paradox at the heart of German Romanticism will not be resolved until the appearance of the sublimest irony of German philosophy—Nietzsche and his particular brand of Persophilia.

ROMANTICISM, MYSTICISM, FASCISM

The more serious question remains: Why is there this organic solidarity between Goethe and Hegel about matters Persian and/or Oriental? This Orientalism had a genealogy entirely different from that necessitated by a discursive domination of the Orient. The experience of the Germans with colonialism was limited and fragmentary, primarily because of the absence of a unified national front and a productive economy rather than a lack of will, as became patently evident the instant Hitler roused Germany with a national cry for European and global conquest. This Orientalism addressed, in absentia and on behalf of an abstracted notion of the European collectivity, the constitutional need of the European bourgeoisie itself, the need not just to produce and dominate the world but also to give itself a sense of destiny and purpose beyond the iron gates of its recent and self-conscious birth. There was an organic solidarity of a different sort between British and German Orientalism. While the British were busy conquering the world (and the Portuguese, Dutch, French, and Spaniards were hard on their heels), the Germans were giving a philosophy and an aesthetics to the logic of that domination.

Paramount in Hegel's mind was to read the entire history of the world, both in its material outline and in its consciousness of itself, as a prelude to the rise of European Enlightenment, to Europe itself, to the very idea of "Europe"—and the more unsure of itself the European bourgeoisie was (or the more amorphous and homeless capital became), the more abstract and universal Hegel's philosophy of history became. That Enlightenment had to be predicated on Greece for its geographical boundaries to be clear-cut, and it had to dismiss the Orientals as incapable of a philosophy, because the very constitution of reason at the center of the European Enlightenment needed the supposition of an unreason much larger in space and modality to be contained in the asylum houses of Europe, as Foucault would later imagine and argue. The Orient was that unreason, the organicity of the world in its infancy. The anxiety of origin was entirely domestic to Europe and was what the very idea of "Europe" needed to sustain itself.

German Orientalism and Persophilia, in both its Hegelian dismissal of the Orientals as incapable of philosophy and in Goethe's admission of Hafez into the bosom of European romanticism, are crucial factors in correcting the lenses that Michel Foucault and Edward Said constructed to reveal the relationship between knowledge and power, not just as a discursive domination of the Orient, but as a multifaceted project constitutional to the very advent of capitalist modernity, the very cast of the European Enlightenment, the very logic of the revolution of capital, the very politics and economics of its extension into colonialism, the very rhetoric of the romantic revolt against the Enlightenment, the very eroticism of romanticizing Persophilia, the very temptations of the collapse of romanticism into mysticism, and the very path that led that mysticism to the predicates of fascism and fundamentalism at both the fictive center and the projected periphery of capital.

The European turn to romanticism as a counter-Enlightenment move was of course not limited to Germany. The universal move against the terror of instrumental reason soon began to implicate Persian poets. As Blake came to replace Pope, and blank verse heroic couplets, Byron, Shelley, and Keats found solace in Hafez, a poet they had read in their early youth, when Sir William Jones's translations in the heyday of the Enlightenment period came home to roost. Jones had explicitly proposed that "if the languages of the Eastern nations were studied in our great seminaries of learning . . . , we should be furnished with a new set of images and similitudes; and a number of excellent compositions would be brought to light, which future scholars might explain and future poets imitate."[38] Romanticism was that future, carrying the unintended consequences of the Enlightenment to its logical and rhetorical conclusions. As moral reaction to the Enlightenment, romanticism echoed the material disenfranchisement from the logic of capital, and the espousal of "Oriental" mysticism was the chief rhetorical mode of that turn, Hafez the brightest eastern star in its firmament.

Here the link between German Romanticism and European colonialism becomes even more evident and critical. What propelled the attraction to Persian poetry from the periphery of academic interest to the centers of economic and intellectual movements in the bourgeois public sphere in Europe was precisely the dual prong of the colonial interest (on the economic front) and the Enlightenment–romanticism seesaw (on the intellectual front). On the economic front, the Pitt's India Act of 1784 became a watershed of immediate colonial interest in Persian language and literature. Herman Bicknell, H. Wilberforce-Clarke, Francis Gladwin, James Ross, Edward B. Eastwick, Edward Rehatsek, and Alexander Rogers were chief among the leading civil servants of the British Empire who devoted abiding and serious attention to Persian language and poetry—that of Hafez in particular. Meanwhile, the giants of European cultural self-redefinition like Goethe and Arnold pushed the limits of attraction to Persian poetry to the center stage of the European literary bourgeois public sphere.

But the question remains as to what it was exactly that these cultural icons of the European bourgeoisie were doing with and to these Persian poets. At the immediate level, Persian poets were being used to learn how to rule India. Hafez and Sa'di were to teach British colonial officers about the manners and customs of Indians, to whom at least since the fifteenth century Persian had been functioning as a lingua franca. But on closer examination, one notices that beyond this immediate practical purpose was a self-universalizing humanism that was being narrated in the language of Persian poetry. British colonial officers and their Indian subjects were now sharing a universal humanism that embraced them both in the bosom of a literary heritage. The institution of Persian Adab, which was neither doctrinally Islamic nor linguistically in the language of the Arabic Qur'an, added zest and momentum to this literary humanism that the British detected in Persian literature, Hafez and Sa'di being chief among the sources they opted to canonize and institutionalize.

If this colonial use to which Persian poetry was put was squarely from within the Enlightenment project as the defining ideological moment of the reign of capital, the counter-Enlightenment movement that manifested itself in romanticism had an equally central role for the Persians. In effect, the romanticist sought to turn the lemon of Persian literary humanism into the lemonade of an equally universalizing cosmic mysticism. The structural continuity that we begin to see among the Enlightenment modernity, European colonialism, and literary humanism coming to terms with romanticism and mysticism integrates the entire spectrum of presumed bifurcation in economic and cultural production in East and West, which is markedly different from the ideological formation of "the West and the Rest" as favored by European philosophers and historians and regurgitated and elaborated even by the postcolonial critics of Orientalism.

The metamorphosis of Persian poets from the Enlightenment to romanticism reveals that the feud between the two movements did not really amount to much, because while the former was promoting a universal humanism that was economically feasible and culturally palatable to the European bourgeoisie, the latter launched a bourgeois-liberal revolt against the excesses of the tyranny of capital. While the anxiety of Enlightenment modernity removed the European bourgeois self-definition from the ecclesiastical church and the medieval aristocracy, that of romanticism removed the instrumental rationalism of the Enlightenment. But romanticism could not replace that instrumental rationalism with anything but an "Oriental" mysticism, and this is where Rumi, Hafez, and Sa'di were now heading in their new European habitat.

German Romanticism and its adaptation of what it called "Persian Sufism" had far-reaching implications for the rest of Europe. In England, Edward B. Cowell, who was Edward FitzGerald's Persian teacher, was attracted to Persian sources through Germans. The same was true of Samuel Robinson. German literary scholars have continued to love and admire Persian poetry as if Sa'di and Hafez were their own poets, for in effect they were—to the point that the last of the great German Persianists could offer a still palpably romantic genealogy of how Sa'di and Hafez have been read:

> At the time that his [Sa'di's] fame grew in Europe [early in the nineteenth century], not many of his admirers asked what lay behind his verse. Did he sing in his ghazals of worldly love, or was it divine love, as the Sufis usually do under the veil of mundane imagery? Or was it, as has been claimed lately, political poetry in the guise of love songs? Perhaps all three interpretations are true to a certain degree, as in the case of Hafez, his great compatriot, for it is the peculiarity of Persian poetry that it oscillates between heavenly and worldly delights and that many images can be understood at different levels.[39]

It is precisely at this amorphous meandering of the mystical and the political that German romanticizing of Persian mysticism had a historic rendezvous with fascism.

THE MOVING SPECTER OF FASCISM

The year of Goethe's publication of *West-östlicher Divan* was no ordinary one. German nationalism was in high gear. Student activism in Giessen and Jena was at a particularly high intensity. A professor of law at Giessen, a hotheaded revolutionary named Karl Follen, had just emerged as the leader of student activists. On 23 March 1819, Karl Ludwig Sand, a follower of Follen's, murdered the popular writer and Russian informant August von Kotzebue in Mannheim. Fearful of a radical trend in the German nationalist uprising, Frederick William III ordered the execution of Sand on 20 May 1820. His execution, however, further aggravated student activism in German universities. On 1 August 1819, Klemens von Metternich met with Frederick William III at Teplitz, a spa in Bohemia, and persuaded him to tighten the state grip on German universities, intensify press censorship, and put an end to his constitutional reform. Metternich arranged for a meeting of the ministers of the larger German states in Karlsbad. The result were the antidemocratic measures known as the Karlsbad Decrees, which Metternich had passed through the Bundestag in a blatantly antidemocratic manner by 20 September 1819. As reported by one historian of the period, Martin Kitchen:

> Under the terms of the Karlsbad decree a federal representative was appointed to supervise each university. All teachers suspected of holding subversive views were to be dismissed. The fraternities were disbanded, academic freedom denied and the universities were brought under federal control. . . . All printed matter of less than 320 pages was subjected to pre-censorship. The longer works could be censored after publication if they contained "breathtaking theories and infectious madness." An Investigation Commission was established in Mainz to track down revolutionaries.[40]

The similarity of these circumstances to the late Pahlavi and early Islamic revolution period marks the historic extension of key events in European social and intellectual history back to the Iranian domain proper. As I will have occasion to explain in more detail later, this confluence of European romanticism and Persian poetic mysticism and their joint proclivity toward political absolutism will have a historical rendezvous in the establishment of the Islamic republic and its innate totalitarian proclivities. What is particularly relevant here is the beginning of the eventual transformation of

German Romanticism into mysticism, in the context of which Hafez and Sa'di were being wholeheartedly received, repeatedly translated, widely emulated, pervasively used as noms de plume, and finally metamorphosed in Rueckert's ghazals and Goethe's *West-östlicher Divan.* Late in the Pahlavi period, this romantic mysticism imperceptively slid into totalitarian fascism, becoming a particularly influential trend that linked the demise of the Pahlavi monarchy to the rise of the Islamic republic.

This fusion of romanticism and mysticism (with a particular penchant for Persian Sufism) eventually found fertile ground in the ideas of the Swiss mystic Frithjof Schuon, passed down to his Iranian disciple, perhaps the most notoriously retrogressive thinker of twentieth-century Iran, Seyyed Hossein Nasr, whose fanatical antimodernism dovetailed perfectly with Ayatollah Khomeini's revolutionary asceticism. While Nasr was weaving together his Islamist romanticism and antimodern mysticism in the bosom of the Pahlavi court and dynasty, and with the figure of the Persian monarch Mohammad Reza Shah in mind, he in fact was inadvertently paving the way for the shah's chief nemesis, Ayatollah Khomeini. The ideological denunciation of modernity had a direct root in these German sources of romanticism, mysticism, and fascism, which S. H. Nasr had received through René Guénon (1886–1951), Ananda K. Coomaraswamy (1877–1947), and particularly Frithjof Schuon (1907–1998), the German-Swiss Perennialist mystic, who had a far more direct influence on the Iranian turn to antimodernism and thereafter to the consolidation of the Islamist ideology.[41] A militant proponent of the esoteric ideas of *Sophia Perennis* and *Philosophia Perennis,* as expounded by these thinkers, Nasr, in a profound and enduring way, laid the ground for Ayatollah Khomeini and his revolutionary asceticism and mysticism.

The fascistic tendencies evident in Nasr's antimodernism and his blind celebration of what he called "Tradition" are far closer to the totalitarian tendencies of the Islamic republic than anything that Jalal Al-e Ahmad or Ali Shari'ati ever said or did, and precisely for this reason Nasr was very warmly welcomed back to Iran by the leading ideologues of the Islamic republic despite his very close connections to the Pahlavi monarchy. At first he did his best to develop his fascistic antimodernism with the Pahlavis and in the midst of the Persian monarchy, but once he had failed and the Islamist revolution happened, the totalitarian tendencies of the Islamic republic blended perfectly with his mystical absolutism, as well as with Khomeini's mysticism and his idea of *Valayati-e Faqih*/Guardianship of the Jurisconsult. The term "*velayat*" in this critical doctrine and the very cornerstone of the Islamic republic contains all the romantic, mystical, and fascistic elements of this genealogy. So, in a very significant way, Nasr is a far more serious theorist of the totalitarian tendencies of the Islamic republic than Ayatollah Montazeri was for the theory of *Valayati-e Faqih,* and precisely for that reason Nasr is becoming increasingly incorporated into the ruling ideology of the regime whereas Montazeri was put under house arrest toward the end of his life and completely discredited.[42]

From the Enlightenment to romanticism to mysticism to fascism, Persophilia became integral to a European social and intellectual trajectory that would eventually alter the course of history around the globe—Iran included. German Romantic poets' fixation with self-annihilation, in which the Persian metaphor of a moth throwing itself at a candle's flame played a central role, had a catastrophic assignation with history. From the ascetic mysticism at the heart of German Nazism, through the doctrine of *Velayat-e Faqih,* to Iranian children throwing themselves under Iraqi tanks, there is thus only one straight and frightful line.

CHAPTER FIVE

From Romanticism to Pan-Islamism to Transcendentalism

AS WE HAVE SEEN, Goethe (1749–1832) was deeply affected by Hafez (c. 1315–1390), a fascination that in turn intrigued Muhammad Iqbal (1877–1938) and led him to rediscover the Persian poet at a critical moment in South Asian history and thereafter have a wide-ranging effect in all Persian-speaking societies, giving renewed reason to consider Hegel's (1770–1831) conception of "the Oriental" in his philosophy of history. But the Persophilia movement was not just eastward from Europe—it was also westward toward North America. Under the influence of European romanticism, Ralph Waldo Emerson (1803–1882), and with him members of the entire American transcendentalist movement, are known for their affection for Persian literature—like others, particularly for Hafez and Sa'di. The feeling was mutual and reciprocated. Especially after World War II there was a marked increase in the interest in American literature in Iran. In the same way that transcendentalism was a contrarian movement at the peak of Enlightenment modernity, the increasing attraction to American literature in Iran had created a paradoxical interest in a country that would become the hallmark of imperialist intervention and the prevention of the rise of homegrown democracy.

Still, through the thick and thin of their historical interactions, the United States would never lose this paradoxical presence in the Iranian literary public space.

The links among these poets and thinkers looping around the globe is one of the most fascinating episodes of Persophilia, connecting Europe, South Asia, the United States, and Iran in a circulatory sphere of cross-references at significant moments of their respective histories when revolutionary ideas were remapping the world afresh. This new cycle reached one of its crucial zeniths in Europe with Goethe's *West-östlicher Divan* (1814–1819), composed under the shadow of Hafez, and continued with Iqbal's European education and subsequent turn to Persian poets, which itself educed a fresh and provocative generation of interest in Hafez's lyricism in South Asia, just as in North America the selfsame German Romanticism extended Hafez and Sa'di into new territories. The cycle became essential to world-historic changes in South Asia, when Persophilia linked the defining moments of the emerging postcolonial history.

THE CENTER CANNOT HOLD

The circularity of Persophilia roaming around the planet from Europe to Asia to America poses a central question to our compartmentalized conception of global capitalism. The navigational routes of Persophilia were paved and facilitated by the increasingly globalized capital of the nineteenth and twentieth centuries. The largely unexamined bifurcation between the fictively presumed "central" domains of capitalist modernity, aka "the West," as rational and progressive and its colonial consequences as "traditional" and thus ipso facto moribund, has resulted in a radically binary false opposition being posited between the economic and social conditions of the two spheres to the analytical detriment of both. We will not have a critical awareness of the rise and demise of *modernity* (as a European imperialist project) as long as we relegate the condition of coloniality to a peripheral status and, at best, try to explain it away with such exoticizing gambits as the "Asiatic Mode of Production" on one side and "modernization theories" or "alternative modernities" on the other. All such heuristic or divisive devices categorically camouflage and distort the circulatory core of capital and the cultures it produces.

The rise of capitalist modernity and its concomitant Enlightenment project, presumed to be centered in a Western European context, and the relegation of its colonial consequences to a wide periphery around the globe are part and parcel of one and the same conceptual hegemony, the understanding of each contingent on an integral grasp of the other. Not only in the dominant, power-basing discourse of capitalist modernity but even in its classical Marxist or the post-epistemic Foucauldian critique, the binary opposition between the *polar* centers of the metropolitan power and the *tropical* outback of colonial territories is very much accepted as valid, and thus left unexamined. Whereas in the Marxist critique of capitalism it was the dismissive gambit of the "Asiatic Mode of Production" that kept the issue at bay, in Edward Said's Foucauldian critique of the discursive constitution of the Orient the very critical act of the deconstructive reading itself in effect paradoxically consolidated the supposition of this binary opposition between "the West" and "the Rest."

If this analytic constitution of a *center* for capitalist modernity and a *periphery* to its logic and rhetoric be true of its economic underpinning, it is equally true of the European project of the Enlightenment, which is coterminous with its rise and confluent with its immediate consequences in the cultural conditions of colonialism. The cultural reproduction of *the real*, very much on the model of the economic production of *reality*, is equally presumed to operate on two adjacent and radically different modalities. It is not until Edward Said's *Culture and Imperialism* (1993) that we begin to notice the political centrality of *the colonial* in the cultural constitution of the European literary imagination as one particularly poignant parameter of the Enlightenment project. But by and large in any critical reading of the Enlightenment—from Theodor Adorno and Max Horkheimer to Ernst Cassirer—we notice a conspicuous absence of any attention to the colonial consequences of the project in cultural reproduction of *the real*. Equally absent on the colonial end of the game is any critique of the cultural reproduction of *the real* in both analytical and organic conversation with the project of capitalist modernity. The perhaps justifiable countercolonial rhetoric of these readings often collapses into the hermetic seal of a rhetoric of *authenticity* and an analytic of *nativism* that divorces the cultural reproduction of *the real* in the colonial realm from the same reproductive acts at the centers of Enlightenment modernity. Instead of any critical undoing of that center–periphery metaphor, the self-authenticating rhetoric of cultural nativism in effect degenerates into an even more radical ossification of it—as we see in the works of critical thinkers ranging from Fanon to Said.

The ultimate objective of investigating such structural affinities between the two conditions of capitalist modernity and the Enlightenment on one side and colonialism and its cultural consequences on the other is to break the artificial and power-basing bifurcation between the "West," as the metaphoric sublimation of the power to produce *the real* and reproduce the cultural, and the "East," as the equally metaphoric realm of Oriental passivity that provides the "West" as much with raw material and cheap labor for its factories as it does with symbolics of submissiveness to its creative fantasies. The objective is to rise against the strategies of the pacification of a whole topography of creative resistance to categorical degradation and begin a kind of comparative cultural criticism that is no longer predicated on the assumption of a binary opposition between a *center* in the West and a globalized *periphery* in the Rest.

Goethe's attraction to Hafez and the company they both subsequently kept in the course of European romanticism would seem a long way from the ideological underpinning of the Islamic revolution in Iran—and yet the winding road has some clear signposts that eventually culminates in the figure of Davud Monshizadeh (1914–1989) and his establishment of a neo-Nazi party, SUMKA, in 1952. The attraction of some leading Iranian intellectuals to German Romanticism and its subsequent transmutation into politicized mysticism, however, was not limited to this blatant case, and pro-German sentiments that had a clearly anti–British colonialism character to them attracted many other leading intellectuals, such as Seyyed Hassan Taqizadeh, and point to a serious structural similarity between the Weimar Republic of the 1930s and the Pahlavi monarchy of the 1960s as two instantaneous preludes to the rise of German Fascism in one case and militant Islamism in the other.[1]

This structural similarity has much to teach us about the Enlightenment project as the cultural condition of capitalist modernity at both its polar centers and its tropical peripheries, a similarity that will perhaps help us collapse that binary opposition between a center and its periphery and work our way toward a more integral grasp of our universal predicament during and in the aftermath of the project. My principal proposition is that the Germany of 1930s had but a taste of the perpetual predicament of colonial territories and reached for similar kinds of responses endemic to colonial conditions. German Fascism put to the same political use the mystical dimensions of German Romanticism that militant Islamism would find useful in Khomeini's mystical asceticism.

Hafez and Goethe were seen as two iconic representations of two cultures presumed to be constitutionally different from and singularly at odds with each other—each the other of the other, each othering the other, the East of it there to Westernize the other, the West of it there to Orientalize the other. Against the continuing legacy of this presumption, the vicissitude of a circular act of transmigration of Persian poets demonstrates the singular gyration of capital and culture in the overriding logic of which there is but one direction—neither Eastern nor Western, neither Northern nor Southern, merely circumambulatory, convulsive, self-generative, substitutional, surrogating. The Enlightenment thinkers found in Persian poetry a universalizing humanism that made their globalizing culture particularly compatible with the planetary claims of mobile capital. European romanticism in general and German Romanticism in particular sought in Persian poets a haven and a refuge from the ravages of instrumental reason constitutional to the working of both capital and the culture of modernity that it entailed. In this context, not only Hegel's *Philosophy of History* but equally important his *Phenomenology of Spirit* found it useful to embrace the poetry of Rumi as the best example of the "Consciousness of One," as best represented in his *Encyclopaedie der Philosophischen Wissenschaften*.

THE WIDENING GYRE

If we were to take a detour from German and European romanticism toward American transcendentalism we would see similar uses to which Persian poets were put by an American version of disenchantment with instrumental reason. In the absence of this perspective it would appear rather odd that the founding fathers of American revolutionary thinking and cultures, from Benjamin Franklin (1706–1790) to Ralph Waldo Emerson (1802–1882), were so enamored of Persian poets. The fascination of Franklin with Sa'di and Hafez in the first issue of a journal he edited and published in Philadelphia was matched by Emerson's enchantment with the Gladwin translation of Sa'di's *Golestan* that had appeared in 1806. The contribution of Persian poets to the eventual transmutation of European romanticism into a nascent and dangerous mysticism became a chief staple of German Orientalism in the wake of a particularly acute ascendancy in European colonialism— almost exactly at a time when in the United States a peculiar brand of Persophilia extended that romanticism into the formation of transcendentalism as a veritable intellectual movement.

While the European Enlightenment was entirely compatible with the project of colonialism, German Romanticism proper and its gradual collapse into mysticism pursued its way toward the rise of fascism. Why was it that Richard Wagner recited, of all things, Hafez's poetry to Frau Cosima Wagner after dinner as we see the great German philologist Hermann Brockhaus, to whom Europe is indebted for his critical edition of Hafez, appear on his doorstep as the German composer's brother-in-law? Yet another young German philologist, Friedrich Nietzsche, met Wagner for the first time at the residence of the same Herr Brockhaus, and from there we can go directly to section 370 of the inimitable *Die Fröhliche Wissenschaft/The Gay Science* where Nietzsche meets Hafez on the site of his own insurrection against Wagner and Schopenhauer as the best representatives of romanticism.

Before you think we are done with this Herr Hermann Brockhaus, we must take a quick look at his critical edition of Hafez turning up (of all places) right in the hands of none other than Allamah Muhammad Iqbal in India in the wake of the Indian independence movement, wherein we can read his *Payam-e Mashreq* as he writes it in dialogue with Goethe's *West-östlicher Divan*. The cycle then comes to a complete closure when the ideals and aspirations of Allamah Iqbal have migrated from the subcontinent back to Hafez's homeland, as the great poet and reformer becomes a paramount figure in the reconstitution of Islamic ideology after the Iranian revolution of 1979. Once we see the same Morteza Motahhari (1919–1979), who adopted Iqbal's ideas in his own ideological articulation of the Islamic revolution, also writing a book about Hafez and arguing against his secularization, we witness the spectacular circularity of culture and capital conflating each other.[2]

Tracing the presence of Persian poets in the active imagination of the very idea of "Europe" as a thin thread holding the circularity of cultural production from Enlightenment to fascism, from Iran and South Asia to the Weimar Republic and Europe, from German Nazism to militant Islamism, is where Persophilia reveals the microcosmic disposition of its significance in the global configuration of power and resistance to power during the nineteenth and the twentieth centuries. A circular reading of capital and the cultures it produces—a circularity that sees the U.S.-led invasion of Iraq and Afghanistan in the light of the same logic with which it sees the presence of the late Palestinian intellectual Edward Said in the academic neighborhood of the U.S. imperialist theorist Samuel Huntington; a circularity that notes the presence of Aramco in Saudi Arabia in the light of the same logic with which it sees the abundance of sweatshops in midtown Manhattan; a circularity that considers the presence of immigrant Pakistanis in England, of working-class Algerians in France, and of guest-laborer Turks in Germany or Latino immigrants in New York or California in the light of the same logic with which it sees the IMF's bailing out of bankrupt economies of the Asian crisis; a circularity that recognizes NATO's global expansion and military thinking in the light of the same logic that facilitates World Bank's globalization of capital; a circularity that sees in the cacophony of postcolonial and cultural studies, partaking like bandits in the hospitable Fifth Column of poststructuralism and postmodernism, as the cultural consequences of a world-devouring colonialism coming home to roost; a circularity that recognizes the ravages of capitalist modernity beyond its sugarcoating by Enlightenment humanism, as it equally recognizes the bogus claim to "authenticity" by multiple "traditions" which that very modernity has engendered and sustained in order to make itself look logical—and thus a circularity that defies the distorting and power-basing binary opposition between "the West and the East," between "modernity and tradition," between "center and periphery," and ultimately between "capitalism and colonialism." The passing love affair of one German poet with one Persian poet is thus the momentous occasion for rereading these otherwise totally nonpoetic and entirely prosaic realities.

My reading of European (and subsequently American and South Asian) Persophilia is thus poised to remedy some of the persistent conservative criticisms regularly raised against, and some of the nativist abuses repeatedly made of, Edward Said's historic diagnosis, by lifting his reading of Orientalism out of the binary opposition that it inadvertently ossifies and placing it in a larger continuum that reaches from the Enlightenment project through romanticism and transcendentalism to the mystical predicates of the rise of fascism in both the centers *and* peripheries of capitalist modernity, and to an analytical degree that makes the very distinction between *center* and *periphery* no longer viable. Some recent studies[3] have taken Edward Said to task for having provided "too political" a reading of European Orientalism, maintaining that there have been numerous occasions of a more "positive" encounter with the East, in effect providing "the West" with alternative models of cultural formations. All of these criticisms will be rendered entirely superfluous when we locate and identify the project of Orientalism, not as a singular act of colonizing discourse formation—a reading of Orientalism for which Said's text may indeed be faulted—but as an integral move constitutional to the European project of Enlightenment in which, for both economic and cultural reasons, attraction to the Orient assumes an integral significance. The use to which Orientalism is then put is not an abuse domestic to Orientalism but to the larger Enlightenment–romanticism trajectory to which Orientalism is integral. The significance of thinking through the specificities of Persophilia as opposed to the generic disposition of Orientalism is precisely this epistemic awareness that the cooptation of non-European cultures enabled (not enriched) the European cultural formations that aided and abetted the aggressive globalization of a Europocentric conception of capital and its colonial consequences.

Once finely tuned through the lenses of Persophilia, Orientalism, in this reading, is no longer an isolated act of simply reading the Orient in order to dominate it, but an integral dimension of the whole vicissitude of the European project of capitalist modernity, of capital and its cultures, of the dialectical formation of the metropolitan and the colonial—all in a singular act of circuitous logic of bloated capital and cheap labor, raw material and market, culture and imperialism. In this reading, Orientalism of the Enlightenment project assumes a rather different character from the one necessitated and promoted during the romantic reaction to it, and both of a slightly different nature from the one experienced during the transcendentalist movement in the United States. The collapse of European romanticism into a visceral mysticism, in turn, required yet a different kind of Orientalism than had been experienced before. Orientalism is not a singular mode of knowledge production, the vicissitudes of Persophilia will teach us, but a transformative metaphor that precisely in its instability has enabled the European cultural domination of the globe.

By honing in on the fate of Persian poets in the course of the historical vicissitudes of the European Enlightenment—through romanticism and transcendentalism, down to the mystical predicate fascism, and from there to the ideological foregrounding of militant Islamism—I propose a much

more animated and multifaceted Orientalism than a flat ideological statement made once and for all irrespective of the historical modulations of
capital and the cultures it procures to camouflage its operations. To be sure,
there has never been an Orientalism that was not politically anchored. But
the strategic location of that anchor has been a subject always predicated
on the European cultural remodulation of the bourgeoisie toward the circulation of capital. By tracing the trajectory of capital and its culture between the metropolitan and the colonial ends of the project of modernity,
the so-called East itself was implicated in the project of Orientalism: the
Orientals began indeed to see themselves in the mirror of the Occident, as
the Occidentals concocted different kinds of Oriental mirrors for their own
changing necessities. The combined insights of Raymond Schwab and Edward
Said have paradoxically blinded us to the far more dynamic disposition of
the circulatory disposition of capital and the cultures it generates in order to
dismantle and devour in order to feed its insatiable appetite for cultural
cannibalism.

MUHAMMAD IQBAL AND PAN-ISLAMISM

The only trouble with that insatiable appetite is that it generates its opposite
force on the colonial sites of its own making. The eminent Indian poet, philosopher, and politician Muhammad Iqbal (1877–1938) became the uncanny
recipient of Goethe's *West-östlicher Divan* at a critical moment in the history of the Indian subcontinent when the very idea of Pakistan as a separate
Muslim nation-state was about to be conceived. It is in this context that he
wrote his *Payam-e Mashreq* (Message of the East) very much as an answer
to Goethe's *West-östlicher Divan,* and in the estimation of one German Orientalist about this book: "Iqbal's dramatic talent shows itself in the 'Dialogue between God and Man' and the conversation between 'Poet and
Houri,' a poem inspired by Goethe."[4] But that very "dialogue" between God
and Man is the key culprit in the de-historicization of fragile humanity in
dangerously mystical terms.

Iqbal is widely regarded as the "spiritual father" of Pakistan as an "Islamic
republic" and a key figure in the articulation of postcolonial Islam as a potent political ideology. He was a poet, a philosopher, and a political activist
all at the same time—and the fusion of these character traits was definitive

to his thinking and legacy. His first poetry books—*Asrar-e Khodi* (1915), *Romuz-e Bikhodi* (1918), *Payam-e Mashreq* (1923), and *Zabur-e Ajam* (1927)— are essential to his philosophical thinking. His Urdu works—*Bang-e Dara* (1924), *Bal-e Jibril* (1935), *Zarb-e Kalim* (1936), and *Armughan-e Hijaz* (1938)—expanded his thinking into further domains and made Persian, Urdu, and English the trilingual territories of his wide-ranging influences. A member of the London branch of the All India Muslim League and a close friend of the founder of Pakistan, Mohammad Ali Jinnah (1876–1948), Iqbal was among the first Indian Muslims who called for the creation of a Muslim state in India—and that proposition was entirely rooted in his singular achievement in the aggressive transformation of the Islamic intellectual heritage into a site of ideological contestation against "the West"—of which he had, despite his longtime education there, an entirely essentialist, ahistorical, and flawed reading.

Influenced and encouraged by Sir Thomas Arnold (1795–1842) when he was at Government College in Lahore, Iqbal was eventually led to pursue higher education in Europe—initially at Trinity College, Cambridge, and then off to Germany, where he earned a doctorate at Ludwig Maximilian University. His doctoral thesis was subsequently published in 1908 as *The Development of Metaphysics in Persia.*[5] It was during his time in Germany that Iqbal discovered Goethe, along with Heine, Nietzsche, and Bergson. Though he was drawn to these European thinkers, it was to the Persian mystic poet Rumi that he was most profoundly attracted. Iqbal would later feature Rumi in the role of guide in many of his poems, which led him to seek a "spiritual" Islam, with dangerously abstract political consequences. His single most important purpose in creating this Islam was to unify the global Muslim community into a single political force. European secularism, Indian Hindu majority, and Arab and Muslim nationalism were the principal sources of his fears and anxieties; and instead of engaging with and absorbing their alterities, he sought to overcome them categorically.

Asrar-e Khodi is decidedly geared toward an articulation of this politically absolutist Muslim self. This self is divinely ordained and yet attained through worldly endeavors. In his *Romuz-e Bikhodi* he complements that endeavor by way of the dissolution of this self in the divine totality that manifests itself in the body of the nation, the *ummah*. When Iqbal modeled his *Payam-e-Mashreq/The Message of the East* on Goethe's *West-östlicher Divan*, he was in effect offering "Eastern" solace to perceived "Western" decadence.

This "Eastern spirituality" was manufactured in response to a frightfully limited and equally artificial conception of "Western materialism," the principal culprit in agitating the passively or defiantly colonized mind of the non-European thinkers who encountered Europe. The same spirit informs his *Javed Nama/Book of Javed* (1932), named for and addressed to his son, in which he combines his understanding of Ibn Arabi and Dante as narrative ruses to visit the world to come. Guided by Rumi, Iqbal navigates through various heavenly spheres to visit the Divinity. All of these works ultimately led to Iqbal's major opus in English, *The Reconstruction of Religious Thought in Islam* (1930–1934), in which he finally offers his conception of Islam—radically politicized, essentialized, and stripped of all its inner dimensions—as the blueprint of a new plan for the formation of a Muslim state. The road to the absolutist propensities of the nightmare of political Islamism was paved with every good intention.

Why did Iqbal write his major philosophical and poetic oeuvre in Persian? When he turned to Persian as the preferred language for his philosophical writing, the language was deeply rooted in the subcontinent. The 1835 Macaulay edict put an official end to the centrality of Persian language and literature in India, but by no means an effective end. In two prominent South Asian poets, Mirza Asadallah Ghaleb (d. 1869) and Muhammad Iqbal, the fate of Persian poetry was given yet another twist in its unending back-and-forth saga with colonialism and its causes and consequences. Ghaleb was particularly proud of his achievements in Persian poetry, and Iqbal, "the spiritual father of Pakistan," opted for Persian in 1915 when he turned his attention to *Asrar-e Khodi*. Iqbal's turn to Persian, as opposed to Urdu or English, marks a critical moment in the history of the Indian subcontinent. In contrast to the limited locality of Urdu and the colonial cosmopolitanism of English, the regional universalism of Persian that embraced the eastern part of Islamic civilization and was the lingua franca central to the last three Islamic empires—the Ottomans, the Safavids, and the Mughals—appealed to him most. In the Persian language, as a result, Iqbal's emerging pan-Islamism assumed both a political and a cultural cohesion—thus enervating the transnational public space of South and eastern Asia all the way to the extended Muslim world.

It is important to note that it was to Rumi that Iqbal immediately turned as his guide upon his return from Europe and the rediscovery of his cultural heritage. From the midst of that heritage, and now in the figure of

Rumi who figures prominently in *Asrar-e Khodi,* Iqbal began to construct a literary mysticism (with a potent penchant for poetry) that befitted the pan-Islamism of his political agenda. Iqbal opted for the metric model of *mathnavi* in *ramal mosaddas* as his formal homage to Rumi and as he sought to revive the Persian poetic passion for his reading of a postcolonial consciousness. But in the explosion of the First World War, and as Iqbal was composing *Asrar-e Khodi,* Hafez went down on the chart of the top-ten Persian poets, because this time around his excessive drinking and merry-making habits were no longer palatable to the ascetic revolutionary disposition of the Indian Islamist reformer, who had now manufactured a far more effective Rumi from his pious remembrances of the mystic master.

For the particular direction that this absolutist Islamism took we need to examine its German Romantic origins. All was rose, nightingale, and candle in the German reception of Persian poets, and the mere metaphors soon assumed deadly consequences in Europe itself. In Schimmel's assessments of Muhammad Iqbal's fascination with Hafez we read a curious reference: "He [Iqbal] had carefully studied the different editions of the Divan-e Hafez and preferred that of Hermann Brockhaus with the Turkish commentary of Sudi."[6] Now who exactly would this Herr Hermann Brockhaus be other than the brother-in-law of none other than Richard Wagner; and who would accompany the young Friedrich Nietzsche on his first visit to Herr Richard and Frau Cosima Wagner as a graduate student other than this very Hermann Brockhaus; and whom would Wagner consult when naming one of his most celebrated operas, *Parsifal,* other than that selfsame brother-in-law?[7] The possible influences of Persian sources on Wagner when he was composing *Parsifal,* plus the charges of racism and anti-Semitism against both Wagner and *Parsifal* in particular, pushes the domain of European Persophilia right into the bosom of the most horrid chapters of European history, with which the whole notion of Indo-European languages is now charged; and the extension of that absolutist politics now extends from Europe to a climactic inaugurating moment of militant Islamism in South Asia.

The crucial question here is why the critical edition of Hafez the great Indian reformer preferred to all others was none other than that of Hermann Brockhaus, and why he should like its English rendition by Wilberforce Clarke better than those of others.[8] Wilberforce Clarke was a civil servant in the service of the British East India Company whose translation of Hafez had appeared in 1891 as one endeavor among many geared to teach British colonial officers not just Persian but also about the manners and customs of Indians.[9] Hermann Brockhaus was a leading German Orientalist actively involved in translating Oriental sources at the height of romanticism. As the historians of the period report: "German philosophy, now given over to organicism, intuitionism, and even mysticism, found an ally in Persian Sufism. Meanwhile German philologists such as Tholuck, von Hammer-Purgstall, Brockhaus, and Rosenzweig-Schwannau were producing texts and translations of Persian literature for the use of not only German but also English and American writers."[10] The copy of the Hafez in Iqbal's hand, as a result, directly linked a founding figure of political pan-Islamism to German Romanticism and British colonialism.

Upon closer examination, however, more revealing information is discovered about Herr Hermann Brockhaus. Wilhelm Halbfass, in his *India and Europe: An Essay in Philosophical Understanding,* reports a "symptomatic coincidence" in the relationship between Richard Wagner and Friedrich Nietzsche and their mutual attitude toward Schopenhauer: "Nietzsche himself left a description of how Wagner, during their first encounter, proclaimed Schopenhauer to be 'the only philosopher who has recognized the nature of music.' It is a symptomatic coincidence that this meeting took place in the house of the Indologist H. Brockhaus, Wagner's brother-in-law, having been arranged by another Indologist who had studied with Nietzsche, E. Windisch."[11] It must have been through his brother-in-law, Hermann Brockhaus, that Wagner developed an interest in Hafez. We read in Cosima Wagner's *Diaries,* the entry of Saturday, 3 April 1880, the following note: "A drive with the children to the Sejanus grotto; everything in bud, but it is still windy. In the evening a merry meal and whist, during which R. quotes Hafiz's line, 'Sinning, to be a sinner,' and says how intoxicating the Anacreontic style becomes when transposed to the Orient."[12] The proximity of Nietzsche to Brockhaus may also account for his immediate attention to Hafez when, in *The Gay Science,* he distinguished between two modes of *immortalization* in the context of German Romanticism—one healthy and promoted by gratitude and love ("an art of apotheoses, perhaps dithyrambic like Rubens or blissfully mocking like Hafez") and the other pathological and tyrannic ("Schopenhauer's philosophy of will or Wagner's music").[13]

Neither Wagner nor Nietzsche, of course, needed this immediate proximity to Hermann Brockhaus to be familiar with Hafez. As early as 1812–1813, Joseph von Hammer-Purgstall's translation of Hafez had appeared in

Stuttgart and Tübingen in two volumes as *Der Divan von Mohammad Schemseddin Hafiz*. Halfway through the century yet another German translation, this time in three volumes, had been published by Vinzent Ritter von Rosenzweig-Schwannau in Vienna in 1856–1864. But the fact that between 1854 and 1856 Hermann Brockhaus published in Leipzig his critical edition of Hafez in three volumes makes him a particularly indispensable figure to be put at the doorstep, as it were, of two iconic figures in the link between German Romanticism and European fascism.[14]

By the time Iqbal received his Hafez in its critical German edition by the same Hermann Brockhaus and its English translation by Wilberforce Clarke, the world of his physical location demanded a different kind of reading of Persophilia in which Hafez was more a hindrance than a paragon. In Iqbal's revolutionary demands for an active reconstitution of the Muslim subject, Hafez figured very poorly. Iqbal was after a postcolonial Muslim subject (or Self, as he called it), and the Hafez that Brockhaus and Wilberforce Clarke had handed him was too intoxicated, exhilarated, out of control. Iqbal wanted an upright, righteous, and principled Muslim to find the dignity of a place for himself in the modernity of the world colonially imposed upon him. Hafez was no such Muslim—he was too unruly, subversive, dismantling all the metanarrative that a Muslim polity demanded.

The more Iqbal objected to Hafez, the more he was convinced that he had to rescue the Persian language from this mutinous Persian. Iqbal's prose and poetry, as a result, becomes replete with an actively revisionist reading of classical Persian poets—Sana'i, Rumi, Fakhr al-Din Iraqi, and Naser Khosrow in particular. In both *Asrar-e Khodi* and *Romuz-e Bikhodi,* Iqbal's fixation is with defining the Muslim Self in the community of the faith that he is now seeking postcolonially to imagine. Persian is the universal language of that Self, and Rumi the sublime guide who will lead Iqbal to define that necessary subjectivity. But, and here's the rub, the captured colonial imagination of Iqbal and the romanticism from which he received his European Hafez, could not help but define that Self in frightfully absolutist terms. This paved the way for the catastrophic partition of India and the separation of millions of Muslims from their cosmopolitan context, and decades later, for the even more catastrophic constitution of an Islamic republic in Iran by some well-intentioned Iranian followers of Iqbal like Morteza Motahhari and Ali Shari'ati, who, as they sought in earnest to define an anticolonial subjectivity beyond the reach of their phantom fears of "the West" in fact plunged that subjectivity even deeper into their own politics of despair.

EMERSON AND TRANSCENDENTALISM

Equally crucial is the Western migration of European Persophilia from German Romanticism to American transcendentalism, a journey that was narrated precisely around the edges of Persian poetry and Euro-American Persophilia.[15] The route of this passage is quite revelatory. As Yohannan noted: "The leading popularizers of Persian literature in England and America in the mid-nineteenth century often took their cue from the Germans. Edward B. Cowell, who taught FitzGerald to read Persian, owed his later interpretations to German sources; Samuel Robinson, a businessman who was an amateur of Persian, owed both texts and translations to them."[16] In this passage inter-European exchanges were critical: "The two most widely read anthologies of Asian literature—Louisa Costello's *The Rose-Garden of Persia* in England, and William R. Alger's *The Poetry of the Orient* in America—contained numerous English translations of German versions of Persian poetry."[17] This fascination was not limited to Hafez; Rumi was equally admired and assimilated. But Hafez was the prince of the romantics: "Even in Transcendentalist America, which was generally resistant to such tendencies, the wine of Hafez was no longer simply 'Moor's best Port,' but stood for intellectual emancipation and expansion of the mind."[18] Ralph Waldo Emerson had great admiration for Sa'di's poetry, whose *Golestan* he had read in Gladwin's translation (1806).[19] Emerson compared Sa'di's "practical wisdom" to that of Benjamin Franklin,[20] thus effectively assimilating him into the American pantheon of wise and judicious framers of the Constitution that defined them all as a people. The journey of Persian poets to North America thus began in earnest at the very roots of American moral and intellectual history, with wide-ranging implications well into its most defining moments.

It was not just in the content of Hafez's ghazals but, even more important, in their formal defiance of instrumental reason that Persian poets appealed to their romantic and transcendentalist readers. As a result, the question of the unity or lack thereof in Hafez's ghazals soon became a defining moment in both the European romanticization and later in American transcendentalization of the Persian poets. When in 1947 the British Orientalist A. J. Arberry brought this romantic cycle to its end and published fifty of his translated ghazals, he opted to compare the Persian poetic form to the sonnet rather than the ode. In his own translations he "sought contrapuntal musical effects, accepting two or more themes in one poem. The later Beethoven sonatas were his models rather than the more formally correct earlier ones."[21] Other translators have been also hard at work to find a proper metaphor for the way Hafez's ghazals should be read. For different lyricists at different times, "the *ghazal* was, like the courtyard in Persian architecture, inward-facing, rather than linear and dramatic as is most Western literature," or else like "spokes radiating from a hub or focal point," or yet like "the arabesque patterns of a Persian miniature and not the thematic Aristotelian structure of a Western ode."[22] This comparative appropriation of Hafez into the Euro-American trajectories of romanticism and transcendentalism made the Persian poets definitive to their Persophilia and pulled it in the decidedly opposite direction to where Iqbal was pushing it in his pan-Islamist project. Iqbal wished to oppose the colonial extension of the capitalist modulation of instrumental reason with an equally absolutist mysticism, while Emerson and the transcendentalists were in search of the poetic dismantling of that very reason. Thus Rumi became far more attractive for Iqbal's project, whereas Hafez was more at home with Emerson and the transcendentalists.

The defining moment of German Romanticism and its attraction to Persian poetry became a moral and material disillusion with bourgeois Enlightenment and instrumental modernity. While Louisa Costello's *The Rose-Garden of Persia* marked the extension westward of German Romanticism, William R. Alger's *The Poetry of the Orient* marked the entrance of Persian poetry, through German Romanticism, into American transcendentalism. It seems that the Persian ingredient of German Romanticism was the chief attraction for its transmission both to the rest of Europe and to the North American continent. Benjamin Franklin went so far as to take a parable on toleration from Sa'di's *Bustan*, which he had received from the Dutch Orientalist George Gentius's Latin translation, but via the English divine Jeremy Taylor, and "tried to pass it off as a missing chapter of Genesis."[23] A compelling point of attraction to Persian poets for the American transcendentalists was what Emerson described as their inconsecutiveness: "Wonderful is the inconsecutiveness of the Persians."[24] Echoing the sentiments of Emerson, the American Orientalist E. P. Evans also believed, as early as 1884, that "the *ghazal* of Hafez can never be acclimatized and thoroughly naturalized in Western literature."[25] But if so, whence the attraction?— except to manufacture something out of the discrepancy that American society, culture, and soon history badly needed but lacked.

In a major study of American transcendentalism, Arthur Versluis traces the place of Persian and other "Asian religions" in the manifold of the intellectual movement that transformed the continent, all the way from its earliest origins in German and British romanticism to the works of Emerson, Thoreau, Alcott, Melville, and Brownson. In his study of the "Patterns in Literary Religion: The Orient and Second Cycle of Transcendentalism," Versluis pays particular attention to the work of Samuel Johnson (1822– 1882) on "Oriental Religions" (1872–1885), wherein we learn about his fascination with Zoroastrianism as a religion of "Personal Will." Johnson provided an exceedingly positive, life-affirming, and iconoclastic reading of Zoroastrianism and Manichaeism. Versluis concludes:

> In regard to Manichaeism, he is by no means willing to acquiesce in denying its legitimacy, quite to the opposite. The "extreme intolerance" of Christianity, Judaism, and Islam for Manichaeism was simply "a war of narrow dogmatism against universal tendencies, however imperfect their expressions, however distorted by the false light of the day." In Johnson's view, Manichaeism, far from being yet another heresy, was, like Gnosticism, worthy of investigation and even admiration, not least because of its "boldness," its eclectic "breadth," and its adherents' fearlessness and rationality.[26]

In a robust and prolific way, American Persophilia of this pedigree was to have a profound and lasting influence in the most critical episodes of American history. Henry David Thoreau's "Civil Disobedience" (1849) deeply influenced Martin Luther King Jr. when he wrote his "Letter from Birmingham Jail" (1963) in the heat of the Civil Rights Movement, while Thoreau himself cited Sa'di sympathetically in his *Walden* (1854), and, indeed, in his journal we see him so thoroughly identifying with Sa'di that he writes of his complete *metempsychosis with the Persian poet:*

I know, for instance, that Sadi entertained once identically the same thought that I do, and thereafter I can find no essential difference between Sadi and myself. He is not Persian, he is not ancient, he is not strange to me. By the identity of his thoughts with mine he still survives. It makes no odds what atoms serve us. Sadi possessed no greater privacy or individuality than is thrown open to me. He had no more interior and essential and sacred self than can come naked into my thought this moment. Truth and a true man is something essentially public, not private. If Sadi were to come back to claim a personal identity with the historical Sadi, he would find there were too many of us: he could not get a skin that would contain us all. The symbol of a personal identity preserved in this sense is a mummy from the catacombs,—a whole skin, it may [be], but no life within it. By living the life of a man is made common property. By sympathy with Sadi I have embowelled him. In his thought I have a sample of him, a slice from his core, which makes it unimportant where certain bones which the thinker once employed may lie; but I could not have got this without being equally entitled to it with himself.[27]

The cycle keeps turning and widening, for Martin Luther King Jr. was also deeply influenced by Gandhi, as is evident from his trip to India and is recorded in his "My Trip to the Land of Gandhi" (1959).[28] But a compatriot of Gandhi, Rabindranath Tagore (1861–1941), would inadvertently allow his own love for Hafez to be abused by the Pahlavi regime for yet another, this time monarchical, predisposition toward an absolutist state. As one historian of this encounter puts it:

> The emerging interwar ideology of "Pahlavi nationalism" sought to dissociate Iran from the Abrahamic-Islamicate "civilizational ethos" that was now understood to have long dominated Iranian culture, and instead sought to associate Iranian nationalism's claim of cultural authenticity to a newly emerging notion of "Indo-Iranian civilization" rooted in the pre-Islamic culture of Zoroastrianism and Aryanism. Tagore's visit to Iran was seen as an opportunity for his Iranian hosts to present him to the Iranian public as a living personification of this newly conceived idea of national authenticity.[29]

From Hafez to Goethe to Iqbal to Wagner to Nietzsche to Emerson to Tagore to Thoreau to Martin Luther King Jr.—the widening gyre of Persophilia expanded "East and West," thus dismantling them both figuratively and factually and multiplying, in both size and significance, the European bourgeois public sphere in known and unknown, liberating and troubling proportions.

CIRCULATORY CAPITAL AND ITS CULTURES OF RESISTANCE

From such a half-hidden, half-visible history of Persophilia, the circulatory course of capital and the cultures it occasioned and facilitated eventually assumed a decidedly global disposition. Goethe discovered Hafez during romanticism in Europe, from which site it went to India via Iqbal and to America via Ralph Waldo Emerson. In America, this Persophilia moved from Emerson and Thoreau with his notion of "civil disobedience" and ultimately reached Martin Luther King Jr. and the Civil Rights Movement. Meanwhile, in India, Gandhi thought he had picked up the very same idea of "civil disobedience" from Thoreau and pushed it forward through Ahimsa just as his compatriot Iqbal had caused a transmutation of Germanic Romanticism into political pan-Islamism. Tagore had come to love and admire Hafez entirely independently of Goethe or Iqbal, but the Pahlavi monarchy used that love for its own Aryanism, while Martin Luther King Jr. brought Thoreau and Gandhi together in his own version of "civil disobedience." Persophilia was adapted in Germany, reclaimed in India, and introduced in America. This panorama projects the complete circulatory disposition of capital—linking King and the vastly liberating Civil Rights Movement to Gandhi and the tradition of nonviolent civil disobedience he put into effective practice against British colonialism. Yet, paradoxically, it was also linked to Iqbal and the political pan-Islamism he so adamantly championed, and thus paved the way for the militant and catastrophic severing of Muslims from the cosmopolitan context of their historical worldliness.

While in its North American sojourn, German Romanticism transmuted into transcendentalism and from there eventually informed the civil disobedience ideas of key thinkers from Thoreau to Martin Luther King Jr., the direction that it took via Iqbal into political pan-Islamism first became evident in the calamitous partition of India and the formation of Pakistan, and later in the establishment of the Islamic republic of Iran, some of whose chief ideologues were deeply influenced by Iqbal. Iqbal's pan-Islamism was particularly influential in the paths taken by postcolonial nation-states.

The transmutation of mystical asceticism into pan-Islamism and from there to militant Islamism had its fair share of anticolonial struggle, while its totalitarian tendencies were checked and balanced by non-Islamist—mainly anticolonial nationalist and third world socialist—ideologies and movements. The instant it succeeded in Iran it brutally outmaneuvered all its rivals, and its totalitarian fangs came out, as it monopolized, brutalized, and sought (in vain) to pacify the multifaceted cosmopolitan revolutionary culture that had occasioned the revolution in the first place. It was precisely this lesson that Egyptian revolutionaries misread some thirty years later when they sided with the military coup in their country against the Muslim Brotherhood and President Morsi. The lesson was misread because Islamism as a militant postcolonial ideology had long since exhausted itself, as I have argued in detail in my *Islamic Liberation Theology* (2008), after the cataclysmic events of 9/11/2001 and the collapse of the Twin Towers, which I read metaphorically as the collapse of the "Islam and the West" binary that, paramount in the colonially agitated minds of thinkers like Iqbal and his followers, had generated Islamist ideology in the first place.[30]

Back in Iran in the aftermath of the militant Islamization of the 1977–1979 revolutions, a genealogy was manufactured for its immediate foregrounding that included Jalal Al-e Ahmad and Ali Shari'ati. In my *Theology of Discontent* (1993), which I began to write soon after the revolution, I tried to unpack the specific peculiarities of these thinkers and the way they could be read retroactively and syntactically as the forerunners and the preparatory stages of the Islamic revolution in Iran.[31] But in a later generation of scholarship, and as the disillusionment with the militant Islamization of the 1979 revolution became rampant, these figures were unfairly and inaccurately plucked out of the nuanced trajectory I had offered and squarely blamed for the totalitarian and nativist tendencies of the aftermath of the violently over-Islamized revolution.[32]

Here we need to make a critical distinction between (1) the panoramic stringing of a trajectory of thinkers and activists who have had historical implications beyond their immediate intentions and audiences, and (2) misplaced blame assigned to any one such person as the primary culprit of a massive social revolution. Even Khomeini himself, as I have argued in detail,[33] was not sure that his ideas and pronouncements would actually lead to a revolution that would topple the Pahlavi monarchy. Such an eventuality was simply beyond the imagination of any revolutionary thinker at the time, including Al-e Ahmad and Shari'ati. When we look at these seminal thinkers today, we see that, while such leading ideologues as Khomeini, Taleqani, Bani-Sadr, Bazargan, and so on were all in their own way system builders, Al-e Ahmad and Shari'ati were most decidedly iconoclastic, fragmentary in their thinking, allegorical, polyfocal, and above all self-critically subversive in their thinking. It is categorically wrong to blame or associate them (through Ernst Jünger and Martin Heidegger) with Nazism, and thus with the totalitarian predicates of the Islamic republic.[34]

The genealogy of the historical formation of the public sphere in postcolonial conditions such as that of Iran, Pakistan, or India requires careful unpacking of the dialectical disposition of the manufactured "center-periphery" through which the European bourgeois public sphere began to move and expand around the globe and become the catalyst of similar formations beyond its immediate or even distant control. That dialectic is predicated on such phenomena as Persophilia through which aspects of non-European cultures were creatively appropriated and subsequently, through the circulatory disposition of capital and its varied cultures, began to circumambulate the globe in creative and significant ways.

CHAPTER SIX

Nietzsche, Hafez, Mozart, Zarathustra, and the Making of a Persian Dionysus

NIETZSCHE (1844–1900) RECEIVED HAFEZ mostly through Goethe, and the two poets became the epitome of the iconoclastic philosopher's notion of a Dionysian revolt against an entire history of Greek metaphysics as European philosophers before Nietzsche had received and dwelled on it. It was also this very Hafez who became definitive to Nietzsche's Zarathustra, the Persian prophet, in his conclusive philosophical treatise. Throughout his philological career and even before exploding into an iconoclastic philosopher, Nietzsche had an enduring fascination with things Persian, from the title of his seminal book, *Thus Spoke Zarathustra* (1883–1885), to his deep and lasting admiration for Hafez. Of the entire range of prophets in the biblical tradition why would he choose the Iranian prophet of Zoroastrianism for the name of his philosophical protagonist? Why not Moses, Jesus, or Buddha? The name of Zarathustra was at once foreign and familiar to his European audiences—a liminal sentiment that perhaps best identified and idolized what he had in mind. The choice coincided with the already deep-rooted fascination of German Romanticism with things Persian, particularly pre-Islamic Iran—things that would later be identified as

"Aryan" and "Aryanism" that in Nazi Germany would degenerate into murderous racism and in Iran usher in the politics of pre-Islamic history and historiography from the late nineteenth to the mid-twentieth century and be of particular use to Pahlavi dynasty propaganda machinery actively seeking a pre- and non-Islamic mode of legitimation for itself. But in the figure of Nietzsche the three iconoclastic figures of Zarathustra, Hafez, and Dionysus would eventually come together to make up the thrust of Nietzsche's subversive philosophy. He thus brought the Persians back to European philosophy precisely to the path from which Hegel had sent them out.

Because Nietzsche had invoked the pre-Islamic Persian prophet, his philosophy initially appealed to the politics of pre-Islamic history, and yet after the Islamic revolution in Iran the counter-ethical frivolity of Nietzsche rubbed the custodians of the Islamic republic the wrong way. So Nietzsche provides a radical contrarian position in both the Pahlavi period and that of the Islamic republic—with the Persian translation of *Thus Spoke Zarathustra* (made between 1970 and 1976) as the key dividing force.[1] From the politics of imagining pre-Islamic Iran during the Pahlavi period to the postmetaphysical frivolity of Nietzsche's counter-ethics dismantling the ideological juridicalism of the Islamic republic, the attention of the subversive German philosopher to things Persian became the site of spatial agitation contesting the ruling ideologies in the Iranian public sphere of both the Pahlavi dynasty and the clerical theocracy.

HAFEZ AS NIETZSCHE'S DIONYSUS

Nietzsche's coming to Hafez and then to Zarathustra was no whimsical Persophilia. There was a redemptive freedom, an "inconsecutiveness" as Emerson would call it, about the Persian poets that appealed to the romantic soul that Nietzsche had received and overcome. It is ultimately in Nietzsche's revolt *against* romanticism that we see the particular way in which Hafez was being reconfigured as late as the early 1880s. "It may perhaps be recalled, at least among my friends," Nietzsche felt compelled to confess in section 370 of *The Gay Science,* written in 1881 and published in 1882, "that initially I approached the modern world with a few crude errors and overestimations and, in any case, hopefully. Who knows on the basis of what personal experiences, I understood the philosophical pessimism of the nineteenth century as if it were a symptom of superior force of thought, of more audacious courage, and of more triumphant *fullness* of life than had characterized the eighteenth century, the age of Hume, Kant, Condillac, and the sensualists."[2] There is a profound sense of disappointment in what Nietzsche had hoped romanticism would achieve and an equally deep sense of disappointment in himself for having fallen for that false promise. It is precisely to the cutting edge of Nietzsche's self-criticism that already by 1881 we have the sharpest and most accurate critic of romanticism: "Thus tragic insight appeared to me as the distinctive *luxury* of our culture, as its most precious, noblest, and most dangerous squandering, but, in view of its over-richness, as a *permissible* luxury."[3] Here is the origin of Nietzsche's discovering in Hafez (and then, through Hafez, in his Zarathustra)—yet to be fully known to himself—a sense of tragedy, not as a byproduct of bourgeois morality, but by a far more daring look into the abyss.

Luxurious and permissible, European romanticism was the limit of toleration that the material achievements of Enlightenment modernity could stand without radically collapsing onto its foundational predicates. Nietzsche gives us his own biographical example that was symptomatic of partaking in that luxurious and permissible radicalism of his age: "In the same way, I interpreted German music for myself as if it signified a Dionysian power of the German soul: I believed that I heard in it the earthquake through which some primeval force that had been dammed up for ages finally liberated itself—indifferent whether everything else that one calls culture might begin to tremble. You see, what I failed to recognize at that time both in philosophical pessimism and in German music was what is really their distinctive character—their *Romanticism*."[4] Through romanticism and against romanticism, Nietzsche was finding his way to a superior insight. Hafez and Zarathustra were waiting for him. In Hafez he would find a way back to his initial impetus for looking in romanticism for a kind of radicalism that was not there—a suspension of belief in reason and progress without losing hope and collapsing into despair—and in his Zarathustra he would bring that discovery to philosophical fruition.

The historical context of this disillusion is important to note. In the same year that Nietzsche wrote this passage on romanticism in *The Gay Science* (1882), Otto von Bismarck (1815–1898) had announced publicly that his administration would pursue no colonial policy. He lied. Bismarck actively intervened on behalf of German companies facing financial crises in the South Seas. He was aggressively involved in establishing German colonies in South-West Africa, East Africa, Togo and Cameroon, New Guinea, the Bismarck Archipelago, the Solomons, and the Marshalls. Finding commercial outlets to alleviate the great depression was a primary reason behind these colonial expansions. Despite their burden on the military budget, these colonies provided the German factories with raw material, cheap labor, a more expansive market, and strategic locations for access to Africa and the Pacific for even more luxurious outlets. But Bismarck's colonial projects were equally instrumental politically in diverting attention away from domestic European feuds and toward a more global vision of the German and European destiny, converted to a campaign slogan that he used effectively in the course of the 1884 election to his full advantage. The fact that Bismarck ultimately failed in his colonial policies and by 1890 had to exchange with the British his holdings in Zanzibar for Helgoland only testifies to the superior will and economic might of the British rather than to any unwillingness on his part to partake in the global booty.[5]

It is in the context of this colonial project that we need to read Nietzsche's critique of romanticism in general and his distinction between two kinds of "sufferings" in particular:

> What is Romanticism?—Every art, every philosophy may be viewed as a remedy and an aid in the service of growing and struggling life; they always presuppose suffering and sufferers. But there are two kinds of sufferers: first, those who suffer from the over-fullness of life—they want a Dionysian art and likewise a tragic view of life, a tragic insight—and then those who suffer from the impoverishment of life and seek rest, stillness, calm seas, redemption from themselves through art and knowledge, or intoxication, convulsions, anesthesia, and madness.[6]

This is Nietzsche at his ironic best, and thus his conclusion that "All romanticism in art and insight corresponds to the dual needs of the latter type, and that included (and includes) Schopenhauer as well as Richard Wagner, to name the two most famous and pronounced romantics whom I *misunderstood* at that time—*not*—incidentally, to their disadvantage as one need not hesitate in all fairness to admit."[7] This would make of European romanticism an art of the "impoverishment of life." But invert Nietzsche's irony and there is little doubt as to where art is a luxury for the overfull and where a necessity for the impoverished. Nietzsche spoke ironically in the case of the overfulls but spoke prophetically of the art of the impoverished, those on the receiving end of European colonial projects—and precisely for that reason we might consider him a "postcolonial theorist" (before the term appeared). Indeed, we need to ask, along with Nietzsche, "is it hunger or superabundance that has here become creative?"[8] From our end of the colonial game we have not a moment of hesitation to see what art is created out of overfullness and what out of hunger, what out of a painless mental gesticulation toward immortality and what out of a painful struggle toward the restitution of dignity. Nietzsche is categorical in his condemnation of the overfulls, and yet we can echo his words for the mystically minded natives at the colonial end: "The desire for destruction, change, and becoming can be an expression of an overflowing energy that is pregnant with future (my term for this is, as is known, 'Dionysian'); but it can also be the hatred of the ill-constituted, disinherited, and underprivileged, who destroy, must destroy, because what exists, indeed all existence, all being, outrages and provokes them. To understand this feeling, consider our anarchists closely."[9]

From this characterization of his anarchist contemporaries, Nietzsche then proceeds to distinguish between two kinds of *immortalization,* and it is right here that he begins to redeem and claim Hafez and Goethe by placing them next to Rubens and appropriating them all back from the fate of European romanticism. First the life-affirming immortalization, the one identified with Dionysus: "The will to immortalize also requires a dual interpretation. It can be prompted, first, by gratitude and love; art with this origin will always be an art of apotheoses, perhaps dithyrambic like Rubens, or blissfully mocking like Hafez, or bright and gracious like Goethe, spreading a Homeric light and glory over all things."[10]

An art of apotheoses, perhaps dithyrambic like Rubens, blissfully mocking like Hafez, bright and gracious like Goethe, spreading a Homeric light and glory over all things, this is no mere verbosity or sudden strike of Persophilia. In the judgment of none other than Walter Kaufmann (perhaps the most crucial figure in adjusting our reading of Nietzsche in the twentieth century), this is in fact the final and most accurate conception of Dionysian revolt central to Nietzsche's later philosophy. As Kaufmann put it:

These final lines of one of the most important sections of the whole book are profoundly revealing both for Nietzsche's style and temperament and for the meaning of the Dionysian in his later work. Now the Dionysian is no longer contrasted with the Apollonian; it is contrasted instead with the romantic and the Christian. In all of the books after Zarathustra, the "Apollonian" is hardly ever mentioned, . . . while Dionysus and the Dionysian assume momentous importance for Nietzsche. The Dionysus whom Nietzsche celebrates in his late works is not the counterpart of Apollo. . . . Anyone who wonders what Dionysus represents in the late works where he is apotheosized by Nietzsche could hardly do better than to begin with section 370 of *The Gay Science*. Here the Dionysian is associated with superabundance . . . and contrasted with a desire for revenge that is born of the sense of being underprivileged—what Nietzsche elsewhere calls ressentiment.[11]

Here Hafez is redeemed, not just from the mystical depths of the European romantic usurpation of him, facilitated by German Orientalists, but also from the fate that will await him when he returns to his homeland via Brockhaus's critical edition and Allamah Mohammad Iqbal's (failed attempt at) his remystification. To anticipate what will happen to Hafez once he returns home, we can do no better than to take with us the second kind of immortalization that Nietzsche identifies. While the first Dionysian immortalization is immediately identified with Rubens, Hafez, Goethe, and Homer, the second is one of *ressentiment* and is immediately identified with Schopenhauer and Wagner. As Nietzsche outlines the chief characteristics of this second, deadly, immortalization, he as a German very much anticipates the rise of Hitler five decades into its appearance, while in the very same passage I can read a nasty streak in militant Islamism of the twentieth century and beyond:

But it [immortalization] can also be the tyrannic will of one who suffers deeply, who struggles, is tormented, and would like to turn what is most personal, singular, and narrow, the real idiosyncrasy of his suffering, into a binding law and compulsion—one who, as it were, revenges himself on all things by forcing his own image, the image of his torture, on them, branding them with it. This last version is romantic pessimism in its most expressive form, whether it be Schopenhauer's philosophy of will or Wagner's music—romantic pessimism, the last great event in the fate of our culture.[12]

NIETZSCHE, ZARATHUSTRA, HAFEZ, AND MOZART

It is with the figure of Hafez as Dionysus that we need to trace the meaning of Zarathustra in Nietzsche's most seminal work. Nietzsche's interests in ancient Persia extended well into India and China, using them as reference points for criticizing the Greco-Roman heritage as manufactured and perceived by his contemporary European culture.[13] His knowledge of Persia was obviously informed by his philological studies and knowledge of Greek and Latin sources. In ancient Iran he sought and found heroic people best suited for his philosophical aspirations: "Nietzsche's deepest interest and admiration for the Persians manifest themselves where he discusses their notion of history and cyclical time. This Persian concept of time resembles to some degree his own concept of the circle of the Eternal Recurrence, expressed in a highly poetic and dramatic manner in his Zarathustra."[14] Nietzsche in effect brings Persians back into European history in a cyclical and millenarian framing: "I must pay tribute to Zarathustra, a Persian (*einem Perser*): Persians were the first to have conceived of History in its full extent."[15] Nietzsche's interest in ancient Persia provides him with the opportunity to reimagine world history, with the Persians rather than the Greeks or the Romans as its victors: "It would have been much more fortunate had the Persians become masters (*Herr*) of the Greeks, rather than have the Romans of all people [*gerade die Römer*] assume that role."[16] Such superlative praise for the Persians, however, must be read more in the spirit of Nietzsche's provocative speculations that paved the way toward his Dionysian philosophy rather than as a blind appreciation of an imperial heritage, as it has been by generations of chauvinist Iranians.

Ignorant of what exactly it was that Nietzsche was doing with his Zarathustra, the name of the ancient Persian prophet on the title of his book gave Iranian supremacists ample reason to launch their Aryanism for a reclaiming of ancient Iran via Nietzsche's prophet. This was entirely inimical to Nietzsche's philosophy, as indeed were his sister Elisabeth Forester-Nietzsche's misguided efforts to turn him into a proto-Nazi philosopher compatible with her own (and her notorious husband's) anti-Semitism. Both European Nazis and Iranian Aryanists seized Nietzsche's Zarathustra for their own maleficence. Nietzsche had scarcely anything to do with it.[17] His interests in the Persian prophet had much deeper roots in his philological studies and philosophical projects:

Nietzsche made several references to "Zoroaster" in his early writings. This familiar name in European languages, of Greek origin, was used in his notebooks of 1870–71, about a decade before writing *Also Sprach Zarathustra*. There he speaks with great admiration of Zoroaster and his religion and, in a short note, as elsewhere (see above), implicitly expresses his sympathy for the historically not improbable possibility that Zoroastrianism could have well triumphed in ancient Greece: "Zoroaster's religion would have prevailed in Greece, if Darius had not been defeated." . . . Also in his posthumously published work of the same period, *Die Philosophie im tragischen Zeitalter der Griechen (Philosophy in the Tragic Age of the Greeks)*, he refers to the probable influence of Zoroaster on Heraclitus.[18]

It was perhaps all but inevitable that Nietzsche had to pronounce the killing of the Judeo-Christian god by the Persian prophet—both familiar and foreign, both prophet and not-prophet, both here and there—with the liminality of the space in between where he could jolt his European culture.

Hafez of course remains central to his thinking, which he ultimately identifies with his conception of Dionysian joy: "The name of Hafez, usually in association with Goethe, appears about ten times in his writings. He admires both poets for reaching the zenith of joyful human wisdom. For him Hafez exemplifies the Oriental free spirit who gratefully receives both the pleasures and sufferings of life."[19] This vision of Hafez dovetails seamlessly with the image he creates of Zarathustra. In the judicious words of Jenny Rose, who has made a thorough study of the image of Zoroaster in Europe: "In *Thus Spoke Zarathustra*, Nietzsche speaks as an ecstatic visionary offering a new way of life. His representation is distinctive from all that had preceded it. His Zarathustra is portrayed as the Superman—the transformer par excellence, who, by his teaching and example, transcends and also rejects the shared narrative of the past and the present, creating a new future independent of what has gone before."[20]

The manner in which in Nietzsche, Hafez, and Zarathustra come together is rooted in the varied ways the Persian prophet was received and conceived throughout European history. Long before Mozart and Nietzsche's mutual but varied reception and celebration of him, the figure of Zarathustra had deep-rooted resonances in European cultural history: "From the Hellenic period to the Renaissance and on to the time of Nietzsche," according to Rose, "Zarathustra could be said to appear in different guises to successive epochs and cultures, each time as a Wise Man who provides the questioning individual with answers relevant to that particular period in human history."[21] The European image of Zoroaster extends well into Judeo-Christian traditions: "Some Near Eastern texts portray Zarathustra as a prefiguration of Christ emanating from within the Jewish tradition. In the Mishna, the Tannaitic literature, and the Gemara, Zoroaster is likened to Nimrod, and in early Christian texts, he is identified with Nimrod, Cush (Nimrod's father), Chaim, or Misraim (respectively grandfather and uncle to Nimrod). . . . From the time of the Italian Renaissance onwards, European Christian scholars perceived the Iranian prophet as part of a chain of continuity running thus: Zoroaster–Greeks (Plato)–Moses–Jesus."[22] When Nietzsche opted for Zarathustra as his preferred philosophical prophet, the figure was thoroughly embedded in Christian tradition. Nevertheless, "it is with Nietzsche that the question of Zarathustra's relationship to Christ is openly tackled."[23]

The figure of Zoroaster remains rather consistent throughout ancient, medieval, and modern European history. The Greek and Latin classical sources were pretty much influential in Europe well into the fifteenth century. "In the later fifteenth and sixteenth centuries, magic and astrology began to be seen once more as forces working toward human liberation from the 'normal' order of nature, which was regarded as just one cause-and-effect dimension. . . . This is both a Zoroastrian and a hermetic notion."[24] It is this complicated, familiar and yet foreign, figure that finally reached Mozart and Nietzsche. "Whether portrayed as a precursor of Christianity or as an opponent of its doctrines, Zoroaster remained, for the French literati of the eighteenth century, a figure of authority and wisdom, a 'law-giver' and liberator."[25]

Long before Nietzsche's Zarathustra, the image of a wise and enlightened liberator had come down to inform Mozart's *The Magic Flute* (1791). "The conception of Zoroaster as a wise and virtuous ruler, who leads his followers from the dark veils of ignorance to a higher truth, had existed in European literature since classical times. *The Magic Flute* continues to represent him in a similar manner. Sarastro's closing words in the opera are: 'The rays of sun drive out the night/Annihilate the illicit power of the hypocrite.' "[26] In this particularly popular opera for which Mozart had opted for a German libretto, the known and familiar figure of Zarathustra assumes a central role. This image of Mozart's Sarastro could not have been too far from Nietzsche's mind when he configured his own Zarathustra.

It is critical to keep in mind, however, that this figure of Zarathustra was as much a product of the *contemporary* times as a figment of historical imagination. "For Goethe and the English Romantics, then," Rose notes, "focus was not so much on the present, but on the allure of ancient wisdom from both 'East' and 'West,' and on medieval aesthetics. . . . Zoroaster, as 'Persian Mage' seems to have represented for them a timeless embodiment of ancient authority and arcane knowledge, much as Sarastro had been depicted in the *Magic Flute* several decades earlier."[27] That timelessness was made timely by Nietzsche in his defiance of the Greco-Roman heritage he wished to dismantle.

The figure of Sarastro in Mozart's *The Magic Flute* is at once benevolent, omnipotent, and dramatic—in effect an operatic precursor of Nietzsche's Zarathustra. He has inherited the position of the head of the Temple from Pamina's father, much to the chagrin of the Queen of the Night (Pamina's mother), who had hoped she would inherit it. He has also removed Pamina from her mother's care. He is a source of light and good, though powerful and assertive. Pamina refuses her mother's order to murder Sarastro. The Queen of the Night's music is also vindictive and vengeful, whereas Sarastro's music is calm and composed. Nonetheless, he has to earn the audience's trust, for his character is not a cliché but thematically dramatic. Nietzsche's Zarathustra is the philosophical culmination of Mozart's operatic prefiguration of Sarastro.

DIONYSUS AT LARGE

Nietzsche, Hafez, Zarathustra, and Mozart finally came together to posit the Dionysian revolt against the instrumental reason that the defiant philosopher had seen as the perhaps inevitable outcome of Platonic metaphysics. They all merged to inform the prophetic figure of Zarathustra in his magnum opus. Nietzsche's Zarathustra is a figure of defiance, of tragic ecstasy, of both recognizing the fragility of now yet paradoxically dwelling in it.

As Kathleen Marie Higgins puts it in her *Nietzsche's Zarathustra*, "Zarathustra's perspective at the end of the book represents Nietzsche's view of what it is to be serious about life."[28] That "seriousness" requires a kind of frivolity, or what Hafez would call *Rendi/Liberated Knavery*. It was this *Rendi* of Hafez that Nietzsche could see and celebrate through Goethe's understanding of him. *Rend* and *Rendi* are almost impossible to translate as Hafez uses them. *Rend* is a superman in the way Nietzsche uses it—someone who has mastered and overcome morality, and thereby achieved a superior sense of right and wrong. In overcoming hypocrisy, the *Rend* posits the measures of a renewed pact with what is right and wrong. They characterize a defiant trickster whose knavery does not rise out of malice but out of a joyous reading of the tragic disposition of life and morality. "Full engagement in the present," Higgins writes, "while it involves recognition of the ends toward which immediate activities are directed, involves the appreciation of the immediate contents of the present as well."[29] This is what Persian Sufis called to be *Ibn al-Waqt*, "the son of the moment," and which Hafez perfected in his lyrical poetry. "The present moment," Higgins continues her reading of Nietzsche's Zarathustra, "at any point in time however distant from the attainment of some projected goal, affords an experiential richness that itself makes life meaningful."[30] That also is the very emotive universe in which Hafez's ghazals breathe and mean and signify. Higgins suggests: "The central 'tragic' message of Zarathustra is that meaning in life is to be found in simply loving life for its own sake. The meaning we can find in this way is not a secure possession. It is a dynamic matter of attitude, intuition, and subtlety—of the elusive thing named by the word 'balance.' "[31]

Hafez is the sublime poet of that balance, of that tragic sense of knowing and losing at one and the same time. Nietzsche published his *Thus Spoke Zarathustra* between 1883 and 1885, by which time FitzGerald's translation of Omar Khayyám had already been out since 1859 but not yet available to Nietzsche's universe. In Khayyám, Nietzsche would have found an even more compelling Dionysian figure than he had rightly detected in Hafez. But his antennae were spot on, and the kindred soul of Hafez he had breathed into his Zarathustra became his final and foremost Dionysian testament.

That joyous defiance was detected in Hafez and invested in Zarathustra—so that the diverse figures of Hafez, Rubens, and Goethe all come together to inform Nietzsche's Zarathustra, with Mozart's German opera as their operatic precursor. It was this Dionysian force that in turn went to Iran and bloomed in the poetry of Ahmad Shamlou (1925–2000), the rebel poet of Iranian defiance against tyranny and the terror of absolutism, while the romantic mysticism of the Germanic tradition passed down through Iqbal to inform the mystical fanaticism of Seyyed Hossein Nasr (b. 1933), who first provided his services to the Pahlavi monarchy, and yet inadvertently paved the way for the militant Islamization of the Iranian revolution of 1977–1979.

You might say that the split image of Hafez both as romantic and antiromantic in Europe—on its Hegelian and Nietzschean divide—returns to Iran as both political mystification (Khomeini as facilitated by, however inadvertently, Seyyed Hossein Nasr) and poetic emancipation (Shamlou as facilitated by, quite decidedly, Nima Yushij). While the romantic incorporation of Hafez eventually yielded to further mystification and eventual fascism, its Nietzschean form had exactly the opposite, liberating, effect. Nietzsche frees Hafez from romanticism and Zarathustra from Aryanism and combines them both into his conception of the Dionysian, which is no longer contrasted with Apollonian but with the Christian and the romantic and with their identical sense of *ressentiment*. It is this Nietzschean Hafez who returns to Iran as the spirit of Ahmad Shamlou and the entire Nimaic poetic movement he represented.

As it bordered on mysticism, German Romanticism was picked up by Iqbal and taken to India, while just about a generation earlier it had been taken as transcendentalism to America. Iqbal navigated and wrote the foundations of pan-Islamism with his Hafez and Rumi, while Emerson and Thoreau gave birth to the most intellectually invigorating American intellectual movement of their time—and thus one could say that Americans did much better with Hafez than his own fellow Muslims, were it not for the gamut of poets ranging from Faiz Ahmad Faiz (1911–1984) to Ahmad Shamlou whose poetic combination of lyricism and defiance became definitive to their generation. At the emerging heart of capitalism, American transcendentalism became the rebellious measure that challenged the dominant instrumental rationalism, while at its colonial edges pan-Islamism became one potent ideology of resistance to the selfsame globalized capitalism, yet at the heavy cost of producing a debilitating metanarrative. The pan-Islamism of Iqbal ebbed into militant Islamism as an anti-imperialist ideology before it degenerated into an absolutist creed of the Taliban, the Salafis, the Wahhabis, and Shi'i clericalism, whereas American transcendentalism extended to inform the civil rights and antiwar movements of the 1960s, with Osama bin Laden and Malcolm X at the two opposite ends of the spectrum. Iranian, and by extension Indian, social and cultural history would have been at the mercy of this pan-Islamist mysticism of Iqbal at one end of it and Seyyed Hossein Nasr at another had it not been for the miracle of the Dionysian spirit of joyous revolt intuited by Nietzsche and Mozart in Europe as it exploded in Iran upon the Nimaic poetic revolution and its most forbidden fruits—Ahmad Shamlou, Forough Farrokhzad, or Sohrab Sepehri.

As Ayatollah Khomeini and his devout followers marched on to craft and empower a brutish Islamic republic to rule the pious and the infidels alike, the defiant spirit of Hafez and Nietzsche were on the opposing front. Ahmad Shamlou published his own rendition of Hafez's ghazals, as did a leading ideologue of the Islamic revolution, Morteza Motahhari—two radically different Hafezes at the service of two equally radical versions of truth on earth. The Islamists won politically; Shamlou lived and loved and lasted triumphantly.

Both the political victory of the Islamists and the moral triumph of Shamlou spoke the same truth. "But when Zarathustra was alone," we re-call the inaugural moment in *Thus Spoke Zarathustra,* "he spoke thus to his heart: 'Could it be possible! This old saint in his woods has not yet heard the news that God is dead!' "[32] It is precisely that Dionysian moment that is resurrected at the height of Shamlou's equally defiant song,

Man bi-nava bandegagi sar-berah nabudam

I was no miserable, obedient, servant—
And the path to my promised paradise
Was no tight rope of obedience and servitude—
A different God I deserved,
Worthy of a creature
Who does not bend his neck in humility
For a meager living—
And thus a different God I created.[33]

CHAPTER SEVEN

Edward FitzGerald and the Rediscovery of Omar Khayyám for Persian Nihilism

IN 2010, POLITY PRESS published a comprehensive edited volume on "cosmopolitanism."[1] Garrett Wallace Brown and David Held's comprehensive volume, *The Cosmopolitan Reader,* is vast and definitive in its coverage. After a major introduction, they divided their volume into six hefty sections and twenty-six sumptuous chapters in which we can read anyone from Immanuel Kant to Martha Nussbaum to Jürgen Habermas to Jacques Derrida and learn all we wish to learn about "cosmopolitanism."

The peculiar thing about this volume is that if we go down the list of the contributors we see plenty of Immanuels, Marthas, Garretts, Charleses, Davids, Jürgens, and Jacques, and scarcely anything else—it would appear that no Chinese, Indian, Muslim, Latin American, or African ever had any idea remotely resembling the thing they call "cosmopolitanism." The book's subject is cosmopolitanism all right, but by and about and for the entity that insists in calling itself "the West" so authoritatively that it no longer even bothers to place that designation on the cover—no "European cosmopolitanism," or "North American cosmopolitanism," not even "Western cosmopolitanism"—just "cosmopolitanism," for the whole world to read about and learn. It is "The" cosmopolitan reader period, upon which claim presides one monumental figure of Immanuel Kant, and if it were to be extended to anywhere beyond the nose of this "West," it would do so by asking how the world at large can help authenticate and corroborate it as the defining moment of all history and all humanity. In short, this volume claims "cosmopolitanism" all for itself the way the Roman, the British, or the American empires have claimed the whole world for themselves. The book about cosmopolitanism is not cosmopolitan. It is in fact decidedly provincial—so provincial that it universalizes itself without the slightest consciousness.

THE THREE-DIMENSIONAL SUBJECT

In a book published in 2010, the entire gamut of non-European civilizations— from the Hebrews to the Egyptians, Chinese, Ethiopians, and Persians—are all referenced and contained in the vast expanse of just one single sentence in a five-hundred-page tome.[2] The move beyond that single sentence and toward the major point of the volume is simple. The editors begin with Diogenes and the philosophy of the Cynics and come down to the cosmopolitanism of Zeno and Cicero, from which they dutifully leap to the Stoics before turning to the Christianization of the Roman Empire and consider Augustine, before they come down to Locke, Voltaire, Kant, and Thomas Jefferson, by which time they are home free with their contemporary cosmopolitan theorists and philosophers—again, all of them without a single exception Roberts, Thomases, Davids, Patricks, Marys, and Daniels. The more you read such volumes, of which there are quite a handful, and what they contain, the more you realize the astonishing parochialism of these thinkers, who fancy not even the faintest idea about the world that lies beyond their European noses. According to them, no Chinese, no Asian, no African ever thought of the world at large, or felt at home in that world, or sought to configure it imaginatively, philosophically, aesthetically in her or his imagination. This cosmopolitan imperialism moves with ease and confidence from a presumptuous politics of political domination into the vast and veritable terrain of literary and philosophical imagination, evidently entirely unperturbed by, or even aware of, the limits of its own imagination.

As best represented in this volume, "cosmopolitanism" is unabashedly Eurocentric and self-indulgent, confident and self-sufficient, and yet paradoxically parochial and provincial in its confidence that what it imagines as "the world," and the manner in which it occupies that world, is "The" world and nothing else. The task at hand for the rest of the world, as a result, is to overcome the unsurpassed provincialism of this way of thinking and map out the alternative worlds that have existed and continue to exist, though they are hidden and glossed over under the generic hegemony of the entity that calls itself "the West." Thus relegated to the terra incognita of "the Rest," these alternative worlds are categorically denied and disallowed articulation, self-historicization, and agential consciousness. The point here is not merely to document and navigate these alternative worlds, but to assay their abilities to map out a different topography of human history and destiny.

In two previous books—*Shi'ism: A Religion of Protest* (2010) and *The World of Persian Literary Humanism* (2012)—I have detailed the scholastic and humanist, respectively, contours of one among many other similar worlds thus camouflaged, seeking to unearth the historical process through which one particular mode of worldliness is posited and crafted. But, like all other worlds, this world is the result, not just of its own worldliness (vast and imperial in its own genealogy as it was), but is also influenced by the worlds into which it was cast by the force of historical destiny. While my book on Persian literary humanism traced the origin of this worldliness to forces domestic to the Persianate imperial universe, the book on Shi'ism marked the relevance of a scholastic heritage to which Iran was integral. I have intended this third book, on Persophilia, as a tracing of the manner in which the varied readings of aspects of Persian culture and civilization were received in Europe and in turn went back to Iran to affect it in profoundly enduring ways, particularly in the formation of a postcolonial subject.

I have intended this book in particular to be the antidote to the thing that primes itself as "the West" and then subjugates the rest of the world to "westernization." To dismantle that false, falsifying, and debilitating binary, I excavate the varieties of Persophilia that have been definitive to major social and intellectual movements in Europe and in turn contributed to the formation of a multifaceted public sphere and postcolonial subject formation in the larger context of the Persianate and Iranian universes. This third volume, as a result, in effect complements those two by adding a third dimension to the formation of a public sphere and a postcolonial subject that inhabited a cosmopolitan worldliness I have detected and theorized in a Persianate world of which Iran has always been the epicenter. Here my objective has been to show how the transnational expansion of the European literary public sphere through the global reach of European imperialism and cultural hegemony became the intellectual, moral, and imaginative machinery of colonial and postcolonial change around the globe, but with specific dispensations in every country and clime around the world. Once the echoes and reflections of this Persophilia reached Iran and its environs, it mixed and matched with historic developments internal to its worldliness and created an alternative universe, now categorically camouflaged under the false rubric of "tradition versus modernity," or "Islam versus the West," in the making of which nativist and self-styled "westernized (colonized)" minds of inorganic Iranian intellectuals have been as much at fault as the cultural officers of European colonialism.

THE ELLIPTICAL CURVE

The elliptical curve this extended shape of Persophilia followed back to Iran itself is varied and multifaceted. Among its spiral variations perhaps the most spectacular is the case of FitzGerald's rendition of the *Rubáiyát of Omar Khayyám* (1048–1131), the Persian scientist and mathematician who left behind a few meditative quatrains—the exact number and content of which vary from one edition to another. These quatrains had been known, loved, admired, imitated, and canonized by Persian literati long before FitzGerald paid any attention to them. But when he did, the result catapulted his rendition into such fascinated global approval that it could not have left even Khayyám's own birthplace untouched. Hollywood cast Cornel Wilde in the leading role in William Dieterle's *Omar Khayyám* (1957) from one end of the globe; the legendary Egyptian singer Umm Kulthum (c. 1904–1975) sang an Arabic rendition of it to spectacular reception; and Omar Khayyám clubs popped up all the way from North America to Europe to India. From legendary American general Omar Bradley (1893–1981) to an offspring of Ezra Pound (1885–1972), Omar Shakespear Pound (1926–2010), prominent Americans named their beloved sons after him.

The English translation by Edward FitzGerald (1809–1883) made of Omar Khayyám a European and subsequently a global sensation that renewed Iranians' own interest in their medieval poet, which in turn brought his iconoclastic ideas to the attention of the founding father of modern Persian fiction, Sadegh Hedayat (1903–1951), and, because of him, to the forefront of the modernist movement in fiction, poetry, and even drama and film. Hedayat was vital to the Persian literary and cultural effervescence of the twentieth century, and Khayyám was central to his thinking—indeed, arguably he would not have been vital had Khayyám not been so definitive to the European context that welcomed Hedayat in his formative years in Paris.

Khayyám had, of course, been known and much loved and celebrated by all Persian-speaking people throughout the ages. But his discovery by FitzGerald, and his subsequent transformation into a global phenomenon under the aegis of British imperialism, placed the Persian poet under a new limelight for his own people—from Tajikistan and Afghanistan and India to Iran and the Arab world. This development, in a circuitous but inevitable way, resulted in the momentous appearance of a decidedly agnostic streak in the emerging Persian literary public sphere that swiftly transmuted into a productive nihilism. Sadegh Hedayat published a critical edition of Khayyám. Very aware of FitzGerald's translation and having lived in Paris, Hedayat's other exposures to European literary movements (that included but was not limited to Kafka) eventually gave momentum to his own subversive nihilism; that nihilism remained quintessentially Khayyámesque and definitive to his own fiction and, under his extended shadow, to Persian literary modernity for the longest time.

Among the British, and by extension the world at large, no other text reveals the European romantic fixation with Persian poetry better than the phenomenal career of Edward FitzGerald's *Rubáiyát of Omar Khayyám*, which first appeared in 1859. A contemporary of Wordsworth (1770–1850), FitzGerald epitomized not just the British but, by the testimony of other European translations of his reading of Omar Khayyám, a continental fascination with an active romanticization of the medieval Persian poet. The success and popularity of FitzGerald's translation cannot be attributed to anything other than the translator's poetic gift and the commensurability of the spirit of his translation with the romantic age in which it was produced. The effect of FitzGerald's rendition was so overwhelmingly powerful that all other Persian poets, Hafez in particular, began to be assimilated, backward in Iranian literary history and forward in their European reception, into a latter-day Omar Khayyám. In the words of John Yohannan:

During the vogue of the Rubaiyat in the late nineteenth and early twentieth centuries, all other Persian poets except Ferdowsi were soon in its rather garish light. Hafez was viewed as a later 'Omar, a skeptic and a hedonist; not merely his roba'is, but also his ghazals were rendered as quatrains (by, for example, Clarence Streit). The same was done, by Thomas Wright, to Sa'di, whose homely philosophy hardly lent itself to such accommodation. Lesser figures like Baba Taher and Kamal al-Din were pulled completely out of their orbits by the magnetism of 'Omar.[3]

What we are witnessing here is the changing fate of Persian poets in perfect harmony with the changing economic and moral atmosphere of Europe and in perfect discord with whatever it is that they signified for their more immediate readers. The successful commensurability of Hafez with European romanticism can also be judged by failed translations of other Persian poets. Not all of FitzGerald's translations were as successful as that of Omar Khayyám. His rendition of Abd al-Rahman Jami's *Salaman and Absal,* in his own estimation, was "in too Miltonic a blank verse"[4] to make it palatable to his readers. But a far simpler explanation will also do. FitzGerald was adamant to read the poetic materialism of Khayyám into the romantic defiance of his age. He simply could not do the same with one of the most passionate love stories of Jami, who in turn was equally adamant in mystifying the medieval Persian tale of illicit love. That insistence on mystification persisted well into subsequent generations of translators—all the way from Europe to North America—reaching the age of New Age mysticism. The publication in 1967 of Robert Graves and Omar Ali Shah's new translation of Omar Khayyám's quatrains on the basis of a presumed newly discovered manuscript gave a new twist to the fixation with Persian poetry as symptomatic of a new fad in the heart of the counterculture movement of the 1960s. In the Graves/Ali Shah reading, Khayyám was rechristened as a born-again Sufi perfectly matching the spirit of the sixties. Khayyám was being taken for yet another ride, and we can now understand what the British poet Basil Bunting (1900–1985) meant when he said that what he was doing with Persian poetry was not "translation" but an "overdraft":[5] "In its heyday, the Rubáiyát factory ground out not only endless reissues of FitzGerald's four—or five—editions, but also numerous new translations and adaptations, some of which were so tendentious and eccentric as to deserve a lunatic fringe tag."[6]

EROTIC ASCETICISM

FitzGerald had nothing to do with this mystification. His Khayyám was translucent, worldly, fragile, vulnerable, seizing the moment for what it was—the ephemeral, the precious, the fleeting. Did his own life, and what we might term his "ascetic homosexuality," have something to do with his Khayyám? Romancing Persia may in fact have found its homoerotic disposition right here in FitzGerald's Khayyám.

The relationship between FitzGerald and his immediate Persian teacher has received considerable attention from subsequent generations of scholars. FitzGerald befriended Edward Byles Cowell (1826–1903) and knew him and his bride, Elizabeth Charlesworth, just around the time they were getting married (1847), when FitzGerald was thirty-eight, Cowell twenty-one, and his bride thirty-five. In the austere but suggestive language of A. J. Arberry, who has closely examined this relationship through their extensive correspondences, "the oddly-assorted trio deepened their friendship."[7] Edward Byles Cowell was a renowned translator of Persian poetry and a professor of Sanskrit at Cambridge University, evidently with a prodigious command of many languages. The trio would read poetry, translate Persian into English, and, through the Persian lyrics, grew ever so emotionally close to each other. Soon Cowell was admitted to Oxford, and, again in the suggestive language of Arberry, "from whatever motives, [FitzGerald] strove his utmost to dissuade him" from going, and when he failed, would visit him there regularly. It was at this time, 1852, that Cowell encouraged FitzGerald to learn Persian, and he eagerly followed his friend's wishes.[8]

FitzGerald and Cowell continued to correspond, with the aging pupil and the youngish tutor weaving their love of Hafez, Sa'di, and Khayyám together as they paced up and down the Persian poetic pantheon. At the time, FitzGerald frequented Alfred Tennyson regularly—as the two of them were making translations from Hafez and sending them to Cowell for his consideration and corrections. When Cowell's own translation of Hafez appeared, FitzGerald was so delighted that he wrote to his friend Thomas Carlyle, asking him to read it.[9] Subsequently, and with some trepidation, FitzGerald dedicated his translation of *Salaman and Absal* to Cowell and his wife, who were of course pleased; and Mrs. Cowell took the liberty of showing the translation to none other than the illustrious Max Müller (1823–1900), the preeminent philologist of his time, who was equally pleased with it.[10]

Yet another anxiety of separation from his beloved Persian teacher was awaiting FitzGerald. Cowell was offered a teaching post at Presidency College in Calcutta, which he accepted despite FitzGerald's plea that he not go, even offering to help the young scholar financially if that was a consideration.[11] "The strange friendship of this oddly assorted trio," Arberry notes, "was to continue until the poet dies."[12] The Cowells sailed to India in August 1856, and about three years later FitzGerald published his first edition of Omar Khayyám's *Rubáiyát,* to which he had devoted his attention while deeply missing his friend, to whom he now habitually referred as his Sheikh and/or Master, and to whom he evidently had originally dedicated the first editions of his now world-renowned translations.[13]

Was, in his own shy and reticent way, FitzGerald in love with Cowell, or perhaps projecting onto him other male friends to whom he was attracted, such as William Browne, whose tragic early death had left a lasting effect on the poet, or the fisherman Joseph Fletcher, to whom he was also attached?[14] Is his translation of Omar Khayyám a disguised expression of his yearning for his beloved Persian teacher who had twice abandoned him, once for Oxford and again for Calcutta? Persian poetry is particularly attuned to homo-erotic suggestion. The absence of gender-specific pronouns in the language makes Persian lyricism particularly open to a transgendered reading. Khayyám's poetry in particular has a pantheistic disposition that embraces the world in lieu of any specific erotic fixation. His quatrains are not lyrical, they are contemplative. His libidinal yearnings sublimated into a fixation with the fragility of life, Khayyám's verses exude an ascetic eroticism that may have particularly appealed to FitzGerald.

HEDAYAT'S KHAYYÁM

The transhistorical fusion of Omar Khayyám and Edward FitzGerald was so thorough that some critics occasionally referred to the English translation of the quatrains as "the Rubáiyát of FitzOmar." Scarcely had a poet and a translator so seamlessly intertwined to become a single soul in two distant bodies. Be that as it may, FitzGerald's Khayyám was not an overnight success. Even its British audience took a long time to discover and warm up to it. But eventually it became a global sensation. Between 1859 and 1889 five editions of FitzGerald's *Rubáiyát* were published—four in his own lifetime and the last after his death. Soon Europe exploded with other translations. Adolf Friedrich von Schack published a German translation in 1878. Friedrich Martinus von Bodenstedt published yet another in 1881. Two English editions by Whinfield appeared in 1882 and 1883. J. B. Nicolas published its French translation in 1867. Justin Huntly McCarthy published a prose version of the poems in 1889. [Richard Le Gallienne did a verse translation in 1897—followed by another in 1897.] Another French translation, this one by Franz Toussaint, came out in 1924.

This last translation by a European, and a French one in fact, brings us down to the time of Sadegh Hedayat (1903–1951) in Paris. By far the most significant literary figure of his time and much beyond, Hedayat had a lifelong fascination for Khayyám. In fact, his vastly influential literary career began with a book he wrote on Khayyám in 1923, just before his book on *Favayed-e Giahkhari/Benefits of Vegetarianism* (1927), followed by his own version of the quatrains in 1934, just before the publication of his universally celebrated masterpiece, *The Blind Owl* (1936).[15]

Hedayat's reading of Khayyám framed the rest of his life and thinking in a fragile and ferociously nihilistic mode, a disposition that was the paramount mode of his reading of the iconic poet and that became definitive to his own thinking. Hedayat was neither a pessimist nor an optimist—he was a nihilist of unsurpassed sardonic brilliance. Subsequent generations writing in Persian or any other language have made of him what best suited their own needs for an enabling foundational myth.[16] In terms domestic to Hedayat's own literary productions, a deeply and pervasively nihilistic disposition dominated his entire thinking from the very outset. This nihilism extends from his prose to his politics—from his notorious racism, anti-Semitism, and Islamophobia to his fascination with pre-Islamic Iran, to his inroads into Persian folklore, to his vegetarianism, and above all into the labyrinth of his literary masterpiece *The Blind Owl* (1936).[17] Throughout these works a delicate ferocity overshadows his prose and politics—Omar Khayyám coursing through his post-optimist veins.

Hedayat's Khayyám prefigured his own ascetic eroticism, his repressed or sublimated homosexuality, refusal to marry or have children, subversive attitudes toward everything, anti-Semitism, hatred of Arabs and Muslims, and in fact hatred of just about anything else. Yet in his pessimism and sardonic literary consciousness Hedayat generated a creative disposition that would define a whole generation of literary creation from which the luminary figures of the subsequent generations—Ebrahim Golestan, Sadegh Chubak, Houshang Golshiri, and Mahmoud Dolatabadi—would eventually emerge.

Since the time of Hedayat many of his books have been banned and accessible only through the underground. This fact raises certain serious questions regarding the impact of such underground literature in the formation of the (literary) public sphere. By "public sphere," Habermas proposed, "we mean first of all a domain of our social life in which such a thing as public opinion can be formed."[18] Otherwise private persons come together to create this public sphere: "a portion of the public sphere is constituted in every conversation in which private persons come together to form a public." A free and unhindered public sphere is obviously the *conditio sine qua non* of this public sphere, for "citizens act as a public when they deal with matters of general interest without being subject to coercion; thus with the guarantee that they may assemble and unite freely, and express and publicize their opinions freely." Habermas then offers "newspapers, and periodicals, radio and television" as examples of means for the dissemination of ideas that make the public sphere possible and meaningful.[19]

This definition of the public sphere, as Habermas knew well, is too European and too bourgeois. When we extend it to non-European and especially colonized spaces, we need to consider the significance of the "underground" in the making of that "public sphere"—namely, banned books, banned music, banned films, and so on, which precisely by virtue of having been banned have a disproportionately higher impact in the formation of the public sphere. This "parapublic sphere" (as we might call it) is integral to the formation of the public sphere. The formation of the Iranian public sphere, like that of many other places in the postcolonial world, is entirely contingent on the formation of this parapublic domain where the visual and performing arts, as well as literary and poetic discourses, become definitive to the nature and disposition of the public sphere and in fact have an organic connection to it. In this parapublic domain things are said much more bluntly, and thus without them the coded discourse of the public domain may in fact remain un-decodable. One must account for the nature of the public sphere in tyrannical and colonized societies by a careful consideration of such parapublic domains; for it is in the healthy symbiotic relationship between these two adjacent spheres that the very nature of the "public" in the public and parapublic sphere is constituted.

It was on that liminal sphere between the public and parapublic, between the permissible and the banned, that Hedayat took FitzGerald's Khayyám and mixed it with Kafka's fright and Nietzsche's nihilism—and from the sight of their fusion he saw through a vision of the abyss, a nightmarish vista of the Iranian encounter with the colonial modernity from which it has yet to recover. Reza Shah was the epitome of a tyrannical take on that colonial modernity (which he turned into a state-sponsored modernity). But in the Tudeh Party, to which he was initially attracted, Hedayat soon found the selfsame fright on an even grander scale. He turned to pre-Islamic Iran in order to discredit and dismantle Islam, and in his literary work he placed the moral cadaver of his country on an anatomy table and carved it to pieces, for the whole world to see. The Islamized revolution of 1977–1979 gobbled up all the alternatives to its own ideology and created a monstrosity. This monstrosity is the interpretation of Hedayat's nihilism—no hope, no salvation, no way out—leaving mere shadows dancing on his grave. There was something primordial, something archetypal, in the Nimaic revolution in Persian poetry, and later in Kiarostami's cinema, from which seeds of defiant hope could grow to fight against both the Islamophobic nightmare that Hedayat had dreamed and its Islamist interpretation that Khomeini delivered.

CHAPTER EIGHT

Matthew Arnold, Philosophical Pessimism, and the Rise of Iranian Epic Nationalism

WHY WOULD MATTHEW ARNOLD (1822–1888), one of the most widely celebrated public intellectuals of the Victorian era, adopt the most famous episode of Ferdowsi's *Shahnameh* as the theme of his most renowned poems, "Sohrab and Rustum" (1853)? What did he see in this tragedy that appealed to his senses and sensibilities as a cultural critic? The Europeans' discovery of the *Shahnameh,* which predated Matthew Arnold's poem and outlasted it, had an obvious impact on Iranians' reception of their own monumental epic, which in turn they began to appropriate for both monarchic and anticolonial nationalism—and thus Ferdowsi's epic became a contested site of Iranian nationalized identity. When Iranians saw one of their literary masterpieces enter the European imperial stage like this, that staging became a conduit of self-consciousness in precisely the global terms that the European imperial imagination in which the Persian epic was staged had made possible.

"AND THE FIRST GREY OF MORNING FILL'D THE EAST"

Predicated on a wider reception of *Shahnameh* in Europe, Arnold's poem made one particularly powerful episode of Ferdowsi's masterpiece even more widely popular. Long before Arnold turned to it, *Shahnameh* had repeatedly been translated into multiple European languages. William Jones had translated it into English (1774), L. M. Langles into French (1778), Friedrich Wall into German (1793), and later Friedrich Schlegel into German (1800), and Jules Mohl into French (1831).[1] All these previous translations had made Ferdowsi's magnum opus available to Europeans in their own languages. Arnold's adaptation, very much like FitzGerald's *Rubáiyát,* was not a direct translation, for in fact Arnold did not even know Persian. His "Sohrab and Rustum" was a free adaptation done in free verse, and yet composed with such verve and power that it made Ferdowsi sing in English what he had composed in Persian centuries earlier.

Arnold's "Sohrab and Rustum" has been widely praised and celebrated by British literary critics. "In Matthew Arnold's style and in his manner," one such critic offered, "he seems to me to recall the great masters, and this in a striking and in an abiding way. . . . To recall them at all is a rare gift, but to recall them naturally, and with no strained sense nor jarring note of imitation, is a gift so exceedingly rare that it is almost enough in itself to place a writer among the great masters."[2] Others have called the poem, "the noblest poem in the English language," or suggested that "it is the nearest analogue in English to the rapidity of action, plainness of thought, plainness of diction, and nobleness of Homer."[3] A reading of Arnold's poem, with its compellingly simple, precise, and evocative phrasing, justifies these praises:

> And Rustum to the Persian front advanced,
> And Sohrab arm'd in Haman's tent, and came.
> And as afield the reapers cut a swath
> Down through the middle of a rich man's corn,
> And on each side are squares of standing corn,
> And in the midst a stubble, short and bare—
> So on each side were squares of men, with spears
> Bristling, and in the midst, the open sand.
> And Rustum came upon the sand, and cast

His eyes toward the Tartar tents, and saw
Sohrab come forth, and eyed him as he came.[4]

But the more compelling question is what is the place of this poem in Arnold's work and why did he choose this particular episode from the *Shahnameh* to turn into one of the masterpieces of English poetry? Any answer to this question must address two elements: (1) the original story in Persian; and (2) the general context of Arnold's own work at the time when he turned to this particular story based on an account of it by Charles Augustin Sainte-Beuve, a prominent French literary critic and a *Shahnameh* enthusiast.[5]

There are a few tragedies in Ferdowsi's *Shahnameh* that are pinnacles of his masterful storytelling. Chief among these are the stories of Siavash, followed by those of Rostam and Esfandiar, and above all of Rostam and Sohrab (or, as Arnold preferred, "Sohrab and Rustum," placing the name of the murdered son first and that of the murdering father second). In Siavash it is the multiple persecutions of a young and innocent prince that are at the heart of the tragedy. In Rostam and Esfandiar it is the equally innocent but ambitious tragedy of Esfandiar, manipulated by his conniving father, that carries the story to its tragic finale, when the *Shahnameh* hero Rostam kills yet another valiant prince. But in Rostam and Sohrab the tragedy of all tragedies lies in the fact that the *Shahnameh* hero inadvertently kills his own son—an action that prompts Ferdowsi to step out of the narrative and compose one of his most powerful lines about greed and the blindness of humanity.

Why would Arnold be particularly interested in this story? Much of the scholarly and critical attention of the last generation was primarily concerned with Arnold's prose work, that of *Culture and Anarchy* (1867–1868) in particular. But in a recent major study, *Overcoming Matthew Arnold: Ethics in Culture and Criticism,* James Walter Caufield radically alters the received conception of the English poet and critic, puts his prose and poetry together, and takes substantial issue with the way he has been portrayed by previous scholars and critics. Caufield picks up on a critical sentence early in *Culture and Anarchy*—in which Arnold states that he is "a Liberal tempered by experience, reflection, and renouncement"—and paints a radically pessimistic picture of the prominent poet and critic. Caufield believes that over the decades an undue emphasis has been placed on Arnold's notion of "Culture" at the heavy expense of what he terms "Conduct"; this leads him to place Arnold within a Christian ethic of renunciation, thereby linking him to a philosophical pessimism extending all the way back to Schopenhauer on one end and to Levinas, Agamben, and Vattimo on the other. Caufield's contentions are quite serious and transformative:

> Just as Hellenism and Hebraism form the twin sides of the "Culture" medal, so the dialectical relation of culture to conduct structures the whole of Arnold's thinking. Twentieth-century criticism generally neglects "Conduct" in favor of a prolonged focus on "Culture," with its "too exclusive worship of fire, strength, earnestness, and action," and now the predictable return of the repressed "Conduct" emerges, for instance, in the rise of identity politics, in such theoretical constructs as Judith Butler's idea of "resignification," or in the "narcissistic" tendency of cultural studies "to create its analytic object as a subject: to establish what is spoken of as the entity that speaks of it." In an effort to restore approximate equipollency to these sides of Arnold's thought, this book shows how his ethic of "renouncement" conjoins the self-abnegation of Christian altruism to the will-denial of Schopenhauerian pessimism. This moral amalgam, the first principle in all of Arnold's work and the logical corollary of his philosophical pessimism, lies at the heart of Arnoldian "Conduct," the ethical end of "renouncement" toward which the "experience" and "reflection" of Liberalism naturally lead.[6]

The Christian ideal of renunciation thus becomes central to Arnold's work, which in turn gives his moral outlook an entirely pessimistic and, one might add, tragic disposition. Tracing his thesis back to the works of Alan Grob, *A Longing Like Despair: Arnold's Poetry of Pessimism* (2002), and James C. Livingston, *Matthew Arnold and Christianity* (1986), Caufield concludes: "pessimistic renouncement is the key to Arnold's entire *oeuvre,* both poetry and prose."[7] In this reading of Arnold he was instrumental in the ethical turn in philosophy of the post-Holocaust era of Agamben and Levinas, thus giving a whole new meaning to his attention to the tragedy of Sohrab and Rustum, in fact making it the cornerstone of his ethical theory of *culture* now embedded in *conduct.*

SHAHNAMEH AS A "NATIONAL EPIC"

Caufield's scholarship places Arnold's philosophical pessimism right at the doorsteps of Carlyle and Goethe, and thus along with FitzGerald smack in

the middle of European romanticism. In clarifying his point about the root
of Arnold's thoughts in Schopenhauer he points out:

> I am not claiming that Arnold read Schopenhauer and embraced his pessi-
> mistic metaphysics. After all, the tropes of suffering and self-sacrifice are the
> generic stuff of Christian and Classical rhetoric—"a graft of stoicism with
> Pauline Christianity," as Jacques Derrida puts it—and Arnold's most imme-
> diate inspiration for "renouncement" might well be Thomas Carlyle, who is
> himself quoting Goethe when he says, in *Sartor Resartus* (1833): "Well did
> the Wisest of our time write: 'It is only with Renunciation (*Enstagen*) that
> Life, properly speaking, can be said to begin.'"[8]

But again, as Ferdowsi was taken in that direction in Europe, the shadow
of his European reception had yet another rendezvous with proto-fascism
in Iran, advocated and promoted by the ruling Pahlavi monarchy, and yet
creatively and provocatively opposed by a new generation of poets, novelists, literary critics, filmmakers, and dramatists. The result of this critical and
creative encounter between the Pahlavi era elite and counter-elite was the
enrichment of the literary public sphere. A new generation of Iranian scholars
and literati who read that European reception as a signal to the pre-Islamic
Iranian heritage—now articulated in racist, anti-Arab, anti-Turkish, Persian
hegemonic, and patently Islamophobic terms—became the harbingers of a
new kind of Persianate chauvinism in Iran. A racist triumphalism ensued and
began to partake in an imperialist complex that informed Persian ethnic nationalism, which in turn alienated both the other ethnicized minorities and
the powerful socialist sentiments that were now emerging in earnest in Iran.

The *Shahnameh* was no "national epic" of any postcolonial nation-state.
It was the product of a transnational imperial age in which many postcolonial nations, Afghanistan and Tajikistan included, had a fair share. But the
violent appropriation of the text by a new generation of Iranian literati sought
to turn it into a cornerstone of the new nation-state—and it succeeded. As
Reza Shah took full advantage of this ethnic nationalism—as did his son
Mohammad Reza Shah, and after him even the Islamic republic—the
counter-elite, now widely popular with a young and restless generation, began
to lay its own claim to ancient Iranian history, heritage, and the *Shahnameh*
in particular. The more Iran plunged under the reign of monarchic tyranny
(1926–1979), the more that racist triumphalism located itself in the domi-

nant political culture. Now imperial history was revived to inform this racist triumphalism and thus ever so angrily alienated the vast non-Persianate population of Iran as a postcolonial nation-state—ranging all the way from Azerbaijan through Kurdistan to Baluchistan and Khuzestan. Pahlavi-sponsored Persianate chauvinism thus became the single most damaging factor in alienating a vast population from their own cosmopolitan heritage.

Before the advent of the European reception of the *Shahnameh,* Iranians and other Persian-speaking people had last noted their imperial epic noted and celebrated from within the dynastic milieus of their own empires—from the Ghaznavids in the tenth to eleventh centuries to the Safavids in the sixteenth through eighteenth centuries. But this time around they had to reconfigure that very same epic from the depths of other empires, the European empires. Suddenly a familiar text had assumed foreign significance, and that foreignness became the condition under which the new hermeneutic circle enabled a literary public sphere in which this cultural icon assumed a new significance. Generations later this would also become the case with Iranian cinema when the global reception of one of their cultural products generated a new hermeneutic circle. But at this very nascent period, seeing *Shahnameh* on the globalized stage radically renewed the historic import of the literary masterpiece for Iranians themselves, who began to pull and push it in various contested directions and thereby organically expanded their literary public sphere. This is a particularly important case in which "*Literarische Öffentlichkeit*/literary public sphere," in Habermas's formulation of it, becomes integral to "*Politische Öffentlichkeit*/political public sphere." Before its European reception, the *Shahnameh* was primarily a dynastic object—a text principally (but never exclusively) used and abused as an apparatus of legitimacy for one triumphant dynasty or another. But after its European reception, the *Shahnameh* returned to Iran as an icon to be claimed and counterclaimed in the public sphere. This fact, this catalytic impact of the European bourgeois public sphere around the world, almost entirely neglected in Said's otherwise legitimate critique of Orientalism, is a critical factor in the creation of the postcolonial public sphere in countries like Iran and beyond.

As Europeans were picking up the *Shahnameh* to read and translate, the state of *Shahnameh* studies in Ferdowsi's own homeland was limited to very small learned cliques. But the eventual awareness of its European acceptance combined with the nascent ethnic nationalism suddenly catapulted the aging text into the political limelight. Even before Reza Shah established the Pahlavi dynasty in 1925, by 1922 "Mohammad Taqi Bahar, the most influential poet of the time and a politician-journalist, urged Reza Khan (later Reza Shah), who had recently seized power, to prove his asserted nationalism by celebrating Ferdowsi and building a worthy mausoleum for the 'resurrector of Iranian national identity and people.'"[9] The organic link between the European reception of the *Shahnameh* and its appropriation by the Persianate nationalist project proceeded apace:

> By the early twentieth century, European studies (particularly by Mohl and Nöldeke) about Ferdowsi and his achievement, and French, German, and English renditions of the *Shahnameh* had made Ferdowsi a household name in the scholarly circles of Europe. Persians, aware of these developments and spurred by the patriotic sentiments motivated by the Constitutional Revolution and the works of fervently nationalistic poets and scholars, began to voice the necessity of the official recognition of Ferdowsi as the true "resurrector" (after the Arab conquest of Persia in the seventh century) of Iranian identity.[10]

In 1934, Reza Shah saw to it that the millenary celebration of Ferdowsi in Tehran and Mashhad dovetailed with the ideological foregrounding of his monarchy. The gesture would be renewed decades later when, in 1972, a year after the notorious celebration of twenty-five hundred years of Persian monarchy under Mohammad Reza Shah, an annual lecture series on Ferdowsi and the *Shahnameh* was established at Mashhad University. The advent of the Islamic revolution in Iran would not in any way diminish the significance of Ferdowsi in nation building, when in 1990 yet another ostentatious celebration was organized by the Islamists to celebrate the millenary anniversary of the composition of the *Shahnameh*. Expatriate Iranian literati opposing the Islamic republic would of course not be left out, and they too began to organize symposia and conferences and to publish learned journals on their national poet.[11]

This picture of the reception of Ferdowsi's *Shahnameh* in the Iranian literary public sphere would not be complete without simultaneous attention to the significance of the *parapublic sphere* in which, when Ferdowsi's epic was dragged into a state-building project, poets and literati like Mehdi Akhavan-e Sales, Siavash Kasra'i, or literary critics like Mostafa Rahimi and

Shahrokh Meskoub pulled him in another direction. A poem like Siavash Kasra'i's (1927–1996) *"Arash-e Kamangir/*Arash the Archer" (1959) became far more effectively popular with the younger generation than anything that the Pahlavi monarchy could do to appropriate the *Shahnameh* for its own lacking legitimacy. In this widely popular poem, Kasra'i gathers the young and the old on a cold winter's night around a fire where Amu Noruz is telling the story of Arash the Archer, a legendary hero who throws his arrow so hard and so far (for where his arrow lands will determine the Iranian border), that he perishes from that heroic throw. Kasra'i, though, turns the poem into a description of masses struggling against tyranny.[12]

Turning to ancient history and to the *Shahnameh* in particular became a poignant literary device that attracted many progressive and antiestablishment intellectuals and thinkers. Shahrokh Meskoub's (1924—2005) *Moqaddameh'i bar Rostam va Esfandiar/An Introduction to Rostam and Esfandiar* (1963) and *Sug-e Siavash/Mourning Siavash* (1971) were typical examples of learned essays written by the leading literati in which the social and political issues of the day were discussed in the form of learned commentaries on Ferdowsi's poem. In a similar vein, Simin Daneshvar's (1921–2012), *Savushun/Mourning Siavash* (1969) became a vastly popular novel that linked the thematic symbolism of the death of a tragic hero in *Shahnameh* to the history of contemporary Iran.[13] The untimely death of its young protagonist, Youssef, resonated with the theme and rituals of tragic heroism in modern Iranian history. The same was the case with Mehdi Akhavan-e Sales's (1928–1990) *"Khan-e Hashtom/*The Eighth Task"—a poem of extraordinary verve and power in which the poet links the *Shahnameh* heroes to contemporary figures of Iranian democratic struggles. Also in the same genre is Mostafa Rahimi's *Tragedy-ye Qudrat dar Shahnameh/The Tragedy of Power in Shahnameh* (1990), in which one of the most prominent contemporary thinkers turned the stories of "Rostam and Esfandiar" and "Rostam and Sohrab" into a salient critique of power.[14] As the Pahlavi regime was busy appropriating the *Shahnameh* for its own propaganda purposes, a far more potent force was at work rethinking the text for a critical awareness of the present and future of Ferdowsi's peoples. The ruling regimes had the entire public sphere at its disposal to do as it wished, and yet the moral imagination of the nation at large had crafted a parapublic sphere that was charting the course of history ahead.

A GENEALOGY OF THE POSTCOLONIAL SUBJECT

My work on a genealogy of the postcolonial subject is ultimately geared toward a critical understanding of how the postcolonial person gets to know what s/he knows, and how exactly it is that s/he has become a knowing subject, and thus what exactly it is that s/he can know, and what the limits and the horizons of this knowledge are—all predicated on the nature and disposition of the public sphere this subject has occupied.

If you were to look at a typical calendar by which Iranians measure their daily lives you would see three simultaneous calendars—an Iranian, an Islamic, and a Gregorian. These three calendars place the person marking them in an Iranian, Islamic, and what is commonly called "Western" frame of reference—of timing, of consciousness, and thus of temporal subjection. I have had occasion to think and write of these three calendars as states of multiple consciousness, as opposed to but following the idea of W. E. B. Du Bois's notion of "double consciousness."[15] But here I wish to suggest that these three books, of which this is the third, also refer to these triple states of consciousness, of postcolonial subjection, of how exactly it is that a human being is termed an "Iranian" subject, a subject that knows herself or himself as Iranian, as a postcolonial person. My contention throughout these three volumes has been that this postcolonial subject is formed and placed on the veritable domain of the *public sphere,* and through these books I have sought to excavate and document the manner in which this subjection has had a *scholastic* (Shi'i), a *humanist* (Persian literary humanist), and now a pointedly *postcolonial* ("Western" anchored) disposition. While the other two accounts were formulated in terms domestic to the imperial domains of the Islamic and Persianate empires, this third volume navigates the terms of the emplotment of that subject (formation) inside the European imperial contexts, with their penchant for things Persian and in and through their Persophilia.

How are human beings made into subjects? Modes of identification that historically posit human beings as particular subjects vary from one social setting to another. My theoretical premise here is that in the colonial and postcolonial sites these modes of subjection are a combined but inconclusive dialectic of perceived and received *history* from one side and the catalytic impact of the globalized *geography* of European imperialism and its contingent public spheres (public spheres it inevitably and inadvertently enables) on the other. The public spheres that are thus generated at the postcolonial sites are intrinsically dialectical, inconclusive, tenuous, and self-transformative. In Foucault's work, particularly in his study of asylum houses and sexuality, he paid particular attention to what he called "the dividing practices" that condition the formation of the subject—mad/sane, sick/healthy, and so on. Such "dividing practices" in the colonial world were under the shadow of such binaries as "the white and the colored," or "the colonizing and the colonized," or "the West and the Rest." But a key idea of my present book is that there is a subterranean link between the public spheres in the colonizing world and the emerging public spheres in the colonized world, and that this link enables a particular view of history that overcomes those "dividing practices" to reveal a far more organic link in the structure and function of the globalized power of capital, that in fact sees those dividing practices as a particular strategy of domination and alienation. Exposing those structural links, and thus revealing the organic idiomaticity of those public spheres and the forms of subjection they enable beyond the colonially manufactured civilizational divides and national boundaries is the central task of any emancipatory scholarship that seeks to de-alienate and liberate the world from the terms of its own enchantments.

The genealogy of subject formation is predicated on the interpolated layers of the public sphere that conditions it and its historical topography. My principal concern in this particular book is with how the European fascination with things Persian—Persophilia—was effectively rooted not so much in their imperial will to rule the world—which fact I take for granted—but far more tightly woven into the social and intellectual movements that were definitive to the rich, diversified, and multivariate formations of their bourgeois public sphere. It is predicated on this bourgeois public sphere, then, that European imperialism—in both its manners and its material forces, its culture and its capital—became the vehicle of the expansion and extrapolation of that transnational public sphere to both colonial and postcolonial sites.

The combined effect of the European public sphere—in which Persophilia thrived—and European imperialism eventually and inevitably came together to facilitate the formation of a transnational public sphere that thrived on formal congruity but structural opposition to that very imperialism that had facilitated its formation. The same paradox that Habermas detects in the formation of the European public sphere expands and multiplies in the rest of the colonial world and becomes the engine of postcolonial history. While the bourgeois intellectuals around the colonial world consider the phenomenon of *modernity* globally and categorically victorious and thus call for the *modernization (Westernization)* of their nativized homelands, anticolonial and postcolonial thinkers, who too are the products of the same paradox, thrive on these very public spheres, poised and inclined to split that sphere up to include the marginalized and the subaltern. But the task ahead is not just to expose and oppose the structural limitations of the bourgeois public sphere, but, far more important, to reveal the hidden worlds, the underbellies, and the geographies of liberation that this structural violence of the bourgeois public sphere seeks to conceal and yet ever so consistently reveals, enables, and disables at one and the same time, on the site of what in this book I have called the *parapublic sphere*.

This structural violence at the heart of the European, transnational, and postcolonial public sphere designs the engine of world history, which is now fought no longer exclusively in terms of labor and capital and the mobilizing cultures it generates in the bourgeois public sphere. As the French Revolution of 1789 and the wider European revolutions of 1848 exposed the inner dynamics of the European public sphere, and later Hannah Arendt theorized and expanded it into the making of the American Revolution, the wave of anticolonial uprisings around the globe were active testimonials to the normative and transformative efficacies of the transnational public sphere and the particular terms in which it was being articulated and dialectically expanded.

As evident in the case of Arnold, European social and intellectual movements liberated and released Persian poetry and prose precisely at the moment when they had started to exit the monarchic courts of the Qajars and had commenced twisting and turning themselves for their own purposes and in their emerging public sphere, now dubbed "*mellat*/nation." The paradoxical twist that this prose and poetry endured was historic in its consequences. The European take on Persian cultural heritage forced a necessary epistemic violence upon it that gave Persian literary humanism in particular, in its own natural habitat, a robust boost in the emerging Persianate public spheres. Persophilia was integral to the most subversive European social and intellectual movements at a time when the inner tensions and contradictions of globalized capital and the transnational public sphere had occasioned much moral and imaginative tumult. It was, therefore, not an exclusive prerogative of the European imperial will to dominate but was equally definitive to the compelling urge to subvert and revolt. While Edward Said in his *Orientalism* rightly emphasized the European will to dominate, I have detected in European Persophilia a strong element integral to the varied forms of resistance to power.

The presence of Persophilia in thinkers ranging from Montesquieu through Goethe, Hegel, and Nietzsche to Arnold was not a result of the European will to dominate or further the cause of imperialism, but, quite to the contrary, was the sign of the will to resist domination, totality, and absolutism. Exposure to these subversive and defiant moments on the site of the globalized European public sphere in turn enabled kindred souls on the colonial site to craft, define, and populate the structural extension of these public shares into the farthest corners of the globe—and thus, as it sought to dominate the world, European imperialism was unintentionally the very vehicle and conduit that carried the seeds of its own negation and contradiction by enabling a *public sphere,* a range of defiant *public intellectuals* and, above all, the articulation of their *parapublic reason.* If we were to place Nietzsche (of all people) and his kindred souls in the bosom of the European will to conquer and dominate and totalize, we have missed not only something very serious in European intellectual history, but far more importantly in what specific terms the anticolonial spirit of the world at large was enabled and enriched.

CHAPTER NINE

James Morier, *Hajji Baba of Ispahan*, and the Rise of a Proxy Public Sphere

ABOUT A DECADE AND A HALF after the publication of Edward Said's groundbreaking *Orientalism,* the eminent Marxist theorist Aijaz Ahmad published an unsettling critique of it in which he first performed a sociology of knowledge on Said's generation of immigrant postcolonial critics and demonstrated how his book in fact glosses over the critical questions of class and gender in the interest of ethnicity—a phenomenon predetermined by the particular moment in history when *Orientalism* was published, and also by the position of the "ethnic intellectual" in the North American and Western European milieu.[1] Ahmad proposed:

> The perspectives inaugurated in Orientalism served, in the social self-consciousness and professional assertion of the middle class immigrant and the "ethnic" intellectual, roughly the same function which the theoretical category of "third world literature," arising at roughly the same time, was also to serve. One in fact presumed the other, and between the two the circle was neatly closed. If Orientalism was devoted to demonstrating the bad faith and imperial oppression of all European knowledges, beyond time and history,

"third world literature" was to be the narrative of authenticity, the counter-canon of truth, good faith, liberation itself. Like the bad faith of European knowledge, the counter-canon of "third world literature" had no boundaries either, neither of space nor of time, culture or class; a Senegalese novel, a Chinese short story, a song from medieval India could all be read into the same archive: it was all "third world." Marx was an "orientalist" because he was European, but a Tagore novel, patently canonical and hegemonising inside the Indian cultural context, could be taught in the syllabi of "third world literature" as a marginal, non-canonical text, counterposed against "Europe."[2]

What Ahmad in effect does in this critique of *Orientalism* is to dismantle the East–West binary projected in Said's critique and offer factual evidence for an alternative reading of reality that brings both the East and the West into an economy of class struggle that has already overcome any such invented civilizational divide. By placing the two almost simultaneous ideas of "third world literature" (on which Ahmad had written an equally critical perspective)[3] and "Orientalism" together, Ahmad points to a kind of cultural essentialism that glosses over the more enduring class struggle that offers a different map of the world.

The circulatory disposition of capital and labor, in turn gendered and class-based beyond any fabricated marker of race and ethnicity, places Persophilia (or Orientalism in general) in that economy of the public sphere which can no longer be merely bourgeois in its colonial extensions. Once we limit the critique of Orientalism only to its European site in bourgeois production, we inevitably remain at the mimetic level and dwell almost exclusively on the train of a critique of representation. Here is where Ahmad's critique of Said's *Orientalism* becomes poignant and inevitable:

> Said quite justifiably accuses the "orientalist" of essentializing the orient, but his own processes of essentializing "the west" are equally remarkable. In the process, Said of course gives us that same "Europe"—unified, self-identical, trans-historical, textual—which is always rehearsed for us in the sort of literary criticism which traces its own pedigree from Aristotle to T. S. Eliot. That this Athens-to-Albion Europe is itself a recent fabrication, as a whole range of writers from Amin to Bernal have recently emphasized, and any Aeschylus-to-Kissinger narrative is therefore also equally a fabrication (or a fabricated reflection of a prior fabrication), is something that seems not to have occurred.[4]

But once we move beyond the European site of Orientalist (or in my case Persophilia) production and trace its consequences and influences all the way to the colonial sites of labor and revolutionary resistances, then that public sphere of which Habermas has written perforce entails *parapublic sphere,* in which revolutionary ideas can also partake of these European traces of Persophilia and, by way of performing an epistemic violence on them, put them to good revolutionary uses. Consider the most significant revolutionary ideas and movements of nineteenth- and twentieth-century Iran. Almost all of them have been influenced by their encounter with European ideas in one way or another aware of Persian culture. From the court-initiated reforms of the Qajar period to the revolutionary disposition of the Constitutional Revolution of 1906–1911, from Nimaic revolution in poetry to Hedayat's inauguration of Persian fiction, from the visual to the performing arts, scarcely any aspect of Iranian culture has been spared an awareness of European ideas already embedded within varied aspects of Persophilia. The flawed phenomenon code-named "westernization" (alternatively called "modernization") categorically glosses over and conceals the organicity of a transnational public sphere in which European intellectual movements meet their unintended consequences.[5]

One must read Aijaz Ahmad's take on *Orientalism* more as a corrective lens to Edward Said's work rather than its negation. Without doing epistemic violence to the critical factors of class and gender, one might argue, and performing what Gayatri Spivak calls a "strategic essentialism" on the racialized condition of knowledge production conducive to the European colonial project, one might surmise and suggest, Said could not have highlighted the European practice of self-projection at the heavy cost of denying it to others. But, at the same time, Ahmad is correct in pointing out how bourgeois intellectuals (and not just those who have migrated to the metropolitan centers in North America and western Europe, as he suggests), are historically conditioned to gloss over the fact that they are the beneficiaries of the selfsame colonial conditions, and thus camouflage the domestic and regional relations of power they have enjoyed by turning the light on an us-against-them battle irrespective of class and gender. Bringing both class and gender back into the analysis does not so much negate Said's reading of the colonial condition of knowledge production as it augments and supplements it. But what both Said and Ahmad would benefit from considering is

that European imperialism is not the only imperialism the world has produced, and that the inhabitants of other empires that European empires conquered have had alternative strategies of resistance to imperial domination
beyond the race, gender, and class consideration, and squarely on the premise
of the global organicity of their rising public spheres.

JAMES MORIER'S ADVENTURES

The advantage of bringing Aijaz Ahmad's criticism to bear on Edward Said's
Orientalism is to allow for a more global condition of knowledge production and reproduction in which (in fact through Edward Said's own theory
of "traveling theory) "the West" (as a metaphor of domination) is neither essentialized nor privileged, but simply marked as a site of knowledge production that through its imperial hegemony facilitates the globalized traveling
of such knowledge. But the class and gender issues that Aijaz Ahmad brings
back into the equation now allow the local and regional operations of capital and its colonial consequences to generate their own take on that knowledge. The result is the equal de-essentialization of "the East" and the exposure
of a palpable and living world far truer to lived experiences than such false
and falsifying binaries.

To make this point patently clear one can scarcely refer to a more poignant case than that of James Morier's (1780–1849) *The Adventures of Hajji
Baba of Ispahan* and the manner in which its Persian translation served precisely the opposite purpose of its author's intentions. Morier's satirical caricature of a Persian charlatan became widely popular in Europe when it was
first released and eventually turned out to be a landmark in the genre of European picaresque novel. But that success pales in comparison with Mirza
Habib Isfahani's Persian translation of the same book, which became an inspiration for the revolutionaries that were bringing down the Qajar dynasty
(1785–1925). Mirza Habib Isfahani (1835–1893) was no ordinary intellectual. He was a close comrade of Mirza Aqa Khan Kermani (1854–1897),
Sheikh Ahmad Ruhi (1855–1896), and Khabir al-Molk (d. 896)—three
radical revolutionaries of their time, who were finally arrested by the Ottoman
authorities and extradited to Iran where they were instantly executed, an event
that many historians consider a turning point in the history of the Constitutional Revolution (1906–1911) in Iran.

It would not be an exaggeration to suggest that Morier's *Adventures of Hajji Baba of Ispahan* in its Persian translation was the instrumental foreground of the Constitutional Revolution. The text became integral to a rising travel literature—either from India (like Abu Taleb Makki's travelogue) or from Iran (Haj Sayyah's)—that was definitive to the intellectual effervescence of the Constitutional period and contributed massively to the formation of the Persian literary public sphere. The Constitutional Revolution would subsequently become the turning point in the effective formation of the bourgeois public sphere (and its subversive shadow in the parapublic sphere), and people like Mirza Habib Isfahani the very prototype of public intellectuals chiefly responsible for cultivating a renewed pact with Iranian cosmopolitan worldliness. In the preparatory stages of the revolution and thereafter, and as indeed is evident from the popularity of Isfahani's translation, what Habermas calls *"Literarische Öffentlichkeit*/literary public sphere" assumed a definite and pronounced historical presence in Iran.

One of the most distinguished literary figures of the late nineteenth century, Mirza Habib Isfahani was born near Chahar Mahal, was educated in Isfahan and Tehran, spent a few years in Baghdad, and upon his return to Tehran was accused of having composed a satirical poem against Mirza Hasan Khan Sepahsalar, a leading Qajar aristocrat.[6] In 1866, Mirza Habib escaped the tyrannical reign of the Qajars altogether and sought refuge in Istanbul, where he worked as a teacher, a translator, a manuscript copyist, and also as a bureaucratic functionary, whereby he earned a meager living to support himself and his family, and soon commenced a writing career chief among the manifestations of which were a series of Persian grammar books on an entirely new and systematic model. The very grammatical foundation of contemporary Persian prose is almost entirely indebted to his groundbreaking work on Persian grammar in the 1870s. Furthermore, Mirza Habib's literary output between his arrival in Istanbul in 1866 and his death in 1893 laid the foundation of modernist Persian literature for decades to come.

By far the most spectacular achievement of Mirza Habib Isfahani was his Persian rendition of James Morier's *The Adventures of Hajji Baba of Ispahan* (1824). Ever since the publication of the English version of the novel by James Morier in 1824 and of its Persian version by Mirza Habib Isfahani in 1886, much discussion and controversy has been generated by these two books.[7] At the beginning of his, James Morier says he has translated it from Persian.

Was that only a literary trope or did he mean it literally? To add credibility to this doubt we know for a fact that Morier was a bureaucratic functionary and colonial officer with only a modest and clumsy command of Persian.[8] His English diction of *The Adventures of Hajji Baba of Ispahan* is full of verbatim and entirely ludicrous translations of Persian phrases. Are these to be read as an indication that he was indeed translating from Persian, or are they the marks of a narrative affectation feigning an "Oriental" phrasing? How could a bureaucratic functionary with a meager command of Persian and very limited exposure to Iranians during his short sojourns in Iran have written such a book—to be sure, full of Orientalist clichés and yet with psychological and sociological meanderings embedded within the condition of coloniality he purposefully or inadvertently portrays? That dilemma has baffled literary historians for decades. Some have suggested that James Morier's is actually a translation and not an original work. Others have wondered how a text of such astounding colonial racism in its English original could, in its Persian translation, become so seminal a text in the course of the Constitutional Revolution. Still others have even accused Iranians who admired Mirza Habib Isfahani's translation of "masochism"!

Much of these controversies revolves around a single and singularly baffling fact: while James Morier's original is a horrid piece of racist farce, Mirza Habib's translation is a literary gem of unsurpassed beauty, grace, elegance, and in fact is foundational to both Persian literary modernity and a preparatory text to the course of the Constitutional Revolution of 1906–1911. How could an Orientalist novel of the worst kind in its English version become a text inspiring to the moral imagination at the core of the Constitutional Revolution?

Here, following Umberto Eco's hermeneutics, we might distinguish among the *intentio auctoris*/intention of the author, the *intentio lectoris*/ intention of the reader, and the *intentio operis*/intensions of the text.[9] Whatever Morier, as a colonial officer, may have intended by this text, Mirza Habib Isfahani, as a reader of the text, altered that purpose, and so did his Persian readers readying themselves to topple a medieval monarchy.[10] Morier's English version is a piece of Orientalist racism rarely matched in literature, clearly intended to demean, denigrate, and discredit a people in order to rule them better. It marks the moment when the height of European Persophilia (produced on the map of the European bourgeois public sphere) degenerated into racist bigotry of unsurpassed conceit (in the hands of colonial officers). The laudatory reception of Mirza Habib's version, however, is due to two fundamental facts: (1) Mirza Habib's Persian version radically domesticates the diction of the novel with such astounding literary felicity that he effectively mutates the racist piece of nonsense into a literary masterpiece in its new habitat; and, equally important, (2) it is the presumed authorship and thus reception of the text by the leading Iranian revolutionaries that reconfigured the text into a radical tract for revolutionary mobilization. Mirza Habib was no ordinary translator. He was a close friend and comrade of the two leading revolutionary activists living in exile in Istanbul—Mirza Aqa Khan Kermani and Sheikh Ahmad Ruhi—the Iranian Marx and Engels of the time. These three comrades—Mirza Habib, Mirza Aqa Khan, and Sheikh Ahmad—collaborated with each other, read each other's work, and copyedited each other's writings. The first copy of Mirza Habib's translation of *The Adventures of Hajji Baba of Ispahan* that reached Iran and India was in fact in Sheikh Ahmad Ruhi's handwriting, to the point that people thought it was his book and thus its first published versions were misattributed to him. Sheikh Ahmad Ruhi was no run-of-the-mill activist. A year after the publication of *Adventures of Hajji Baba of Ispahan* in Persian, he and his comrades were cold-bloodedly murdered by the Qajar executioners.

It was the presumed authorship of that novel, and the radical character of its reception, that turned its advent into a defining moment both in the rise of the literary public sphere in Iran and in its centrality to the Constitutional Revolution, not a nonsensical notion about "the masochistic Persian modernists." Morier's text reads as a bigoted tract racially characterizing an entire nation as deceitful and thus in need of political domination and colonial control. In his translation, Mirza Habib turns the text into a piece of not just cultural auto-criticism but a sociological examination of clerical and courtly corruption. James Morier was a colonial officer par excellence. Mirza Habib was a leading public intellectual in close collaboration with two radical revolutionaries of his time. It was the authorship of these two texts that accounts for how they were read and received, not a transhistorical delusion about Iranian self-hatred.

A PROXY PUBLIC SPHERE

Mirza Habib Isfahani belonged to a generation of Iranian intellectuals who had left their homeland, mastered European languages abroad, and were eager to effect change in their country. Having breathed in a different intellectual climate, they there and then put their learning to work by translating what they considered important and timely European books into Persian. Isfahani had a comfortable command of English and French (in addition to Persian and Turkish), and among his major achievements while he was in Istanbul was his translation of Molière's (1622–1673) *Le Misanthrope* as well as Alain-René Lesage's (1668–1747) *Gil Blas,* the novel that was instrumental in making the picaresque genre a major European literary sensation. The location of Isfahani and his comrades in Istanbul reveals the extraordinary significance of this major cosmopolitan city in the rise of the Iranian public sphere. The *liminality* of Istanbul as a critical space between Europe and Iran and the *proxy public sphere* it enabled for expatriate intellectuals like Mirza Habib Isfahani posits an entirely different geography of liberation and cultural transmutation that almost instantly dismantles the fictive binary between West and East and mitigates the criticism that Aijaz Ahmad brings to bear on Edward Said; for on this site the binary completely collapses and reveals the significance of a major Muslim empire, the Ottoman territories, as the birth canal of much that we know and understand from the conditions of postcoloniality.

When we move from Europe to colonial contexts, we may thus talk not just of *parapublic spheres,* namely the formation of a powerful underground literary culture, but also of *proxy public spheres,* namely the formation of liminal public spheres in countries adjacent to Iran but organically linked to its nascent public sphere. Istanbul is a key location in this regard. But so are Tbilisi, Cairo, Mumbai, and other major and minor Asian and African urban centers with a sizeable bourgeois class and corresponding weakening of the dynastic elites. Isfahani's Persian translation of Morier's *The Adventures of Hajji Baba of Ispahan* was published in Calcutta and Lahore as well as in Tehran and thus had simultaneous impacts on multiple sites. It is in this vein that we may in fact consider cities like London, Berlin, or Paris as the extension of these liminal spaces, for without places like Istanbul as a major traffic zone the expatriate intellectuals in London, Paris, or Berlin would have been unable to evade governmental censorship and still reach their audiences farther to the east. Periodicals like *Akhtar, Habl al-Matin, Iranshahr,* and *Kaveh* were instrumental in disseminating these transformative ideas and thus generating a constellation of proxy public spheres under the feet of the tyrannies that were ruling over the region at the time. Because of a sustained history of domestic tyranny and colonial interference such *proxy public spheres* around and *parapublic spheres* inside recently formed nation-states would combine and become critically important for the history of revolutionary uprisings in the country.

It is impossible to exaggerate the significance of Mirza Aqa Khan Kermani, Sheikh Ahmad Ruhi, and Khabir al-Molk to the history of Iranian encounters with colonial modernity and the prerequisite formation of a public sphere in which they articulated their ideas. The most prominent among the three was Mirza Aqa Khan Kermani, a leading intellectual of uncommon learning who had to abandon his homeland and find refuge in the much more hospitable and cosmopolitan environment of Istanbul. Mirza Aqa Khan was born and educated in Kerman. By the time he was twenty-five years old, he had already mastered all the major classical fields of Islamic learning, published his first book, *Ridwan,* and learned English well enough to translate a book on astronomy into Persian. Motivated by his precocious mind and impatient disposition, Mirza Aqa Khan Kermani soon got into trouble with political authorities in his native Kerman, moved to Isfahan for a short while, and soon after that to Tehran. From there he was finally forced into exile in Istanbul, where he lived his most fruitful and exciting years.

From the vantage point of expatriate intellectuals like Mirza Habib Isfahani or Mirza Aqa Khan Kermani, the Istanbul of the late nineteenth century was the capital city of a cosmopolitan worldliness whose significance went beyond the Ottoman Empire proper and reached widely and deeply into central Asia, Iran, all the way to South Asia and North Africa. One might, in fact, think of a cosmopolitan crescent that began in the farthest reaches of central Asia, went west toward the Ottoman territories, turned south, and stretched all the way to Egypt and North Africa, with Istanbul as the cosmopolitan capital of this vast, multicultural, and worldly terrain. While for the late nineteenth century Turkish intellectuals like Namik Kemal (1840–1888) London (or similarly Paris) was the center of the universe, for Iranian intellectuals of the same period Istanbul was a far more exciting, hospitable, consequential, and effervescent cosmopolis. This is not to say that colonizing capitals like London or Paris did not cast their magic spell over Iranian intellectuals as well.

This is simply to identify and suggest Istanbul as the cosmopolitan center of an entirely different normative and moral imaginary far closer to home and far healthier in its worldly offering of a hospitable space for critical and creative thinking and action—and thereby a liminal public sphere that acted as a catalyst in generating and invigorating the nascent Iranian public sphere. Istanbul was both home and not-home. To live and write in Istanbul did not mean one was in a state of permanent exile from home. You could both live and work in Istanbul and feel connected to home. A generation or two later, if an Iranian intellectual moved to Berlin, London, or Paris (or, years later, to New York or Chicago), there was a sense of almost permanent removal from one's homeland—a feeling with which the debilitating ideas and sentiments of *exile,* of *exilic conditions,* or worse of *diaspora* were identified. In contrast, Istanbul for Iranian intellectuals of the late nineteenth century was a liminal space, a space where they were close enough to home to feel implicated in its destiny yet far enough to allow them a freedom of emotive navigations around their normative and moral imagination.

It was no accident that Mirza Aqa Khan and his comrades chose Istanbul as the center of their intellectual life and political activities. While in Istanbul they collaborated with the leading intellectual organ of the time, *Ekhtiar,* and earned a living as teachers at an Iranian school. A particularly important event in Mirza Aqa Khan's life while he resided in Istanbul was his acquaintance with Seyyed Jamal al-Din al-Afghani (1831–1897), by far the most globally celebrated Muslim reformist of his time. The two revolutionary intellectuals struck up an immediate friendship and camaraderie in their mutual struggles against tyranny throughout Muslim lands. Istanbul was a natural habitat for the reformist and radical movements that al-Afghani and Mirza Aqa Khan Kermani initiated late in the nineteenth and early twentieth centuries. It was the cosmopolitan effervescence of Istanbul that gave al-Afghani and his comrades that sense of global significance that attended their ideals, aspirations, and activism. A young revolutionary activist by the name of Mirza Reza Kermani, running away from the tyrannies of Qajar Iran, came to Istanbul, met Jamal al-Din al-Afghani, and, encouraged by him, went back to Iran and assassinated the reigning monarch, Naser al-Din Shah (1831–1896), thus triggering a chain of events that ultimately resulted in the Constitutional Revolution of 1906–1911.

That revolution was the most significant event of contemporary Iranian history, Istanbul was a singularly significant site in the intellectual environment that occasioned it, and Mirza Habib Isfahani and his provocative translation of Morier's *Hajji Baba* while in the company of his revolutionary comrades were all definitive to the formation of a proxy public sphere in which these ideas were cultivated. The case of Mirza Habib Isfahani and his friends was not an exception but in fact the rule in making the Iranian (moral, normative, literary, and intellectual) public sphere a possibility. A crucial aspect of living and working in Istanbul for Iranian intellectuals was their easy access to the most progressive and revolutionary ideas that came from European and Russian struggles against their own tyrannies. The literary public sphere that Mirza Habib Isfahani personified in Istanbul was matched by the equally important work of his close friend and comrade Mirza Aqa Khan Kermani, and that not merely as a radical thinker and revolutionary activist but in fact as a literary public intellectual. What made Istanbul a particularly suitable habitat for activist intellectuals like Mirza Habib Isfahani or Mirza Aqa Khan Kermani and their fellow public intellectuals was the cosmopolitan worldliness of the metropolis, which made it possible for them to combine their political activism with astonishing intellectual outputs. It would not be an exaggeration to suggest that had these intellectuals remained within the Qajar territories they would not have been able to realize their potentials as worldly and multifaceted members of a rising intelligentsia. Mirza Aqa Khan Kermani's *Ridwan* (1886), which he wrote on the model of Sa'di's *Golestan,* is an exemplary model of updating the graceful Persian prose of the thirteenth century for effective use in the tumultuous period of Kermani's activism in the nineteenth. In a subsequent work, *Reyhan* (1895), on which he was working when he was arrested and executed, Kermani pushed the boundaries of literary modernity even further; severely criticized the literary stagnation of his time, including his own *Ridwan;* and demonstrated a thorough familiarity with European literary traditions, on whose model he believed that Iran needed to create a literary renaissance. In *A'in Sokhanvari* (1889), he provided a literary history of Iran, while in *Nameh Bastan* (1895), which he modeled on Ferdowsi's *Shahnameh,* he introduced contemporary historical criticism to pre-Islamic Iranian history. At the end of this book, Kermani included a critical essay on poetry and poetics, plus a number of poems on more contemporary political issues.

Paramount in Mirza Aqa Khan's literary prose, as for example is evident in his *Ayeneh Eskandari* (1891), a book he wrote on the history of Iran, is his elegant blending of graceful Persian prose and poetry with radically progressive and deeply cultivated criticism, at once deeply political and marshaling highly effective and contemporary arguments. Kermani put his politically effective and radically charged prose to good historical use and wrote extensively on medieval and modern Iranian history. The points of all his historical writing were in effect a diagnosis of the maladies of tyranny and his way of trying to find a path out of the historical predicament of emerging nation-states. Such titles as *The History of the Qajars and the Causes of the Rise and Fall of the Iranian Nation and State* (1893) or *On the Civic Duties of a Nation* (1893) are quite clear and rather self-evident as to what sort of historiography engaged and preoccupied Mirza Aqa Khan Kermani. What we witness in all these writings is a relentless mind systematically tackling every aspect of his received cultural stagnation and systematically seeking to remedy its diverse aspects. Kermani wrote on music, painting, sculpture, and dance. He theorized the aesthetic judgment, speculated on the nature of musical composition, and wrote a comprehensive theory of poetics. Having mastered the classics of Persian prose and poetry to a degree rare for his time, he then proceeded to make groundbreaking innovations in prose and poetry, both in his own work and also in theorizing what it was that he thought Persian literature in general needed to experience. What is paramount in Mirza Aqa Khan's progressive literary engagements is his active fusion of radical ideas and formal innovations. Mirza Aqa Khan Kermani was a towering public intellectual who defined and occupied a proxy public sphere for his homeland for generations to follow.

The brutal beheading of three rebellious Iranian intellectuals under a wild rose tree soon after they had been arrested in Istanbul and extradited to their native homeland marks a particularly poignant moment when the *proxy public sphere* of Istanbul finally came into physical contact with the Iranian *public sphere*. The date of this execution is 15 July 1896, and the location of the beheading the city of Tabriz, where the three revolutionary activists had been dispatched from Istanbul. Who were these three, and why were they arrested in Istanbul, sent to Tabriz, and cold-bloodedly murdered in a particularly vicious and brutal way? The story of these three radical revolutionaries (all of them close friends of Mirza Habib Isfahani) and their ruthless end has stayed in the collective unconscious of an entire nation— like an adolescent trauma that simply refuses to let go of the grown-up person it has long preoccupied. Without these three revolutionary thinkers, the proxy public sphere they enabled, and the critical thinking they initiated it would not be an exaggeration to suggest that the Constitutional Revolution of 1906–1911 would have had a far different character.

What we learn from the cosmopolitan environment in which Mirza Habib translated James Morier's *Hajji Baba* and the revolutionary manner in which it was subsequently received is that *parapublic spheres* are organically linked to *proxy public spheres,* and thus Iran is connected to its environs and a liberation geography is formed beyond any particular colonial and postcolonial boundaries. Upon such geographies social movements effect change and thereby cast long and towering shadows over their participants and their next generations, successive and enriching shadows that in turn become the single most important source of legitimacy or illegitimacy for the governments that rule those nations. We might argue that the entire history of Iran during the twentieth and well into the twenty-first centuries is very much under the shadow of the Constitutional Revolution of 1906–1911, entirely informed by these groundbreaking events in Istanbul. After that momentous event, the nationalization of Iranian oil in the 1950s under Premier Mohammad Mosaddeq had a similarly overshadowing impact on Iranian history. It is in that context that the Iranian revolution of 1977–1979 (before it was kidnapped and ransomed by the militant Islamists) was in the same set of extended shadows. But thirty years plus into its history, the Islamic republic categorically lost any credible link with that set of revolutionary shadows and became a complete negation of all of them. It was against this backdrop of the loss of legitimacy that the Green Movement of 2009–2011 became the most serious threat to the Islamic republic by extending those historic shadows into the twentieth century.

Mirza Aqa Khan Kermani's arrest by Ottoman authorities, his subsequent dispatch to Tabriz, and brutal end (he and his comrades were beheaded under a *Nastaran*—wild rose—tree and their heads then stuffed with hay and sent to Tehran for the edification of other revolutionaries) marks a particularly poignant moment in modern Iranian intellectual history when the active formation of a proxy public sphere finally came home to roost. Mirza Aqa Khan Kermani was part of the same intellectual milieu, the same body of public intellectuals, the same transformative proxy public sphere that included Mirza Habib Isfahani and his groundbreaking translation of a racist Orientalist tract and turning it around and against itself. One can in fact argue that Istanbul (along with Cairo and Mumbai) was the birthplace of Iranian (Egyptian, Indian, etc.) cultural "modernity" (if we were to remain limited to that quintessentially European term), a home away from home, where expatriate intellectuals could solicit the collaboration of their likeminded activists all the way from central Asia, down to western Asia and North Africa, thereby forming a proxy public sphere beyond the reach of the censorial limitations of their home country and yet organically linked to the parapublic spheres in which their compatriots were intellectually nourished. In thinking through the history of Istanbul as a cosmopolis, it is crucial to locate it in its own imaginative geography, home to generations of public intellectuals from all over the world—from Mirza Habib Isfahani in the late nineteenth to Erich Auerbach in the early twentieth century. This, I believe, will radically remap the world—up to this time so awkwardly and jarringly divided between a metaphysical "East" and an everlasting "West"— valid only in the colonial imagining of a white supremacist perspective unable to see the world in alternative, more democratically liberating, ways.

CHAPTER TEN

Picturing Persia in the Visual and Performing Arts

IS IT NOT STRANGE that at almost exactly the same time James Morier was writing his *Hajji Baba* to be published in 1824, Delacroix was copying Persian miniatures of the Safavid period that were purchased and made available to him at Bibliothèque Royale? No, it is not. The author of *Hajji Baba* was a nasty colonial officer at the service of the British Empire, while Delacroix was a magnificent painter busy transforming the history of European art. One was promoting the subjugation of nations to British imperialism, the other chief among a succession of revolutionary painters who were changing the very idea of art as it had been known.

The origin of the interest European artists and composers had in Persian themes was much older than Delacroix, rooted in the classical and biblical sources, and climbing all the way to the zenith of operatic productions in the eighteenth and the nineteenth centuries. From George Frideric Handel's *Serse* (1738) to Giacomo Puccini's *Turandot* (1926) and beyond, European opera has been widely attracted to Persian themes, which provided it with unfamiliar tropes and settings made familiar by way of exploring a variety of dramatic sentiments. There is quite a distance between these earliest representations of Persia and Persians in European operatic scenes and Abbas Kiarostami's direction of Mozart's *Così fan tutte* (1790) in Aix-en-Provence in 2008. But the road that connects these two points took a cinematic detour that enabled Iranian cinema and by extension other visual and performing arts to become perhaps the most effective form of cultural production through which the Iranian public sphere became so politically powerful that it landed filmmakers like Jafar Panahi in jail or forced Mohsen Makhmalbaf to join scores of other filmmakers in exile from their homeland.

As early as the early nineteenth century, when students like Mirza Saleh Shirazi traveled to Europe and attended operas in London, Iranians were aware of the art form and eventually of their own cultural reflections in it. From that early awareness, European visual and performing arts would travel to Iran and have a profound impact on the globalization of their Iranian counterparts. Exposure to Italian neorealist cinema was widely responsible for the rise of Iranian cinema. From the time that Puccini adapted a Persian theme—most probably based on an episode in Nezami's *Haft Peykar*—for his *Turandot,* until the time we see the lead character in Bahman Farmanara's film *Khak-e Ashena/Familiar Land* (2008) go to his basement studio in a remote village in the Kurdistan area of Iran and paint while listening to Puccini's *Tosca* (1900), European operatic scenes have, either directly or channeled through Italian neorealism, found a reflection in Iranian cinema. In time, Iranian cinema became the most influential cultural form in twentieth-century Iran and was celebrated globally, where it became the locus classicus of critical and critically acclaimed cultural production.

Global recognition of Iranian cinema became a clear sign of that public sphere having become transnational in nature and disposition. Before directing *Così fan tutte,* Kiarostami had joined the legendary Italian filmmaker Ermanno Olmi and British filmmaker Ken Loach in directing *Tickets* (2005), and after that he went on to direct *Certified Copy* (2010), in which he cast in the leading role William Shimell, a celebrated opera singer known for his interpretations of Mozart's *Don Giovanni*. As people in Europe and North America began to discover, appreciate, and love Kiarostami's cinema, it was perhaps not entirely known to them that aspects of this cinema was coming back to them from their own artistic heritage. What this case clearly indicates is that, while Edward Said's *Orientalism* exposed the imperial modes of knowledge production for colonial domination, and Raymond

Schwab's *La Renaissance Orientale* (1950) examined the phenomenon for the enrichment of European cultures, something far more fundamental has been missed by both Eurocentric perspectives—namely, the *contrapuntal* effects of *traveling ideas* (both Said's own terms) exponentially expanding the public sphere upon which intellectual movements have cross-fertilized each other's cultural productions and moral imaginations.

PERFORMING THE BOURGEOIS IN THE PUBLIC SPHERE

The Orient as a place of faraway intrigues has had a central dramatic role in European visual and performing arts. Within that context, Persia and Persians were of particular significance because of both the classical and the biblical locations of the ancient empire in European Hellenistic and Judeo-Christian sensibilities. Cyrus or Xerxes as powerful emperors, Alexander the Great as the valiant warrior who defeated the Achaemenids, and Esther as the Jewish princess who saved her people from destruction, are all examples of this unique place held by Persophilia in the European visual and performing arts.

Both Persophilia and Orientalism are part and parcel of what European musicologists consider "the exotic" in "Western music."[1] This exoticism is not limited to Persophilia or Orientalism and extends into Eastern European, Russian, or folkloric elements in one way or another alien to the musical idiom of a given composer. The significance of that exotic element cannot be reduced to its political aspects, as indeed its political dimensions can be readily dismissed. Major European composers at various stages of their careers have turned to folkloric, ancient, and distant musical phrases for reasons domestic to their musical repertoire. Be that as it may, when these "exotica" are placed next to each other they do inform of a certain kind of anxiety, fascination, or fixation with things Oriental or, in our particular case, Persian. A judicious consideration of such attractions in European music should not in any shape or form detract from their musicological significance. Major European composers, from Handel to Mozart, were attracted to Persian themes (in musical or story-line aspects of their oeuvres) in the same way they were attracted to Chinese, Indian, Eastern European, or even their own folkloric music or whatever else tickled their fancies. The purpose of the exercise is not to find fault with these fantasies, but to see in what ways they helped generate a particular visual or musical regime that, in turn, played upon the bourgeois public sphere and that, by virtue of European imperialism, had global (intended or unintended) consequences beyond their immediate reasons, purposes, or functions.

As the European bourgeois public sphere expanded exponentially during the age of European imperialism, opera in particular became a singularly popular art form. It is imperative to keep in mind that, long before the French Revolution, the European bourgeoisie was ipso facto a global product. By the time Adam Smith wrote his *Wealth of Nations* (1776) capitalism was already a global phenomenon and "the wealth" it sought to theorize was not a national product. As a result, the European bourgeoisie was, in both material and cultural terms, a byproduct of an already globalized class. The European age of colonialism thus emerged as the logical extension of the capitalist revolution. In this regard, theorists like Rosa Luxemburg understood the limitations of Marx's theories much better than Weber did.[2] As the project of Enlightenment gave the rising bourgeoisie its ideological credence and legitimacy, so was the same bourgeoisie in need of public symbolics of identity and legitimacy. In form and content, eighteenth- and nineteenth-century European art in general, and the opera in particular, was inextricably connected to the consolidation of the bourgeoisie as a self-conscious class. Whereas the church and the court were the principal patrons of art in medieval and Renaissance Europe, in the eighteenth and nineteenth centuries the bourgeois public sphere performed their combined task for the modern visual and performing arts.

The bourgeoisie as a self-conscious class fully recognized its need for *public performances* that substituted for the medieval pageantry that had been constructed around the aristocracy and the church. The definition and occupation of a new set of senses and sensibilities were thus paramount in turning opera into the most successful and popular form of cultural entertainment among the bourgeoisie. Regular attendance in concert halls and opera houses began to fulfill the natural need for public performance in which the bourgeoisie recognized and identified itself. Central to the European project of Enlightenment was the construction of a metanarrative of emancipation, which was based on the two god-terms of Reason and Progress. Reason, or what Weber in his theory of the rise of capitalism called "Occidental Rationalism," was constitutional to the capitalist mode of production. From this economic premise, the centrality of Reason in human affairs was extended into all other social spheres. In *Madness and Civilization* (1961) Foucault extensively documented and argued the process by which madness was defined as a necessary corollary to the constitution of Reason. Having borrowed the term "Reason" and its concomitant "Progress" from the capitalist logic of economic production, the joint projects of Enlightenment and modernity extended them into principal god-terms of a whole philosophical movement against what was now dismissed as "medieval" thinking, now identified as inseparable from theology.

Thus culturally constructed and defined, Reason needed its shadow, its opposite, its negation, its absence, in order to bring it into sharper focus. This much we have already learned from Foucault. Unreason was the opposite of Reason, the opposite of European cultural modernity, the opposite of Enlightenment. Thus it became a principal item in the European project of Enlightenment, not just to define what Reason was, but what Unreason was. Unreason first became the principal characteristic of the ancien régime. The church and the aristocracy became identified with it. But that was not enough. Here is when Foucault noted the sudden emergence of asylums and the cultural construction of "madness." He has already told us how the rise of asylums and the cultural construction of madness contributed massively to the consolidation of Reason as the defining moment of cultural modernity in Europe. But even the invention and confinement of Unreason to asylum houses were not enough. They constituted only a partial containment of the shadow of Reason. Unreason as such required a much larger abode, a much more spacious confinement. As Reason began to be understood as the central defining force of capitalism and its liberal bourgeois project of Enlightenment, "the West" began to be identified as the site of this exclusive possession.

PERSOPHILIA IN THE OPERA

Although the function of exotica, Orientalism, or Persophilia was integral to the operatic sense of drama, it nevertheless had a central role to play in the manufacturing of non-European Unreason. The two sides of the argument must be held together as the central paradox of the European bourgeois public sphere. The study of European Persophilia must thus entail both the narrative impact it naturally had for performative purposes and the operatic energy it thus generated for the further globalization of that drama.

In the case of Persophilia in particular, European opera took its clue from European painting. The origin of Persophilia in European painting from antiquity to the Renaissance and beyond is rooted in the classical heritage and biblical stories. Paolo Veronese's *The Family of Darius before Alexander* (1565–1570), depicting Alexander the Great with the family of Darius III, or Pierre-Henri de Valenciennes's *Alexander at the Tomb of Cyrus the Great* (1796) are examples of one, whereas Rembrandt's *Ahasuerus and Haman at the Feast of Esther* (1660), Jan Steen's *The Wrath of Ahasuerus* (1671–1673), or Théodore Chassériau's *Esther Prepares Herself for Ahasuerus* (1841) are of the other. The Persophilia evident in these works of art have an innate Greco-Judaic frame of reference in them that points to the Greek and biblical sources, long before they were put to any future colonial context. In both of these sources, whether the reference is to Alexander's victory over Darius III or to Esther's heroism, the figure of the Persian is one of royal and imperial power.

From this visual repertoire we eventually come to the rise of opera, where precisely the same themes entered the story lines of the most prolific librettists. Perhaps the most spectacular case is Giuseppe Verdi's *Nabucco* (1841), with its libretto by Temistocle Solera. Inspired by Psalm 137, the opera recollects the story of Jewish exiles after the loss of the First Temple in Jerusalem, but it soon emerged not only as a pinnacle of the composer's achievement as a major European force, but its main chorus became the unofficial national anthem of Italy. The chorus resonates with the cry of freedom rising throughout Europe, soon to be marked by the Spring of Nations, or the revolutions of 1848, on the occasion of which Marx wrote his *Communist Manifesto* (1848). The magnificent chorus sings beautifully of that universal cry for freedom:

Va, pensiero, sull'ali dorate;
va, ti posa sui clivi, sui colli,
ove olezzano tepide e molli
l'aure dolci del suolo natal!

Fly, thought, on wings of gold;
go settle on the slopes and hills,
where, soft and mild, the sweet breezes
of our native land perfume the air!

The longing of the Jews for their freedom from slavery as expressed in this opera was soon to come true when Cyrus the Great set them free from that bondage. This aspect of the story is not in the opera, but it was in the air of the time, thus marking the fulfilled prophecy of freedom not just for the Jews but also in fact for the entirety of Europe, and through that, positing a metaphor for humanity at large. In Verdi's *Nabucco,* as a result, we have a clear case of the Judaic and Persian traces of European culture being put to emancipatory and liberating uses right at the heart of the European revolutions. This is no "Orientalism" at the service of any colonial project. This is Persophilia and Judaica coming together at the most liberating moment of Europe in its modern history.

If Verdi's *Nabucco* was implicitly about Cyrus, the operatic genealogy from which it sprang was far more articulate. Based on Pietro Metastasio's libretto *Siroe,* one opera historian has counted the following number of works in the eighteenth century: Vinci (1726), Handel (1728), Hasse (1733), Piccinni (1759), plus ten other operas not based on Metastasio's libretto. The same holds true for the other Achaemenid monarch, Xerxes, on whom an earlier generation of composers had staged their spectacular renditions: Cavalli (1654), Bononcini (1694), and Handel (1738).[3] In these operas, the figure of the Persian emperor is integral to the dramatic setting of the libretto, giving it a royal texture drawn from the same classical Greek heritage in which Xenophon had written his *Cyropaedia,* a major political treatise read for generations in tandem with Plato's *Republic.* European imperialism was the site, the mechanism, and the machinery of the global dissemination of the bourgeois public sphere upon which these operas were performed—and once they reached the colonial edges of those empires they became the stuff of which postcolonial dreams were made.

Persian imperial history continued to play a central role in European opera to the point where there are scholars who have argued that in fact Puccini's *Turandot* (1926) is based on a Persian story[4]—a suggestion that may in fact lead us to speculate that the brutal execution of the "Persian Prince" early in the first act might be read as a repressed way of citing the origin of the story! It seems to have become something of a rite of passage for a European composer to include something "Persian" in his repertoire. *Persischer Marsch/ Persian March* (1864), for example, was composed by Johann Strauss II on the occasion of celebrating the twentieth anniversary of his musical career. This is not surprising at all, for by the time the Persian prophet Zoroaster played a central role in Mozart's *The Magic Flute* (1791) we might conclude European operatic Persophilia was not anything new or strange. To be sure, the legendary general who put an end to the Persian Empire, Alexander the Great, was equally, if not even more, dear to European opera. Some one hundred operas were composed and performed about Alexander, including those by Leo (1727), Vinci (1730), Handel (1731), Hasse (1731), Gluck (1745), and Piccinni (1758, 1774).[5] But from Cyrus to Xerxes to Alexander to Zoroaster, a flamboyant cast of characters kept European opera lovers busy for generations with a Persia they had received and embellished from their Athens and Jerusalem.

The operatic fascination with things Persian continued well into the twentieth century. *The Rose of Persia, or, The Story-Teller and the Slave* (1899), a two-act comic opera with music by Arthur Sullivan and a libretto by Basil Hood, featured The Sultan Mahmoud of Persia (lyric baritone) and The Sultana Zubeydeh (named "Rose-in-Bloom"; coloratura soprano). "The Persian" reappears as a major character in Gaston Leroux's novel *The Phantom of the Opera* (1910), providing the background of the lead character Erik's history. The trend continued well into the end of the century with Hugo Weisgall's *Esther* (1993), an American opera in three acts updating the fascination with the Jewish savior that dated back to *Esther* (1718), an oratorio by George Frideric Handel, and that was repeated on screen in the luscious cinematic rendition of Michael O. Sajbel's *One Night with the King* (2006), framing the entry of Persophilia into Hollywood that had been already paved by William Dieterle's *Omar Khayyám* (1957), with Cornel Wilde in the title role.

PAINTING PERSIAN

European Persophilia enters a whole new stage with the rise of transformative movements like postimpressionism, fauvism, and abstract art in painting. If we cast a quick look at the modern history of European art we might be surprised at the range and depth of great masters' interest in Persian painting. Eugène Delacroix (1798–1863) was one of these. "In the 1820s he copied Persian miniatures of the Safavid period which were purchased in the 18th century by the Bibliothèque Royale. He may also have looked at travel books for the exotic details in his *Death of Sardanapalus.*"[6] Delacroix was not alone.

Art historians have also discovered that "Degas copied Persian and Indian miniatures and Manet may have based his 1868 *Odalisque* on a Turkish miniature." The list, without being exhaustive, continues to include Pissarro, Toulouse-Lautrec, Redon, Klimt, Franz Marc, "and even a much more recent artist such as Frank Stella."[7] The list includes luminary masters of European art: "Rembrandt, for example, knew Persian miniatures and even copied them as costume studies, and as well, no doubt, from admiration. He thus found a certain stimulation in Persian painting; but to say that he was deeply affected by that art would be to distort the nature of a simple and superficial relation."[8]

It was Paul Gauguin (1848–1903), however, whose fascination with Persian art became quite serious and integral to his work. According to Fereshteh Daftari, who made a thorough study of such influences in a major doctoral dissertation written in the 1980s and later published as a monograph: "The influence of Persian art on the formation of Gauguin's synthetist and subsequent style . . . is apparent in stylistic qualities to be seen in a number of his works. These qualities are: relatively flat areas of pure color with clear-cut boundaries which suggest a compartmentalization of the picture surface; a use of the Persian spatial convention, and a suggestion of additive figure relation."[9]

In a letter dated 25 September 1888, Gauguin refers to Persian carpet as an inspiration for one of his paintings of a face: "Le dessin des yeux et du nez semblables aux fleurs dans les tapis persans résume un art abstrait et symbolique."[10] Along the same lines, he said of his own *Self-Portrait:* "Les yeux, la bouche, le nez, sont comme des fleurs de tapis persan personnifiant aussi le côtè symbolique."[11] At the Louvre, Gauguin would examine Persian artifacts attentively and write in detail about his impressions: "Examinez attentivement au Louvre, dans la galerie Dieulafoi, les bas-reliefs des Lions. Je prétends qu'il a fallu un immense genie pour imaginer des fleurs qui soient des muscles d'animaux ou des muscles qui soient des fleurs. Tout l'Orient mystique rêveur se retrouve là-dedans."[12] As Daftari has carefully documented, by 1896 Gauguin "forcefully states his admiration for Persian carpets which he urges painters to study, especially for their colors." In Gauguin's words: "Les orientaux, les Persans et autres, ont avant tout imprimé un dictionnaire complet de cette langue de l'oeil qui écoute, ils ont doté leurs tapis d'une merveilleuse eloquence. O peintres qui demandez une technique de la couleur, étudiez les tapis, mais, qui sait, le livre est peut-être cacheté, vous ne pouvez le lire. Puis le souvenir de mauvaises traditions vous obstrue."[13]

Gauguin most emphatically preferred the Persians to the Greeks when it came to sculpture, for, as he wrote to a friend in 1897: "Je vois que vous êtes en veine de production; de la sculpture! . . . Ayez toujours devant vous les Persans, les Cambodgiens et un peu l'Egyptien. La grosse erreur c'est le Grec, si beau qu'il soit."[14] Here he exudes a discoverer's joy and enthusiasm in having discovered a source of inspiration for his own work.

Gauguin so thoroughly identified with Persian painting that he evidently used the name of the Persian prophet/painter Mani as the presumably fictive author of a text he found essential to his thinking about painting. As Daftari concludes about this text: "Whether Mani meant a prophet or a painter to Gauguin, it appears that in the 1880's, a decade in which scientific theories were used by artists to elevate the status of the artist, perhaps in order to gain credibility and prestige with Pissarro and Seurat, both of whom were then steeped in color theories, Gauguin opted, in a typical manner, to invent a legend to synthesize his own views and experience of art, among which Persian miniatures may have played a role."[15]

Gauguin was not the only artist who in this transformative period in European art was attentive to Persian visual art. About Henri Matisse (1869–1954) art historians have long believed that "the Persian traits in his pictures are so interwoven with those of the other Oriental traditions and with elements contributed by Matisse himself that they appear as a pervasive quality which cannot be abstracted and identified in isolation."[16]

Matisse's fascination with Persian miniatures becomes evident in a relevant passage in which he writes of the expansive space he sees evident in Persian painting: "Les miniatures persanes, par exemple, me montraient toute la possibilité de mes sensations. Je pouvais retrouver sur la nature comment elles doivent venir. Par ses accessoires, cet art suggère un espace plus grand, un veritable espace plastique."[17] This fascination extended to Persian textiles: "Je me suis dit: si tu aimes les belles choses, va au Louvre au lieu d'obéir à un sentiment de propriété. Tu aimes bien les étoffes persanes? Mais un ciel a des nuages épatants, et tout le temps il change."[18] About the evident influence of Persian painting on Matisse, Daftari concludes: "Matisse's achievement in the early years remains particularly original in the ways he makes use of Persian motifs and stylistic elements without ever succumbing to a mere reproduction of appearances. He draws from miniatures, textiles,

ceramics and metalwork and selects those stylistic elements of Persian art
that would advance his personal vision, his own stylistic development."[19]

Wassily Kandinsky's (1866–1944) attraction to Persian painting was
equally compelling: "Just as open to non-Western traditions as Gauguin and
Matisse and maybe even more cosmopolitan than these two artists, Kandinsky is another painter whose discovery of Islamic art, and more specifically Persian miniatures, sustained him in breaking away from naturalistic
themes."[20] Daftari further adds: "Persian and Indian miniatures may have
suggested certain stylistic features for Kandinsky's Improvisations on the
theme of the Garden of Love. The high horizon line in Kandinsky's and
Kahler's Garden of Love may have been inspired by the all-over patterning
so typical of these Near-Eastern works."[21] Kandinsky considered Persian
painting to be "the most arresting of all and closest to us today," recording for
posterity how, "Standing before it, I felt it had come into being of its own
accord, as if it had come down from heaven, like a revelation."[22] Thus, from
Kandinsky we have a written record of his elated soul once he came face-to-
face with a Persian work of art: "I stood and I looked, and as I did so,
everything that had previously seemed true in our 'decadent' art, everything
to which the soul responded with such joy that it felt like pain: 'this is truth;
this, beauty'—everything else was eclipsed, obscured, forgotten."[23]

PERFORMING ON THE PERSIAN STAGE

As Fereshteh Daftari has documented, most of these exposures of the leading
European painters to Persian art were the result of various art exhibitions in
Europe to which these artists were attracted at various stages of their careers.
But obviously they were not the only visitors to these exhibitions. Iranian
expatriate intellectuals, traveling merchants, and visiting diplomats fre-
quenting major cosmopolitan sites from Calcutta to Cairo to Berlin to Paris
were all integral to the formation of a transnational public sphere in which
these visual and performing arts were staged and from which they were reflected back to Iranian and other similar sites.

In *Colonising Egypt* (1988) Timothy Mitchell demonstrates how the staged
representation of "Egypt" in European world exhibitions in 1889 was something of a premonition or blueprint for the political ordering of Egypt itself
in the European colonizing imagination. This insight is of course entirely

valid for the sort of critics of colonial modernity that Mitchell and others have convincingly undertaken to study in this and similar projects. But the example of Persophilia I am following in this book, plus the fact that Iran was never officially colonized the way Egypt (or India or Algeria, etc.) was, points to the open-endedness of a dialectic between the European public sphere and its imperial extensions around the world. Things never actually ended up the way Europeans had dreamed they would, as the example of James Morier's *Hajji Baba* clearly testifies. Mitchell is correct in extending Foucault's panopticon to Egypt and beyond into the colonial world as a site of surveillance. But that surveillance and its extensions had much more difficulty sustaining itself on the colonial site. The combined insights of Edward Said's *Orientalism* (1978) and *Culture and Imperialism* (1993) have paradoxically given the primacy of action and agency to the entity that calls itself "the West" at the expense of the revolutionary and subversive uses to which ideas of European origin were put there. The incorporation of the colonial site into the European project of modernity is of course critically poignant and valid, but not in the manner in which it robs the colonial world of revolutionary, disruptive, and subversive agency.

There is a critical moment in Mitchell's *Colonising Egypt* in which, upon examining the Egyptian exhibition at the World Exhibition in Paris in 1889, he says, "I am going to return with the Egyptian travellers to Cairo, and examine Middle Eastern life through the eyes of nineteenth-century European scholars, writers, and tourists."[24] The sentence is a bit contorted, for Mitchell will indeed return to Egypt (metaphorically speaking) "with the Egyptians," but he will look at what he sees as a "European scholar, writer, and tourist." Mitchell is of course right that when Europeans visited Cairo they did so with lenses in their eyes installed, as it were, in Paris and at such exhibitions; but generations later, he too scarcely looks at Egypt from the vantage point of those traveling Egyptians (with whom he has metaphorically traveled back to Cairo) or of any other Egyptian for that matter. This choice of vantage point and perspective I attribute to the combined effects of Edward Said's *Orientalism* and later his *Culture and Imperialism,* wherein legitimate criticism of the European mode of knowledge production during the project of Enlightenment (colonial) modernity has assumed primacy and thus blinded critical thinkers to the actual site of the colony, which has remained in the capable but limited care of "area specialists" who have all but a blindfolded vision of what they call "modernity."

I am, of course, in total sympathy with Mitchell's project of considering colonialism as integral to the European project of "modernity" and have in fact done my own share of making precisely that argument. But here in this book my objective and contention are that, once the events such as the World Exhibition in Paris took place in the always already transnational European public sphere, and then traveled to "the Middle East" or anywhere else on the colonial peripheries of such self-centering events via precisely the same sorts of visitors that Mitchell describes (and who had many of their Iranian, Turkish, Indian, Chinese, Japanese, African, and Latin American counterparts), they assume a significance almost independent of their European origins and authorship. Of course, colonialism was integral to the European project of modernity—this is precisely what Fanon had in mind when he said, "Europe is an invention of the Third World"—and particularly in its extension of the surveillance state and the disciplinary formations that enabled it. But because of the loose and undisciplined sites of the colonies, especially in places like Iran where colonialism worked indirectly, the formation of the unruly subject was always in defiance of those colonial designs, and thus they did things with those images entirely counterintuitive to their European origin and purpose. The formation of "colonized minds" was of course as definitive in Iran as it was in Egypt or anywhere else, particularly among organic bourgeois intellectuals (like Daryoush Ashuri or Dariush Shayegan) who spoke of their liberal class interests through that colonized mind. But the paramount forces of history in the colonial world (long before the critic of modernity became philosophically forceful in the aftermath of the European Holocaust) were entirely counterintuitive to that colonized mind.

From that visual and performing tradition we eventually come down to photography and cinema, in which such postcolonial nation-states as Iran began to partake in creative and defiant ways. The Qajar monarch Naser al-Din Shah (1831–1896) was an avid photographer, and his successor, Muzaffar ad-Din Shah (1853–1907), was instrumental in bringing cinema to Iran.[25] These early interests eventually resulted in the rise of a robust art and industry in photography and cinema from which eventually emerged a critical distinction between *modernism* and *realism* as they were conceived and performed in Europe, which in turn resulted in the rise of "Iranian neorealism" in cinema as the most potent aspect of a cinematic movement in the late twentieth and early twenty-first centuries. The first photographic daguerreotype equipment arrived in Iran in 1842 by way of a gift from the Russian emperor to his Qajar counterpart. The daguerreotype eventually came into widespread use during the reign of Mohammad Shah Qajar (1808–1848). Luigi Pesce (Italian, active 1848–1861) is credited with having been the first European to photograph Iran extensively. His "Portrait of Naser al–Din Shah" (c. 1850s) is a significant event in the history of photography. Antoin Sevruguin (1830–1933) was another major photographer with a widespread interest in photographing people and landscapes in Iran.[26] In the history of photography in Iran, the figure of Mehdi Ivanof (1875–1967), known as Russi Khan (Mr. Russian), is linked with the history of cinema. He and Mirza Ebrahim Khan Akkasbashi (1874–1915) were instrumental in introducing cinema to Iran.

The rise of contemporary drama in Iran is equally rooted in this context. Mirza Aqa Tabrizi (fl. 1900s) became the first dramatist who successfully combined Iranian theatrical traditions with the contemporary dramaturgy to which he was exposed through his knowledge of Russian and French. He was a bureaucrat in the service of the Qajar monarchy, in which capacity he worked in Iranian embassies in Baghdad and Istanbul before returning to Tehran to work at the French embassy. His plays had no chance of being published during the reign of Naser al-Din Shah or even Muzaffar al-Din Shah, and it was not until the heated days of the Constitutional Revolution (1906–1911) that they finally saw the light of the day. His plays were initially published anonymously, and then attributed to another prominent expatriate intellectual, Mirza Malkam Khan Nazem al-Dowleh, who at the time was based in Berlin. Subsequent scholarship revealed his identity and consolidated his reputation as a pioneering figure in the rise of contemporary drama.[27] From Mirza Aqa Tabrizi early in the twentieth century down to Gholam-Hossein Sa'edi (1936–1985) later in that century, Persian drama remained deeply cognizant of the Russian and European masters effectively towering over Iranian dramaturgy.

One significant consequence of this trajectory of Iranian visual and performing arts in the framing of its self-reflection in the European mirror and thereafter upon the global stage was the creative mixing of the two traditions of modernism and realism in a provocative and pathbreaking way—bringing together the abstract metaphysics of one with the virtual facticity of the other. If we put Bahman Jalali's (1944–2010) photography, Abbas Kiarostami's cinema, and Gholam-Hossein Sa'edi's (1936–1985) drama

together, what emerges is a visual defiance of the factual registered somewhere between European modernism and realism combined with the effervescence of a *magic of realism* that is akin to, but different from, Latin American "magic realism." In the Iranian case, there is no additional element of
magic to make realism more palpable, but the visual oozing of magic from
the odd authority of the real, the teasing out of a superlative element in the
factual mannerism of reality itself, that transcends it via various narrative
techniques. People in the colonial expanses of the European empires did
not roll backward, pretending they were dead once European ideas reached
them. They were not the mere object of other people's representations; they
were the agents of their own history. They played with those ideas, put them
to good use—their own immediate and more distant use—and in the
playful and deadly serious act of such mischievous somersaults they found
and cultivated their own life-affirming, defiant agency.

CHAPTER ELEVEN

E. G. Browne, Persian Literature, and the Making of a Transnational Literary Public Sphere

IT IS IMPOSSIBLE to exaggerate the importance of the eminent British Persianist E. G. Browne (1862–1926) to Persian literary historiography. His four-volume opus, *A Literary History of Persia* (1902–1924), became the defining moment in the narration of Persian literature not just for Europeans but also, by extension through its subsequent translation and eventual influence, for Iranians themselves, and thus for the eventual rise of their own literary history. While Browne's project reflected the European penchant for nationalizing literary histories prevalent at the time, his *A Literary History of Persia* fit well with the dominant anticolonial nationalism of Iranians evident in the Constitutional Revolution of 1906–1911, for which Browne expressed unrivaled sympathy and solidarity.[1]

Browne's sense of historiography and his lifetime commitment to Persian literary humanism, in turn, deeply affected subsequent generations of Iranian literary scholars, from Mohammad Qazvini, who was Browne's contemporary and collaborator, to Mojtaba Minovi, Seyyed Hassan Taqizadeh, and Kazem-zadeh Iranshahr, all the way to Badi' al-Zaman Forouzanfar and Zabihollah Safa.[2] The genre of Persian literary historiography that

Browne brought to its heights and was based on earlier Persian literary studies by other Europeans, eventually extended into literary criticism and became crucial to the formation of a transnational literary public sphere in which European, Iranian, Indian, and central Asian literary scholars were all equally active and thus contributory to the subsequent and systematic canonization of Persian literary masterpieces for a new generation of readership—a decidedly *public* readership historically cultivated in the expansive and liberating domains of a transnational public sphere.[3]

At times the Pahlavi regime sought to appropriate this literary public sphere, but through the instrumentality of leading public intellectuals—poets, essayists, novelists, dramatists, filmmakers, and so on—that sphere managed to sustain a vast degree of autonomy for itself. After the Iranian revolution of 1977–1979, it became subject to clerical appropriation; but it still remained institutionally robust to the point where the Supreme Leader of the Islamic republic, Ayatollah Khomeini, denounced the whole spectrum of the social sciences and the humanities and demanded that they be "Islamized." During the height of state repression of the Islamic republic, some leading literary scholars left their homeland to reside in Europe and the United States. For example, Zabihollah Safa and Djalal Khaleghi-Motlagh produced some of their greatest works while living in Germany, while Jalal Matini, Heshmat Moayyad, Ehsan Yarshater, and Mahmoud Omidsalar all lived and worked in the United States. This diffusion of Iranian literary scholars throughout Europe and North America in effect replicated and brought to closure the cycle of the literary public sphere that was highlighted by E. G. Browne's scholarship. This entire historic episode introduced literary historiography as a bona fide field of critical inquiry to the public at large and at its farthest remove from both the royal court and the madrasa/mosque scholastic hagiography—so much so, in fact, that the canonization of Persian literature, now available to both a liberal bourgeois and a radical revolutionary claim, was the primary product of a public sphere in which European, American, Iranian, and other scholars were equally instrumental. The recognition and theorization of this *transnational public sphere* is not only quintessential to our understanding of literary historiography today, but it also categorically dismantles the overriding binary of East–West upon which much postcolonial literary criticism is predicated.

FROM AN IMPERIAL HERITAGE

By the time Matthew Arnold read a famous episode of the *Shahnameh* and turned it into a memorable English poem, Ferdowsi, among other luminaries of Persian poetry, were already known, admired, and loved in Europe. A key question that arises from this European familiarity with and scholarship on Persian literature is the process by which this exposure and interest were instrumental in the making of a transnational public sphere in which certain masterpieces of Persian literature were eventually canonized. Today it is impossible to imagine that canonization occurring without a systematic gathering of European, American, Russian, Iranian, Indian, or central Asian scholars come together representing the literary public sphere that made the very constitution of the postcolonial Persian literary heritage possible.

Persian literary historiography is a fairly recent development in the Persianate world, and a direct result of the formation of that transnational literary public sphere—from Europe to Iran and central Asia to India. Throughout its long and varied history Persian-speaking literati have been the most immediate source of knowledge about their own craft. The sites of these literary productions have been multiple and successive imperial courts all the way from the Indian subcontinent, through the Iranian plateau, up to central Asia, and down to the Ottoman domains. Persian poets, in particular, were conscious and aware of their crafts and often referred to their predecessors—such as Ferdowsi referring to Daghighi, or Rumi to Attar and Sana'i, or Jami to Ferdowsi and Nezami, and so on—as they were equally conscious of the royal provenance of their literary milieu. Intertextuality and the courtly domain of poetic or prose production were thus the modus operandi of positing or projecting a literary continuity.

The first genre of writing that could be considered a precursor of modern literary historiography is biographical dictionaries *(Tadhkirah)*, written in the long tradition of similar sources in Arabic and composed by leading members of the literati in order to provide a generational *(tabaghat)* history of various professions—such as medicine, philosophy, law, mysticism, and poetry. These biographical dictionaries—such as Nur al-Din Muhammad al-Awfi's *Lobab al-Albab/The Kernel of Kernels* (composed in 1221), the oldest extant in Persian—are the earliest available sources that later literary historians used in order to write their own accounts of Persian poets and literati. Such seminal texts as Dolatshah Samarqandi's *Tadhkirat al-Sho'ra/Biography of Poets* (composed in the fifteenth century) or Reza Qoli Khan Hedayat's *Majma' al-Fosaha/Compendium of the Most Eloquent* (composed in the nineteenth century)—to give two prominent examples—are chief among the primary sources from which the biographies of prominent poets and prose stylists were subsequently reconstructed. Upward of five hundred such biographical dictionaries have been identified. Most of them were composed in the Indian subcontinent after the sixteenth century, where and when Persian literature found a happy and prosperous residence under the Mughal Empire (1526–1858). In both diction and habitat such sources are definitive to a literary heritage that traces itself directly to the dynastic history of empires in which Persian was the lingua franca. These biographical dictionaries also had the function of creating a long and distinguished history, particularly for the profession of poets, whereby they procured employment at various royal courts.

Major sources for the critical evaluation of medieval Persian poetics were books written on the qualities of eloquence and beauty in poems and how to recognize and evaluate them. Chief among these are Mohammad ibn Omar al-Raduyani's *Tarjoman al-Balaghah/On Eloquence* (composed in the eleventh century), Nezami Aruzi Samarqandi's *Chahar Maqaleh/Four Treatises* (composed in the twelfth century), and Shams Qays al-Razi's *al-Mu'jam fi Ma'a'ir Ash'ar al-'Ajam/A Concise Guide to Excellence in Persian Poetry* (composed in the thirteenth century). These sources deeply influenced the assessment of subsequent generations of literary criticism. Shams Qays al-Razi's *al-Mu'jam fi Ma'a'ir Ash'ar al-Ajam* was particularly influential in providing literary historians with a reliable source of critical assessment of who was considered a master poet, and by what standards. Immediately useful as they undoubtedly were for the professional careers of poets at various royal courts, these sources were also indispensable to the historical process of the eventual canonization of literary masterpieces in the age of empires.

A TRANSNATIONAL LITERARY PUBLIC SPHERE

Based on these and similar primary sources from the age of Persianate empires from India through Iran and central Asia to Asia Minor there eventually emerged a number of by now classic studies of literary history written by leading European Persianists—pathbreaking, highly informative, and exceedingly insightful for the time and the context in which they were produced, but above all for the systematic canonization of Persian literary texts in a transnational public sphere that these European scholars occupied. Canonization was no longer the prerogative of court poets or the Persian literati closely affiliated with the royal courts. European Persianists were not at the service of the Persianate royal courts, nor were their Iranian colleagues; the formative site of their canonization of Persian texts was the European bourgeois public sphere. Europe was being swept away by massive social and intellectual movements—from the Industrial Revolution (1760 to 1840) to the French Revolution (1789 to 1799) to the Enlightenment (from the late seventeenth to the late eighteenth centuries) to the Spring of Nations (1848). It is in this context and in the bourgeois public sphere that these world-historic events had occasioned that European Persophilia in general and the canonization of Persian literary texts in particular need to be located.

The first task of the new generation of scholarship was to prepare critical editions of these old masterpieces. Every major text of Persian poetry or prose that had survived the ravages of the ages reached subsequent generations of scholars in multiple and varied manuscripts. Some of the most spectacular works of scholarship over the last two centuries have been done by scholars preparing the critical editions of major texts in Persian prose and poetry. R. A. Nicholson's edition of Rumi's *Mathnavi,* Badi' al-Zaman Forouzanfar's edition of his ghazals in *Divan Shams Tabriz,* and Mohammad Reza Shafi'i Kadkani's edition of Mohammad ibn Munawwar Mihani's *Asrar al-Tawhid fi Maqamat al-Sheykh abi Sa'id* are among the greatest examples of these scholarly feats. Ferdowsi's *Shahnameh* has gone through successive critical editions prepared by major *Shahnameh* scholars based on multiple manuscripts, the most recent version of which is the result of the monumental scholarship of Djalal Khaleghi-Motlagh, Mahmoud Omidsalar, and Abolfazl Khatibi. Without these patiently prepared critical editions, produced with encyclopedic knowledge of Persian literary history, no subsequent work of interpretative scholarship would have been possible. Critical editions began their original techniques in Europe, and eventually Iranian and Indian scholars joined the enterprise and collectively produced the textual foundation of literary scholarship.

Today our knowledge of Persian literary history is much indebted to these pioneering works by exceptionally competent Persianists—Europeans,

Iranians, Indians, Tajiks, Afghans, and so on—creating and sharing a transnational literary public sphere beyond any particular national or colonial provenance. Accurate as the term is in many of its enduring political consequences, "Orientalism" does not quite express the multifaceted bourgeois public sphere this body of scholarship occupied and constituted. Whatever the political contexts and hermeneutic limitations of these groundbreaking works may be, from the vantage point of subsequent generations of literary criticism and critical reflections on the European colonialism their *historical* significance and their instrumentality in the subsequent postcolonial developments remain compelling. The fact is that our current understanding of Persian literature is very much indebted to the astounding philological skills and exquisite textual criticism of those pioneering European Orientalists and the transnational literary public sphere they enabled. That in any critical postcolonial study one may take issue (as indeed I have) with their fundamentally flawed and even disfiguring assumptions about Persian literary history should not camouflage their revolutionary importance in bringing the Persian literary field outside the Persianate dynastic territories. Where I believe they have gone wrong in their epistemic assumptions and projections about Persian literary humanism is only partially connected to the colonial context within which they were operating.

Take, for example, J. von Hammer-Purgstall's *Geschichte der schönen Redekünste Persiens, mit e. Blütenlese aus 200 persischen Dichtern* (Vienna, 1818), the classical example of European fascination with Persian literature. By the early nineteenth century he had provided the European literati with a vast exposure to the best of Persian literature known to scholars by that time. Hermann Ethé (1844–1917), following in Hammer-Purgstall's footsteps, matched what his predecessor had done earlier in the century and, in his *Neupersische Literatur,* published in *Grundriss der Iranischen Philologie* (Strasburg, 1895–1904), paid particular attention to cultural history and political context in the writing of his account. The later Persian translation of Ethé's book by a leading Iranian scholar, Sadeq Reza Zadeh Shafaq, became an exemplary source of reliable literary historiography for generations of Iranian scholars, in effect framing their subsequent canonization of Persian literature. Some of these nineteenth-century European Persianists were prominent cultural figures of their own time. Italo Pizzi (1849–1920), for example, is now mostly remembered as a friend of Giuseppe Verdi who wrote a memoir on the great Italian composer. Pizzi was also a major scholar of

Persian literature who translated the *Shahnameh* into Italian, published an anthology of Persian poetry, and wrote two major texts on the history of Persian literature, *Manuale di letteratura persiana* (Milan, 1887) and *Storia della poesia persiana* (Turin, 1894).[4]

The nineteenth-century European fascination with Persian literature was as much in the colonial context of European conquests, as Edward Said argued in *Orientalism* (1978), as it was integral to what Raymond Schwab had termed *La Renaissance orientale* (1950). But by the early twentieth century, the public sphere that the earlier Persianists had crafted was extended into academic studies of Persian literature as a bona fide field of scholarship. By the time Paul Horn wrote his *Geschichte der Persischen Literatur* (Leipzig, 1909), Ruben Levy his *Persian Literature, An Introduction* (London, 1923), and Arthur John Arberry his *Classical Persian Literature* (New York, 1958), the scholarly study of Persian literature had reached beyond popular fascination and become a fairly stable academic discipline— in both terms enriching the European and a fortiori a transnational public literary sphere. It was in this context that Alessandro Bausani and Antonino Pagliaro's *La letteratura persiana* (Milan, 1960) became a classic of the genre and a model for subsequent scholarship, adding the momentum of Italian to those of English, German, and French in enriching this Persian literary sphere. Following in their footsteps, Jan Rypka, in collaboration with a number of his colleagues, wrote *A History of Iranian Literature* (London, 1968; initially in German as *Iranische Literaturgeschichte,* Leipzig, 1959). What was particular about Rypka's volume was the inclusion of an extensive chapter on pre-Islamic literary history, capped by chapters on Persian folkloric literature in addition to chapters on Persian literature in Tajikistan and India, as well as an outline of Judeo-Persian literature. Rypka's text thus opened up a far wider field of investigation into the European vision of Persian literature. Soon after Rypka's monumental work, A. M. Piemontese's *Storia della letteratura persiana* (Milan, 1970) pushed this Persianist tradition forward into uncharted territories; while Claus V. Pedersen's *Worldview in Pre-revolutionary Iran: Analysis of Five Iranian Authors in the Contexts of the History of Ideas* (Wiesbaden, 2002) and N. L. Tornesello's extensive work on modern Persian literature in *Oriente moderno* (2003) began to pay closer attention to more contemporary Persian literature. By now, a solidly transnational literary sphere was framing a global reception of its masterpieces.

The undisputed masterpiece of this particular genre of European scholarship on Persian literature is the monumental work of Edward G. Browne, *A Literary History of Persia* (Cambridge, 1902–1924), whose four volumes remain a model of detailed scholarship to this day. Produced by a European connoisseur of Persian literature who solicited the collegial company of his Iranian counterparts, he in fact actively supported Iranians during their Constitutional Revolution of 1906–1911. Today Browne's four magnificent volumes read as a testimony to a period in European scholarly dedication to understanding Persian literature with remarkable linguistic competence, literary taste, and political commitment to the democratic aspirations of the people who produced that literature. The combined effect of Browne's scholarly work on Persian literature and his political principles dedicated to the cause of liberty in Iran during that critical period singles him out as a massively influential figure in transporting Persian literary history outside its dynastic histories and imperial genealogy and right into the formation of a transnational public sphere in which Iran, like all other postcolonial nation-states, was now squarely located.

Not all fascination with Persian literature was in the context of European Orientalism of one sort or another. As I have noted earlier, two other equally if not more important contexts for that attraction were European romanticism and America transcendentalism—two potent intellectual movements with enduring consequences on their domestic turfs in Europe and the United States. While the British colonial interest in Persian literature goes back to Sir William Jones (1746–1794) and the East India Company, that interest was coterminous with the European romantic fascination with the genre as evident in the works of Lady Mary Wortley Montague (1689–1762), Lord Byron (1788–1824), Alfred, Lord Tennyson (1809–1892), Edward FitzGerald (1809–1883), and even Oscar Wilde (1854–1900). During the Victorian era, this romantic interest included writers like Louisa Costello (1799–1870), Samuel Robinson (1794–1884), and the Reverend Edward Byles Cowell (1826–1903), all of whom took Sir William Jones's Orientalist lead and pulled it in romantic and Victorian directions. Two globally celebrated outcomes of this romantic interest were Matthew Arnold's *Sohrab and Rostum* (1853) and Edward FitzGerald's *The Rubáiyát of Omar Khayyám* (1859). The same fascination with Persian literature is equally evident in the rise and ascendancy of American transcendentalism; in 1858, Ralph Waldo Emerson (1803–1882) opined, in an essay published in *Atlantic Monthly*, that names such as Ferdowsi, Anvari, Nezami, Rumi, Sa'di, Hafez, Jami, and even Attar and Khayyám had become common staples of "Western estimation."[5] The active integration of the scholarly work of European Persianists into the major literary and intellectual movements of the eighteenth and nineteenth centuries in Europe and North America meant the organic expansion of that reception into the wider domain of their literary public sphere.

Russian and subsequent Soviet scholars' interest in Persian literary history was a genre of scholarship unto itself, with some similarities to western European Orientalism but not entirely identical with it, in which such significant works of scholarship as E. Berthel's' *Ocherk istorii persidskoy literaturi* (Leningrad, 1928) and I. Braginskiy and D. Komissarov, *Persidskaya literatura* (Moscow, 1963) were produced and subsequently became widely influential. In comparison with western European Persianists, Russian and Soviet scholars' interest in Iranian history and Persian literature in particular was characterized by a wider range of familiarity with primary sources and by a historical materialist disposition. The *Shahnameh* scholarship that was produced in the Soviet Union, in particular, became highly influential for generations to come. The Soviet scholarship on Persian literature was in no significant degree different in its emplotment in Soviet imperial interest in the region, particularly calibrated through the political interests of its Persian-speaking central Asian republics such as Tajikistan. None of these political considerations, however, in any significant degree diminish the enduring scholarly significance of Soviet Orientalists' work on Persian literature. It just frames their epistemic mode of reading and interpretation in a decidedly Marxist narrative, which in turn had a profoundly enduring impact on the organic growth of the transnational public sphere in progressive social and intellectual movements. Leading Iranian literati like Karim Keshavarz (1900–1986) began to translate these sources into Persian, a project that in turn had a catalytic impact on the rebellious disposition of the contemporary interpretation of the classical heritage.

OLD WINE, NEW BOTTLES

Simultaneously with these enduring works of scholarship by European and Russian Persianists, and precisely in that widening literary public sphere they were building, Iranians were equally busy producing their accounts of their literature in the immediate context of a decidedly nationalist historiography in which the heritage of Persian literature was systematically appropriated into the larger and longer process of postcolonial cultural nation building, a project that had its own inherent strengths and insights as well as enduring problems with the transnational heritage of Persian literature and the subnational literatures it had inevitably repressed and concealed. The nature of these categorical problems was quite obvious. A literary tradition that was the successive heritage of multiple transnational empires from India through Iran and central Asia to the Ottoman Empire was now forced into the critical conditions of literary historiography for fragments of those empires in postcolonial nation-states. Both colonial and anticolonial nationalism, as two sides of the same coin, were deeply engaged in producing national identities that inevitably included historical, cultural, literary, and artistic components. Such prominent members of the Iranian literati as Mohammad Ali Foroughi Zoka' al-Molk (1877–1942), Ali Asghar Hekmat (1892–1980), Abbas Iqbal Ashtiani (1896–1955), and Sadeq Reza Zadeh Shafaq (1895–1971) were the pioneering figures in the production of these nationalized literary histories produced on the selfsame public sphere in which European Persianists had been active for a long time.

In this rich and multifaceted body of scholarship, Badi' al-Zaman Forouzanfar's *Sokhan va Sokhanvaran/Literature and the Literati* (Tehran, 1929–1933) stands out as a model of classical learning coming to inform modern scholarship. In the same vein would be Jalal al-Din Homa'i's *Tarikh-e Adabiyat-e Iran/History of Literature in Iran* (Tabriz, 1929) and Abbas Iqbal Ashtiani's series of essays on *Tarikh-e Adabi/Literary History* in *Daneshkadeh* literary journal in 1918. Occasionally this mode of literary historiography would extend to the pre-Islamic period, such as in Muhammad Torabi's *Negahi beh Tarikh va Adabiyat-e Iran pish az Islam/A Glance at the History of Pre-Islamic Literary History* (Tehran, 1989). The most spectacular example of this mode of national literary history is the monumental achievement of Zabihollah Safa's voluminous *Tarikh-e Adabiyat dar Iran/History of Literature in Iran* (Tehran, 1953–1990). In this seminal work, Zabihollah Safa provides a detailed social and intellectual history of successive phases in Persian literary history by way of providing the necessary context in which poets and prose stylists produced their masterpieces. Extensive samples of the works of these poets and literati are then provided, though with little or no commentary. Today this feat of scholarly achievement is best admired for its encyclopedic knowledge of Iranian social and intellectual history, as well as for providing a single-authored vision of a vast panorama of Persian literature. In the same vein, but devoted entirely to modern Persian literature of the last two hundred years is the extraordinary work of Yahya Aryanpour, *Az Saba ta Nima/From Saba to Nima,* and *Az Nima to Ruzegar Ma/From Nima to our Time* (Tehran, 1971–1995), which is the singularly authoritative source of a comprehensive study of modern Persian literature. The combined effect of all these works of scholarship is the canonization of Persian literature on a transnational public sphere that links European Persianists to Iranian literary scholars. Today, the successful canonization of Persian literature would have been inconceivable except in that transnational literary public sphere.

The organic expansion of the transnational literary sphere ultimately resulted in an increasing number of Iranian literary scholars producing their works in European languages, such as Iraj Parsinejad's pioneering study *A History of Literary Criticism in Iran, 1866–1951* (Bethesda, MD, 2002), Kamran Talattof's *The Politics of Writing in Iran: A History of Modern Persian Literature* (Syracuse, NY, 2000), or Mohammad Khorrami and M. R. Ghanoonparvar's *Critical Encounters: Essays on Persian Literature and Culture in Honor of Peter J. Chelkowski* (Costa Mesa, CA, 2007). Equally noteworthy in this category is Hassan Kamshad's *Modern Persian Prose Literature* (Bethesda, MD, 1996). These works reveal the full hermeneutic circle of that public sphere in which literary scholarship had brought the masterpieces of Persian literature out of their dynastic and courtly habitats and established them in the transnational sphere. Now, either in Persian or in any European language, the canonization of its literary masterpieces was in full transnational swing. Within the context of this full circle, an even more monumental, multiauthored compendium under the guidance of multiple editors and the general editorial leadership of Ehsan Yarshater is currently under way. In this unfolding work of extraordinary scholarship, a number of leading European, American, Iranian, and other scholars have gathered together to produce a new account of the Persian literary heritage.[6] That a positivistic disposition characterizes this body of scholarship does not detract from its historic significance in plucking the study of Persian literary heritage from its historical home in the royal courts and setting it down in the academic domain of a transnational public sphere.

Within this sphere, significant developments in the field of literary criticism soon emerged in Persian, which next to critical editions of classical texts is the most spectacular achievement of contemporary Iranian literary scholarship in both prose and poetry, classical and modern. This scholarship would have been impossible even to imagine anywhere outside the literary public sphere systemically cultivated since the Constitutional Revolution. Mohammad Reza Shafi'i Kadkani's *Sovar-e Khiyal dar She'r-e Farsi/Visionary Images in Persian Poetry* (Tehran, 1971) and *Musiqi-ye She'r/The Music of Poetry* (Tehran, 2000) are two excellent examples of contemporary reflections on classical poetics by a leading literary scholar. The same is true of Shafi'i Kadkani's exquisite study *Sha'er-e Ayeneh-ha: Barrasi Sabk-e Hendi va She'r e Bidel/The Poet of Mirrors: An Examination of the Indian Style and the Poetry of Bidel* (Tehran, 2000) or his *Advar-e She'r-e Farsi: Az Mashrutiyat ta Soqut-e Saltanat/Periodization of Persian Poetry: From the Constitutional Revolution to the Collapse of the Pahlavi Monarchy* (Tehran, 1980). An equally impressive body of literary scholarship was produced by Abd al-Hossein Zarrinkub, in *Naqd-e Adabi/Literary Criticism* (Tehran, 1959) and *She'r-e bi-Dorugh, She'r-e bi-Neqab/Poetry without Lies, Poetry without Mask* (Tehran, 1967). Baha' al-Din Khorramshahi's *Hafez-nameh/Hafez Studies* (Tehran, 1987) is an excellent example of the sort of literary scholarship of a quarter of the century, as is Hamid Zarrinkub's *Chashm-Andaz-e She'r-e No-e Farsi/Perspective on Modern Persian Poetry* (Tehran, 1979). In the field of modern fiction, Jamal Mir Sadeqi's *Adabiyat-e Dastani/Fiction as Literature* (Tehran, 1987), Mohammad Ali Sepanlou's *Nevisandegan-e Pishro-e Iran/Progressive Iranian Writers* (Tehran, 1983), and Ibrahim Yunesi's *Honar-e Dastan-Nevisi/The Art of Writing Fiction* (Tehran, 1973) are prime examples of the expansion of the classical to contemporary literary scholarship.

TRANSNATIONAL EAST AND WEST

It is imperative not to limit this transnational public sphere in which Persian literary studies are being conducted and canonized only to Europe and Iran but extend it well into Indian, central Asian, and Arab domains. For instance, scholars from the Indian subcontinent have been instrumental in producing voluminous histories of Persian literature, the most famous of which is Shibli Nu'mani's classic *Shi'r al-Ajam/Persian Poetry* (Lahore, 1924). Yunus Jaffery's edited volume, *History of Persian Literature* (Delhi, 1981), and

Girdhari L. Tikku's *Persian Poetry in Kashmir: 1339–1846* (London, 1971) are two other such excellent studies. A. N. Tarlan's *Iran edebiyati* (Istanbul, 1944) is an equally important book written from the perspective of a Turkish scholar of Persian literature. There is also an extensive body of scholarship in Arabic on Persian literature, for example, Hamid Abd al-Qadir's *Al-Qutuf wa al-Lubab: Mukhtarat min al-Adab al-Farisi* (Cairo, 1955); Muhammad al-Tunj, *Qutuf min al-Adab al-Farisi* (Beirut, 1965); and Amin Abd al-Majid Badawi's *Al-Qissah fi al-Adab al-Farisi* (Cairo, 1964). Arab scholars have also done pathbreaking comparative work on Persian literature, such as Husain Mujib al-Misri's *Bayna al-Adab al-Arabi wa-al-Farisi wa-al-Turki: Dirasat fi al-Adab al-Islami al-Muqaran* (Cairo, 1985), Muhammad Ghunaymi Hilal's *Al-Hayah al-Atifiyah bayna al-Udhriyah wa-al-Sufiyah: Dirasat Naqd wa-Muqaranah hawla Mawdu Layla wa-al-Majnun fi al-Adabayn al-Arabi wa-al-Farisi* (Cairo, 1976), or Husain Mujib Misri's *Misr fi al-Shi'r al-Turki wa-al-Farisi wa-al-Arabi: Dirasah fi al-Adab al-Islami al-Muqaran* (Cairo, 1986). The distinguished Indian literary critic Shamsur Rahman Faruqi has also produced extensive literary critical works on Persian literature in Urdu, among them *Sher, Ghair Sher, Aur Nasr* (Allahabad, 1973) and *Sher Shore Angez* (three volumes; Allahabad, 1991–1993). Considered together, these volumes provide a much larger frame of reference for our understanding of that transnational literary public sphere wherein the masterpieces of Persian literature were canonized.

To be sure, most of these literary historiographies and works of criticism, but by no means all of them, are cast either in European Persianist or in exclusionary nationalist narratives in their methodological underpinnings, produced either out of a Eurocentric cultural fascination with Persian poetry and prose or else as a form of nationalist appropriation in the context of modern nation building and its aggressive nationalization of a patently transnational (primarily imperial) literary heritage. Prominent exceptions to this rule are Mohammad Reza Shafi'i Kadkani from Iran, Husain Mujib Misri from Egypt, and Shamsur Rahman Faruqi from India—none of whose works feed into a nationalist and nativist narrative but instead are directed toward a rich and rewarding textual and comparative hermeneutics. But these sorts of textual hermeneutics are few and far between, still very much located within and assimilated back into a nationalist narrative. Be that as it may, what both these trajectories of at once conflicting yet complementary modes of literary historiography—Eurocentric Persophilia in one direction and bourgeois nationalist in the other—have paradoxically enabled is the transnational public sphere in the making of a postimperial literary heritage. The extensive domains of Persian literature in the Indian subcontinent, Iran, central Asia, and the Ottoman territories provide insoluble problems for any such nationalist historiography, as indeed do subnationalized literary traditions such as those of the Iranian Kurds, the Lors, the Baluchis, or the Azaris. The case of Judeo-Persian literature provides another subnationalized genre that nationalist historiography categorically disregards. What the violent nationalization of Persian literature conceals is the categorically transnational literary public sphere in which the masterpieces of this literature were historically canonized.

PERSIAN GONE PUBLIC

The effective canonization of Persian literature took place in a transnational literary public sphere informed by European Persianists conversant with classical sources and their contemporary Iranian counterparts. European Persianists were busy informing their bourgeois readers of a significant literary tradition about which they knew very little. The critical point here is that, before European Persianists played close attention to Persian literature (in order to learn about it and teach it to their readers), its classical heritage was primarily the prerogative of a decidedly royal, imperial, and dynastic milieu, with certain notable exceptions of which I have taken careful note in my book *The World of Persian Literary Humanism*. Against this background, European Persianists began to pay critical and comparative attention to this literature on the site of the European public sphere, and such eminent Iranian literary scholars as Mohammad Qazvini were in fact in Europe at this pivotal time and were close collaborators and colleagues of such leading European scholars as E. G. Browne; and later, other luminary Iranian scholars like Badi' al-Zaman Forouzanfar considered themselves grateful to scholars like Nicholson. Collaboration between these and other European and Iranian scholars of the Persian literary heritage was the premise upon which the eventual canonization of Persian literature took place.

The result of this close collaboration was twofold: (1) the eventual formation of a transnational literary public sphere that extended from Europe to India and embraced Iran and central Asia, upon which classical Persian literature now received an entirely new readership; and (2) the equally eventual canonization of a body of literary and poetic texts that were now considered the masterpieces of Persian literature. It was these two developments that, in turn, enabled the rise of contemporary Persian literature in conformity with or defiance of figures like Sadegh Hedayat (1903–1951) and Nima Yushij (1896–1960), who were the products of that literary space; this is perhaps best represented by the close friendship and collaboration between Mojtaba Minovi (1903–1976), a leading literary scholar, and Sadegh Hedayat, the founding force of modern Persian fiction, or by the fact that Nima Yushij, the most iconoclastic poet in modern Iranian history, appointed a key literary scholar like Mohammad Mo'in (1914–1971) to be in charge of his poetic legacy. Sadegh Hedayat and Nima Yushij proceeded to revolutionize Persian prose and poetry, inaugurate contemporary Persian fiction, and radically alter the course of Persian poetry—now all accomplished in the solid and confident domain of a public sphere that was made possible by the extension of European literary Persophilia and by the Iranian scholars partaking in the institutional consolidation of that sphere. It is impossible to exaggerate the significance of contemporary Persian fiction and poetry, which in turn informed drama and cinema, to the formation of Iranian cosmopolitan worldliness of the nineteenth and twentieth centuries and beyond, most emphatically evident in the course of the Constitutional Revolution of 1906–1911 and the Iranian revolution of 1977–1979.

The active formation of this literary public sphere was of course predicated on a number of institutional developments early in the nineteenth century, ranging from the eventual expansion of public literacy, to the introduction of printing machinery, to the publication of the first newspapers, to the active simplification of Persian prose (significantly aided by the translation of European literary sources into Persian), to the publication of the first literary periodicals—all of which helped prepare Persian prose to migrate from the court to the newly constituted public sphere. Roughly, from the early nineteenth century, when the first group of Iranian students was sent to England, to the early twentieth century, when E. G. Browne began publishing his voluminous history of Persian literature, is when these institutional changes in Iran dovetailed with the height of literary Persophilia in Europe.

As a self-propelling engine, capitalism not only induces imperialism to spread its wings but also sows the seeds of resistance to it on an equally global scale. That paradox lies at the very core of capitalism and its cultures. Too much plaintive emphasis on and long-winded criticism of imperialism and its hegemonic ability to represent and misrepresent, legitimate as that line of critical thinking is, inadvertently rob the world of the ability to muster defiant agency and subjectness and fashion multiple fronts of authorial autonomy; and thus assign a fetishized authenticity and authorship to the fiction of "the West"; thereby promoting a unidirectional conception of power and governmentality. Every assertion of power engenders resistance to itself; and as those who are disenfranchised by the machinery of globalized capital are numerically far more than those who are privileged by it, both outside and inside the fictive frontiers of "the West," such acts of resistance are bound to generate many forms of cultural defiance staged precisely in that domain occasioned by the European bourgeois public sphere. The case of Persophilia clearly indicates that in the globalized European public sphere not just the overpowering terms of representation, ordering, and disciplining of others were evident and palpable, but in precisely the same space were equally evident the rebellious terms of enabling mobilization, resistance, and the necessary boldness to dare to reverse them. The result should never be judged in terms of the victory of one over the other, of "westernization" versus "nativism," but in terms of the dialectical outcome of power and resistance upon which emerge the terms of progressive parameters of critical thinking and of revolutionary action.

CHAPTER TWELVE

Persica Spiritualis: Nicholson, Schimmel, Corbin, and Their Consequences

THE ARGUMENT I have been putting forward in this book is that the global-ized imperialism that European capitalism had generated economically and culturally sustained was not a one-way street, and that it had all sorts of dia-lectical consequences once it reached the colonial corners of its material imagination. The site of that dialectic is the transnational bourgeois public sphere it created both inside and outside its European territorial boundaries and the fictive frontiers of "the West." Given the uneven and contested dis-position of that bourgeois public sphere and all the parapublic spheres it inevitably generated, what we have is a globalized revolutionary condition rooted in that space but pulling it asunder and working against its stated and projected purposes.

Two sorts of distortions have historically and theoretically camouflaged and concealed that dialogical state: (1) the perfectly legitimate critique of Orientalism, imperialism, and colonialism that paradoxically assigns uni-versal agency to a Eurocentric conception of the world; and (2) the per-fectly natural nativism that propositions such as "westernization" or "mod-ernization" entail and dialogically condition. Both sides of this binary—the critique of Orientalism and the appeal of nativism—are both necessary and even logical for the historical circumstances in which they were launched. But at the same time they have both come together paradoxically to rob the postcolonial person of historical agency and moral and authorial imagination. The historical site of that agency and authorship has been staring at us all along, but we have been too busy with and thus blinded by the fruitful insights of the critique of Orientalism and the false appeal of nativism. The space between the critique of Orientalism and the lure of nativism is the wide and widening transnational public spheres that defy frontier fictions of all nations and their narrations, empires, and their power of representation.

The fact and phenomenon of that transnational public sphere itself has been the locus classicus of both imperial hegemony and revolutionary resistances to that hegemony. Consider the fact that Karl Marx, in his categorically flawed conception of "Oriental despotism" (which seriously compromised his understanding of the self-globalizing proclivity of capitalism beyond its European limits, as Rosa Luxemburg acutely recognized), was a product of European Enlightenment modernity and yet the most potent revolutionary theorist against its ravages. The paradoxical example of Marx is useful only if we limit ourselves to the European site of the always already globalized capitalism. Once we move around the globe, we need to navigate the local and regional consequences of that self-globalizing public sphere that provides the formal contours of its expansions into the colonial site but in no shape or form is in control of its intended and unintended consequences. In this book I have used and navigated the specific case of Persophilia to map out the detailed ways in which a European attraction to things Persian has had catalytic historic effects on the historic site that has called itself "Persia" or, now, "Iran."

ROMANCING RUMI

Romancing the Persian mystic poet Rumi was one such paramount example. Two European connoisseurs of Persian mystical poetry, the British scholar R. A. Nicholson (1868–1945) and the German Orientalist Annemarie Schimmel (1922–2003), had a monumental impact on the global rediscovery of the genre in general and of the poetry of Mawlana Jalal al-Din Rumi (1207–1273) in particular. The tradition of these attentions from which these eminent European scholars drew their own inspirations went back to Sir William Jones (1746–1794), Goethe (1749–1832), Joseph von Hammer-Purgstall (1774–1856), Friedrich Rueckert (1788–1866), and Rainer Maria Rilke (1875–1926), among many others. Nicholson's lifetime achievement was the critical edition and translation of Rumi's *Mathnavi.* Nicholson's connection with the Iranian literary scene was through the greatest doyen of Persian literary historiography and literary criticism, Badi' al-Zaman Forouzanfar. Forouzanfar effectively invented the link between classical literary learning and modern scholarship. His critical edition of Rumi's ghazals, *Divan-e Kabir,* augmented Nicholson's work on the *Mathnavi,* and between the two of them the apparatus of modern literary scholarship was founded for the Persian literati in Iran. The renewed interest in Rumi also emerged from the German Romantic corner in the twentieth century in the vast and variegated scholarship of Annemarie Schimmel, perhaps the last great German Romantic with an abiding interest in the Persian mysticism and its whole extension into the Indian subcontinent.

Schimmel was the European continuation of Mohammad Iqbal's interest in Rumi, and in her scholarship we in fact find a complete circle, when a European Orientalist goes back to her East to recollect the renewed interest in the Persian mystics and bring it back home to German and other European romantics. Though both Nicholson and Forouzanfar were serious scholars with a tangential interest in politics, the next generation of Iranians who followed their work, perhaps best represented by Seyyed Hossein Nasr, court philosopher-mystic at the service of the Pahlavi monarchy, were far less gifted scholars and far more clever in accommodating power and catering to it. Seyyed Hossein Nasr became the chief champion of Persian mysticism, and through his connection with the Pahlavi royal court carried on a sustained conversation with the French mystic-philosopher-Orientalist Henry Corbin (1903–1978). Corbin's interest in Martin Heidegger (1889–1976) was interrupted and replaced by his love and admiration for Shahab al-Din Yahya Suhrawardi (1155–1191). A leading Iranian intellectual, Dariush Shayegan later became the representative of the next generation of such mystic-philosophers, who developed an ahistorical mystical disposition that links Corbin to Persian Sufism and Indian philosophies. Through the intermediary of Corbin, and along with the enduring influences of the French-German–educated Iranian philosopher Ahmad Fardid (1909–1994), Heidegger entered the Iranian intellectual scene, providing leading public intellectuals like Dariush Shayegan with an added mystical momentum. By now the Germanic mystical disposition bordering with metaphysical absolutism had made a solid inroad in Iran.

In the 1960s, the affiliation of the leading Iranian public intellectual Jalal Al-e Ahmad with Ahmad Fardid had introduced Ernst Jünger (1895–1998) and his famous tract *Über die Linie/Crossing the Line* (1949) to Iranian attention and thus initiated a strong streak of antimodernism into Iranian political culture that later resulted in the radical Islamization of the 1977–1979 revolution—almost entirely opposite to Al-e Ahmad's intentions. It is upon that fertile ground of a false and falsifying bifurcation between "tradition and modernism," "Islam and the West," "religious and secular" that we need to understand the next towering intellectual of his generation, Abdolkarim Soroush, who in effect picked up that legacy and became a peculiar combination of Ali Shari'ati, Seyyed Hossein Nasr, and Dariush Shayegan. Soroush became the champion of what in the aftermath of the Islamic revolution would be termed "*Roshanfekr-e Dini*/religious intellectual."

One might thus argue that the line that began with Nicholson and came to Nasr and Corbin provided the modus operandi of the Islamist takeover of the 1979 revolution in Iran. While Al-e Ahmad and Shari'ati may have paved the way for the Iranian revolution of 1977–1979, it was the ideas of Seyyed Hossein Nasr, in particular, that were deep in the roots of the Islamist takeover of that revolution and the formation of an absolutist Islamist state—what he had also tried but failed to do with the Pahlavi monarchy. Before this distorted and maligned backdrop of Iranian political culture, "religious intellectuals" led by Abdolkarim Soroush defined the Iranian intellectual scene for over thirty years in the aftermath of the 1979 revolution and finally degenerated into a figure like Arash Naraqi, who while in exile in a college in Pennsylvania, became the chief theorist of militarism cum "humanitarian intervention" in his own homeland. And thus ended the cycle of mysticism galore that Nicholson had innocently initiated and had inadvertently culminated in an Islamic revolution in Iran at one extreme and in the justification of U.S. militarism on the other, perhaps iconically best exemplified by the figure of Seyyed Vali Reza Nasr, Seyyed Hossein Nasr's son, becoming an adviser to American presidents in their imperial projects in the Muslim world.

The completed cycle, however, liberated the postcolonial person and readied him/her for newer horizons. Central to this episode in modern Iranian intellectual history was the enabling of Ayatollah Khomeini and other Muslim revolutionaries to lead a massively popular and later violently Islamized revolution. This was perhaps the most important manifestation of the Iranian public sphere, but it eventually ran its course and thus, paradoxically, dismantled the ideological domination of that militant Islamism by forces innate to that public sphere.

THE VIEW FROM THE EDGE

The view of the extended shadow of a European reception of a visionary mystic poet like Rumi, seen from the postcolonial end of capitalist modernity, gives the Heideggarian critique of the same project added momentum. What would Martin Heidegger, Jalal Al-e Ahmad, Friedrich Nietzsche, and Ali Shari'ati have in common—what sort of itinerary, archive, allegory, or inventory would that trajectory entail? The public sphere in which transformative ideas take place is not divided along fabricated civilizational divides.

Heidegger's critique of technological modernity took place within the context of German reaction to the immediate consequences of the project at one particularly acute moment and vulnerable spot in its center of gravity. Heidegger was part and parcel of the Weimar culture, "haunted," as Pierre Bourdieu puts it, "by the 'discontents of civilization,' fascinated by war and death, and revolted by technological civilization as well as by all forms of authority."[1] Bourdieu has further demonstrated that Heidegger's antimodernity was predicated on similar sentiments in such figures as Oswald Spengler who were calling for an end to the "alienation" rampant in the very "spirit" of their time, while lamenting the "uprooting" of the Germanic culture. Fritz Lang's "Metropolis" Bourdieu in fact singles out as "that virtual summary of all their fantasized problematic . . . a graphic retranslation of Jünger's *Der Arbeiter* (The Worker)."[2] The antitechnological modernity that finally found its most elaborate philosophical expression in Ernst Jünger and reached its culmination with Heidegger, Bourdieu extensively demonstrates, had its origin in the economic and social circumstances of postwar Germany where the underemployed professoriat became the mouthpiece of a whole generation of dissatisfaction with the catastrophic consequences of the project. The passage from Oswald Spengler's *Man and Technics*[3] that Bourdieu quotes gives a full description of the ideological mood of the era:

The Faustian thought begins to be sick of machines. A weariness is spreading, a sort of pacifism of the battle with nature. Men are returning to forms of life simpler and nearer to nature; they are spending their time in sport instead of technical experiments. The great cities are becoming hateful to them, and they would fain get away from the pressure of soulless facts and the clear cold atmosphere of technical organization. And it is precisely the strong and creative talents that are turning away from practical problems and sciences and towards pure speculation. Occultism and spiritualism, Hindu philosophies, metaphysical inquisitiveness under Christian or pagan colouring, all of which were despised in the Darwinian period, are coming up again. It is in the spirit of Rome in the Age of Augustus. Out of the satiety of life, men take refuge from civilization in the more primitive parts of the earth, in vagabondage, in suicide.[4]

Bourdieu's sociological explanation of this ideological atmosphere that engulfed and animated Heidegger's critique of technological modernity is squarely planted in his assessment of the class structure of postwar Germany: "The 'conservative revolutionaries,' whether they were bourgeois who were excluded by the nobility from the prestigious posts of State administration, or petty bourgeois who were frustrated in the aspirations aroused by their educational success, found a magical solution to their contradictory expectations in the 'spiritual renaissance' and the 'German revolution.'"[5] He further elaborates: "The spiritual revolution which was supposed to 'revitalize' the nation without revolutionizing its structure is what allowed these actual or potential déclassés to reconcile their desire to maintain a privileged position in the social order and to rebel against the order denying them this position, with their hostility to the bourgeoisie who excluded them and their repugnance for the socialist revolution that threatened all the values which helped to distinguish them from the proletariat."[6] Bourdieu continues to observe how the "regressive yearning for a reassuring reintegration in the organic totality of an autarchic agrarian (or feudal) society" was "simply the counterpart of a hostile fear of anything in the present which announces a threat for the future, whether that threat is capitalist or Marxist; they fear the capitalist materialism of the bourgeoisie as much as the godless rationalism of the socialists."[7]

The problem with Bourdieu's reading of the ideological atmosphere that contextualized Heidegger's critique of technological modernity is that it analytically isolates, and thus sociologically explains away, the German crisis as a unique phenomenon. But the predicament is far more endemic to the global condition of capitalist modernity, even though it may have a particularly acute manifestation in the Germany of the Weimar Republic. Both the catastrophic consequences of the technological modernity at large and the conservative revolutionaries' response to them were integral to a constitutional crisis in the very nature of the project, as Horkheimer and Adorno were the first extensively to articulate,[8] and which had now become evident on the German scene. Both Heidegger's critical stance vis-à-vis technological modernity and the economic and social conditions that were conducive to that response were integral to the project of capitalist modernity and its endemic moments of crisis, whether in Germany or anywhere else. The result is that no sociological explanation can diminish the significance of Heidegger's devastating critique of the whole project of modernity, even though, or perhaps particularly because, he was part and parcel of it.

What both the liberal humanist critique of Heidegger's involvement with Nazism[9] and its sociological explanation[10] totally disregard is what his critique of capitalist modernity has in fact made possible. The misplaced criticism of Heidegger's critique of modernity and Enlightenment-based humanism, which invariably collapses into the perfectly legitimate one of his Nazi affiliation, has made the liberal humanists strange bedfellows of such ideologues of capitalist modernity as William Bennett, Allan Bloom, and Dinesh D'Souza. The critique of Heidegger's affiliation with Nazism thus is the very predicate of a political absolutism of equally sinister possibilities. If for no other reason, at least for its reminding everyone of the tremendous critical power that Heidegger's critique of modernity has made possible, William V. Spanos's corrective move ought to be heeded very carefully.

> What has been obscured in the dramatization of this "scandal," especially by those liberal humanists in the United States who have imported the European debate into the North American intellectual milieu, is the ideology informing the attack on Heidegger's personal adherence to the practice in behalf of German National Socialism. Whatever its intention, this negative renarrativization of the itinerary of Heidegger's thought in terms of historical anecdote has as its ideological subtext the discrediting of Heidegger's powerful interrogation of the discourse of humanism as such. More important, it also is at some level intended to delegitimate those later, more radical, demystifications of the privileged concept of Man that Heidegger's interrogation catalyzed.[11]

But what even Spanos does not pay any attention to are the consequences of the emancipation of the subject at the postcolonial end of the game. The Eurocentricity of this entire enterprise is evident even at its most self-critical moments. To be sure, the freedom of the colonial subject has been earned on the backbreaking experience of having been located at the receiving end of the project of European modernity and not by its theoretical articulation at the presumed center of the project. But the destruction of the project internally, whether manifested in the German crisis that gave rise to Nazism or in the monstrous consequences of Nazism itself, has added theoretical zest to the factual evidence of postcolonial emancipation of the subject. But at the globalizing center of European modernity, beginning with the publication of Victor Farías's *Heidegger and Nazism,*[12] the numbingly Eurocentric controversy over Heidegger's involvement with Nazism has been caught in a claustrophobic hermetic seal that categorically disregards, as a psychologically conditioned blind spot, the colonial consequences of Enlightenment humanism and capitalist modernity. From the postcolonial neck of the modernity woods, the "humanism" that Heidegger dismantles as the latest, Enlightenment-induced, version of ontotheological metaphysics has had nothing but catastrophic consequences. The critical edge pointed at Heidegger raises the Holocaust flag as the most damning sign of Heidegger's antihumanism. But equally critical is the structural violence at the colonial edges of the selfsame project.

What this critique "forgets" are the much more atrocious catastrophes that Enlightenment-predicated, capitalist-based colonialism has caused globally. Perhaps Europeans, blinded by the immediate fruits of the joint projects, needed the Holocaust to occur before realizing the catastrophic consequences of technological modernity. But generations of catastrophes in Asia, Africa, and Latin America did not. Only those who were fooled by the lucrative profits of the "bourgeois humanism" of the Enlightenment because they were the material beneficiaries of it needed Heidegger's critical destruction of the illusion; the rest of the world did not. Not just the Holocaust but Nazism, not just Heidegger's support for Nazism but his critical dismantling of the very advent of technological modernity and its ideological foregrounding in Enlightenment (bourgeois) humanism, were part and parcel of the project itself. It is not surprising at all that the chief drummers of Heidegger's Nazi affiliation, people like William Bennett, Allan Bloom, Roger Kimball, Dinesh D'Souza, and others, are the principal ideologues of "Western civilization" and its chief defenders against "multiculturalism." What they rightly detect in what they call "multiculturalism" is the voice of the colonies now having come home to roost from the tropical peripheries of their native tongues into the very center of capitalist modernity.

But even this mobilization of counterintelligence is the handiwork of global capitalism, which has made migratory labor and transnational capital coterminous with each other. The custodians of "democratic modernity" were frightened witless by the Pandora's box of insurrectionary intelligence that, while rooted in the factual experiences of the postcolonial condition takes full advantage of the theoretical emancipations that precisely Heidegger's antihumanism entails, his colossal destruction of the very philosophical basis of modernity made possible. The so-called democratic humanism that the guardians of "Western civilization" advocate is predicated on the havoc that the rapid globalization of capitalist modernity has wreaked on the world at large and yet they opt totally to disregard. But, and here is the whole point of this argument, the disruptive return of the colonial repressed to the presumed centers of the European imagination in the form of labor migration was only a belated sign of realities already present and evident on the colonial ground itself, agitating change and defiance hitherto repressed, denied, and denigrated by the first world theorists of the European crisis of the subject and critiques of bourgeois humanism.

FROM THE RUINS OF MODERNITY

Between the "authenticity" (the traditions that Eurocentric modernity invents in the plural in order to believe and mark itself believable in the singular) of national and religious identity and the colonial constitution of the subject, the postcolonial art that Iranian cinema represents at its best liberates the subject from its agential constitution and sets it free in divergent and unanticipated directions. But because postcolonial poetics must, ipso facto, pass through the very essence of that *danger* that technological modernity has constituted, it can harbor no illusion for the "authentic," as Heidegger did. Iranian cinema at his best posits that defiant subject, the postcolonial poet of the vision of the possible.[13] The fact that this cinema emerged from a violently Islamized revolution makes it a particularly defiant site of subjection and agency. The very formation of "Islamic ideology" both as an ideology of resistance and as a metaphysics of *ressentiment,* and that not just in Iran but along the whole spectrum of anticolonial movements of the last two centuries in North Africa, the Middle East, and the Indian subcontinent, is very similar to the post–World War I German reaction to the project of capitalist modernity, which is replete with a consuming *ressentiment.* Because the colonial world was not the beneficiary of the project, and in fact was on the receiving end of its most calamitous consequences, it too, just like the Germans of the first two decades of the twentieth century, was attracted to mystical notions of authenticity, collectivity, tradition, and so on. Consider the following assessment of Bourdieu about the German condition that bred Heidegger—"Their regressive yearning for a reassuring reintegration in the organic totality of an autarchic agrarian (or feudal) society is simply the counterpart of a hostile fear of anything in the present which announces a threat for the future, whether that threat is capitalist or Marxist; they fear the capitalist materialism of the bourgeoisie as much as the godless rationalism of the socialist"[14]—and see how perfectly it matches with the rhetoric of Islam-e Nab-e Muhammadi (pure Muhammadan Islam) that became the dominant passion of Muslim revolutionaries as they laid total claim to the Iranian revolution of 1979. This search for mystical purification from the real Bourdieu aptly calls "the desperate effort to overcome a set of insuperable alternatives through a kind of headlong flight, whether heroic or mystical." Even more to the point, consider the rhetoric of alternatives available to the German ideologues: "it is no coincidence that the book where Möller van den Bruch, one of the prophets of "revolutionary conservatism," preached the mystical reunion of the Germanic past and the ideal Germany of the future, together with the rejection of bourgeois society and economics and the return to corporatism, was first called the 'Third Way,' and then 'The Third Reich.' "[15]

The leading mobilizing slogan in the course of the Islamic revolution of 1979 was *Na Sharqi Na Gharbi, Jomhuri-ye Islami* (Neither Eastern, nor Western, [but] the Islamic republic). The entire course of the "Islamic" revolution can in fact be read exactly as a "third" way distinctly different from the capitalist and socialist models against which the Germans of Heidegger's generation were reacting. Muslim mystical ideologues, led by Ayatollah Khomeini's ascetic absolutism, in effect crafted a mystic world outside history, to which they could lay total and absolutist claim. Seyyed Hossein Nasr's gnostic, entirely ahistorical, articulation of what he called "tradition" had paved the way for this mystic takeover of a people's worldly cosmopolitanism.

What the comparison of common mystical responses to the calamitous consequences of technological modernity demonstrates is that a momentous crisis at the European heart of that project generated identical reactions to the structurally sustained movements at the postcolonial peripheries of the same project. The notion of the "authentic German" is frightfully similar to "Islam-e Nab-e Muhammadi/The Pure Muhammadan Islam." The absolutist tendencies constitutional to the very project of an "Islamic" ideology are thus equally rooted in the bitter sense of *ressentiment* that disenfranchisement from and in the project of capitalist modernity can and does generate. By something far more than a mere historical coincidence, the same textual source that Heidegger pays homage to as the soul mate of his diagnosis of technological modernity in "Die Frage nach der Technik," namely Ernst Jünger's *Über die Linie,* is the very source that was equally present in the mind of one of the key ideologues of the Islamic revolution in Iran. In his famous letter to Jünger, Heidegger compliments the German nihilist on the occasion of his sixtieth birthday with the homage, " 'The Question Concerning Technology' owes enduring advancement to the descriptions in *The Worker,*"[16] a text on the premise of which *Über die Linie* further examines the consequences of technology. As Bourdieu demonstrates extensively,[17] more than anybody else, the ideas of Jünger were instrumental in shaping Heidegger's conception of the crisis of technological modernity: "Their ideological agreement on this topic is complete."[18]

This is the Germany of the late 1930s, in a moment of crisis at the polar center of capitalist modernity. Let us now cut to Iran of the early 1960s at the tropical periphery of the same project. Jalal Al-e Ahmad, by far the most celebrated public intellectual of the era, and one of the chief advocates of the Islamic ideology as a site of resistance to colonialism, his influential essay *Gharbzadegi* ("West-Strickenness," 1962) being the cornerstone of the whole political culture of the period and beyond, writes in his introduction to this essay a short note about the circumstances of its publication. His initial attempt, he says, to get the first draft of his essay on West-Strickenness published in the official organs of the Ministry of Culture having failed, Al-e Ahmad circulated a typescript copy of it among his closest friends and colleagues.

Among them was Dr. Mahmud Human, who encouraged me persistently to see one of the books of Ernst Jünger, a German author, called *Über die Linie,* which is a discussion on Nihilism, because, as he said, the two of us [i.e., Al-e Ahmad and Jünger] had more or less seen the same phenomenon but from two perspectives, said the same thing but in two languages. Since I do not know the German language, I appealed to [Human] himself, and for three months, about twice a week and about three hours a day, I took much advantage of Human's knowledge and learned much from him. It was in this way that *Über die Linie* was translated by his rendition and my narration.[19]

Al-e Ahmad's "West-Strickenness" subsequently emerged as the chief polemical tract of the 1960s and 1970s, leading far into the anticolonial disposition of the Iranian revolution of 1979.[20] The structural similarity between Jünger/Heidegger in postwar Germany and Al-e Ahmad's response in revolutionary Iran to technological modernity are no mere historical coincidences. Both these societies, at two distinct historical moments and at two distinct locations on the globalizing continuum of capitalist modernity, were on the receiving end of the economic logic of the project—Germany at a critical moment in the center of the gravity, Iran conditioned by its semicolonized status on the same scale. The search for the "authentic German" in postwar Germany finds its precise equivalent in the search for the "true Islam" in Iran. In Nazi Germany, people began to read, in Albertus Magnus through Nicolaus of Cusa to Nietzsche, a narrative of "German" continuity that anticipated the National Socialist agenda of the 1930s—irrespective of who these thinkers were and what they actually wrote.[21] In Iran, precisely the same thing happened: postrevolutionary ideologues began to read from Al-e Ahmad through Ali Shari'ati to Ayatollah Khomeini despite a number of significant differences in their perspectives, arguing for an "authentic, traditional, Islamic" response to colonialism. For the generation of Al-e Ahmad activists, "colonialism" was the target, just as the "bourgeoisie" was for the German "conservative revolutionaries." "Islam" for Islamist ideologues was the same "authentic" identity as "German" was for Jünger's generation of "conservative revolutionaries." In Germany, Nietzsche in particular was actively read as a prophetic voice anticipating much of what was to happen in the Germany of the 1930s. In Sluga's assessment:

The crisis was still a thoroughly German event and was to be resolved through a rebirth of German culture in the spirit of the classical world and with the help of Schopenhauer's philosophy and Wagner's music. Since the end of the age of Greek tragedy, Nietzsche wrote in The Birth of Tragedy, humanity had lived in a false, "Socratic" and Alexandrian world, a world full of philosophical illusion. The spirit of Greek antiquity was to be reborn in Germany out of a renewed Dionysian consciousness. . . . The rebirth of a tragic culture, Nietzsche went on, could occur only in Germany since "out of the Dionysian recesses of the German soul has sprung a power which has nothing in common with the presuppositions of Socratic culture."[22]

Precisely the same spirit of revival and rebellion was evident in the Shi'i triumphalism that found its most articulate ideologue in Ali Shari'ati, who was now championed as having called for a "return" to our "true selves" before they were corrupted by colonialism. Early Islamic history assumed the same symbolic significance for this generation of Muslim ideologues as Greece did for the Germans. Iranians, just like Germans for Germanness, were now given this historical opportunity to revive the virtues of the golden age of early Islam when brotherhood and equity had reigned supreme under the shadow of the Prophet of God. Ali Shari'ati, after Al-e Ahmad the chief ideologue of a renewed pact with revolutionary Islam, invented a whole arsenal of his ancestral faith that he called "The Alavid Shi'ism" and contrasted it with the "Safavid Shi'ism." In this Manichean opposition Safavid Shi'ism, identified with the Safavid dynasty (1501–1722) that had made Shi'ism the state religion early in the sixteenth century, was the very epitome of corruption and decadence, whereas Alavid Shi'ism, freshly minted in the creative revolutionary imagination of Shari'ati himself, became the supreme ideology of revolt and triumph. As you read the following passage from one of Shari'ati's most famous tracts on Alavid Shi'ism, consider the astonishing similarity of his religious nationalism to the ideological predicates of German Fascism already evident in the ideas of Jünger:

Iranian Shi'ism has a superior and brilliant scientific and scholastic status in Islamic history. The majority of great Islamic geniuses as well as the most prominent jurists, scientists, philosophers, historians, non-religious men of science, and even jurisconsults and the founders of the great Islamic schools of law and theology are all Iranian. The same is true about Shi'ism, which has always been identified with Knowledge, Logic, Piety, Depth, and Love of Justice, as indeed someone like the great Egyptian scholar Abd al-Rahman al-Badawi has had to confess irrevocably that everything in Islam is indebted to the multi-faceted and multi-talented genius of Iranians.[23]

This self-congratulatory illusion about "Iranian genius" is no mere accidental religious chauvinism. Shari'ati's political agenda was predicated on a revolutionary ideology that was squarely founded on this premise:

> In addition to its cultural and intellectual aspects, which, as al-Badawi's scholarly assessment puts it, is at the very basis of the perspicacity and morality of the great Islamic civilization, its political aspect . . . in my opinion and the opinion of people like me, in this day and age, is the most brilliant and life-affirming aspect. Because, contrary to Abd al-Rahman al-Badawi's assumption, and the assumption of other university professoriat like him, the political concern of Shi'ism was not a simple political slogan at the ordinary level of historical events. Quite to the contrary, in its political aspect, Shi'ism postulates a political school which is the principal direction and central line of the universal message of Islam, and that message is the salvation of humanity, negation of class struggle and racial and social segregation, and ultimately an attempt in achieving a true leadership for the masses in order to attain equality and justice in social life. That is why the two major slogans of Shi'ism, which are Imamat ("Leadership) and Adl ("Justice"), in the sense that they have been understood in the Alavid Shi'ism and materialized in the character and government of Ali, are more life-affirming and revolutionary than any other slogan for the consciousness of dispossessed people and responsible intellectuals.[24]

Right here a critical distinction ought to be made between Al-e Ahmad and Shari'ati's ideas as they were articulated before the 1977–1979 revolution and the uses and abuses to which they were put in the aftermath of the Islamist takeover of that momentous event. Some leading scholars of Iranian intellectual history have fallen into the trap of confusing the two, and their legitimate criticism of the Islamist ideology and the Islamic republic has been marred by an illegitimate criticism of Al-e Ahmad and Shari'ati, in which they have even accused them of "nativism."[25] The strengths and weaknesses of their ideas, however, need to be evaluated for the time when they were in fact articulated. Their crescendo, as I have argued in my own

Theology of Discontent (1993), can indeed be traced forward to the Islamist dimension of the 1977–1979 revolution. But the specifics of those ideas are hermeneutically time-bound to when and where they were articulated. In this vein, a new generation of scholarship is now turning a far more nuanced and critical eye on this important distinction and teases out a far more accurate picture of the revolutionary character of both of these leading thinkers.[26] Entirely ignored has remained the pivotal role the absolutist "traditionalism" of thinkers like Seyyed Hossein Nasr played at this critical juncture—court philosophers who had put their ideas squarely at the service of the Pahlavi dynasty, as opposed to Al-e Ahmad and Shari'ati, both of whom to their dying days remained steadfastly on the side of their people and their revolutionary aspirations. If they had been alive when the Islamic republic turned viciously ugly, they would have been the first to oppose it and end up in its darkest dungeons. Their ideas were developed in the cosmopolitan context and dialogical atmosphere of the late Pahlavi period and were thus entirely inimical to the totalitarian absolutism of the Islamist state.

COLLAPSING THE CENTER AND ITS PERIPHERIES

The global nature of the crisis and the link of the German predicament to the farthest corners of the colonial extensions of technological modernity are perfectly evident in the Nazi reading of Nietzsche, as it is indeed in the reading of Shari'ati and Al-e Ahmad after the Islamist revolution. As Hans Sluga has demonstrated extensively, from Fichte to Nietzsche there was a gradually universal and globalizing conception of the German crisis extended first to a "European" and then to a "world-historical" condition.

> In such texts as *Human, All Too Human,* and *The Will to Power* they discovered a version of crisis that differed from Fichte's in several respects. The mature Nietzsche saw the crisis as a European event. Fichte had also acknowledged the world-historical character of the crisis, but it was still centered on Germany and was to be resolved through political action in Germany. Nietzsche spoke a radically different language. "For some time now, our whole European culture has been moving as toward a catastrophe," he wrote in the preface to The Will to Power, and this could be overcome only through a new, great, and European form of politics.[27]

"Europe" thus emerges as a colonially conditioned conception of itself precisely because the Nazi reading of Nietzsche had come to see it in clear contradistinction to "non-Europe."[28] "Such a conception could please Nazi readers because National Socialism was not simply an old-fashioned German Nationalism. It represented instead a new kind of Europeanism, for the Nazis not only saw Germany's place in Europe threatened but also Europe's place in the world." But where exactly did that "threat" come from?

> Such threats were coming from America and the Soviet Union, from Asia and Africa. They feared a Europe overwhelmed by outside forces, deprived of its dominion, endangered in its well-being, overrun by alien races. Their goal was not simply to save Germany but to save all of Europe. For that reason they reached out to countries like Great Britain, in the name of common interests. . . . There was, indeed, an internationalist side to National Socialism that took in many different national embodiments of its ideology, and there was, specifically, a European side to National Socialism that made the German form part of a larger European complex. It was precisely to this side of Nazi ideology that Nietzsche's widened sense of crisis could appeal.[29]

The invention of this "Europe" from the heart of Nazism corresponded with the invention of similar "traditions" by absolutist Islamist thinkers like Seyyed Hossein Nasr in Iran; and the turn to mysticism he best represented, the creation of nonexistent "golden ages," and all of these as ideological preparations for retrograde ideals as the first step toward a brutal absolutism, all occurred in the Germany of the 1930s and 1940s as they occurred in the Iran of the 1960s and 1970s, in one case leading to National Socialism and in the other to the Islamic republic, two almost identical cases of absolutist tyranny predicated on a mystical conception of either Germanness or Muslimhood. The structural similarity between moments of crisis at the centers of capitalist modernity at one end of its globalizing continuum, and the constitutionally endemic crisis at the colonially conditioned peripheries of its self-worlding logic at the other, categorically eliminate the division of the world into first and third, or "the West" and "the Rest," or "Islam" and "the West." This continuum of economic reason and cultural response reveals the one, singular, and underlying reality of a globalizing condition that since the very advent of capitalist modernity in the early nineteenth century has defined our global predicament. One can get at the evident logic of this singularity from either end of the continuum, from an Islamist attraction to European mysticism or the German attention to Persian mysticism. Either way, the common ground is the transnational *public sphere* upon which Europe and non-Europe come together to constitute and posit a superior and more accurate site for reading history.

In a major new study, Joseph Massad has persuasively demonstrated how European liberalism manufactured a conception of Islam as its doppelgänger, its absolute alterity, by way of a negational blueprint that in turn defined what liberalism was all about.[30] If that Islam were to be taken away from European liberalism it would not know what to do with itself. European citizens were posited against Muslim subjects, European democracy against Oriental despotism, European civil society against its categorical absence from the Muslim world. A key concept in my argument in this book is that the formation of that public sphere was ipso facto transnational, and that the ideological manufacturing of a nonliberal Islam opposed to European liberalism goes against the grain of the historical fact that its conceptual and territorial expansion indeed posited a trans-European idea of citizenship that in the postcolonial context became even more robust than it had in its European gestation. In short, European liberalism was not fully in control of its own doppelgänger, and the dialectic between the two was the engine of postcolonial history.

Conclusion

AS I WAS WORKING on the last few paragraphs of the last chapter of this book, I received a copy of the most recent book of the eminent Japanese philosopher Kojin Karatani, *The Structure of World History* (2014). It was a pleasant surprise to see how, entirely unbeknownst to me, Karatani had been working on the more philosophical underpinnings of almost exactly the same idea I have been documenting in this book. In his new book, Karatani gives Marx's notion of world history a critical twist, shifting the focus away from modes of production to modes of exchange. His objective in this turn is to overcome the symbiosis of capital/nation-state. To do so, he traces different modes of exchange, particularly those of the nomadic tribes, presenting a pathbreaking reading of the gift-exchange systems. In this crucial argument, Karatani questions the assumptions about sedentary human societies and demonstrates the reciprocal exchanges that took place within the earliest communal formations—and thus he underlines the function of reciprocity in social formations across nations and their fictive frontiers and thereby demonstrates how reciprocity is in fact an impediment to state formation. State (and thus nation-state) emerges after the assumption of a nonreciprocal mode of exchange becomes dominant[1]—therefore citizens within a state are presumed equal in terms of their property ownership. Both these ideas— preference for the nomadic and gift exchange to sedentary settlements and commodity production—are the same that effectively inform my reading of Persophilia as the simulacrum of traveling nomadic ideas and, as such, a mode of cultural gift exchange on the global scene.

PERSOPHILIA AT LARGE

In the phenomenon I have called Persophilia we witness a mode of knowledge production in the context of the emerging European empires of the eighteenth and nineteenth centuries integral to varied social and intellectual movements in Europe during its imperial age. The cycle began naturally at the metropolitan centers of capitalist modernity by generating a new mode of knowledge about the Orient—vast territories at the disposal of commerce, conquest, and acculturation. That mode of knowledge, however, was largely produced on the site of the European bourgeois public sphere and thus did not stay confined to those metropolitan capitals but traveled, including to the places that were the subjects of the new modes of knowledge, namely "the Orient itself."

In his "Traveling Theory" (1982), Edward Said thought through the issue of how ideas (or theories) lose their insurrectionary power when traveling from their place of origin to other contexts. Years later, in his "Traveling Theory Reconsidered" (2000), he corrected his own insight and suggested that ideas might actually benefit and be expanded to unanticipated dimensions when traveling to other climes. I have a similarly open-ended idea in mind when I suggest that the European Persophilia had its own rhymes and reasons when it emerged in Europe and later in North America, but that the subjects of Persophilia, seeing themselves in European mirrors—in positive or derogatory terms—carried those ideas into dimensions and directions far beyond the expectations and even the intentions of their authors, as is perhaps best evident in James Morier's *The Adventures of Hajji Baba of Ispahan* and its translation by Mirza Habib Isfahani. The subjects of Persophilia thus eventually crafted a *public sphere* in which they mapped out the course of their own future, in part determined by the text and context that had come its way and in part by the free will and agency of those who peopled that public space. The question here is less one of revolutionary ideas becoming domesticated or domesticated representations becoming revolutionary, than the power of representations evident in the European bourgeois public sphere traveling to the actual sites of their fantasies and assuming a life of their own far beyond the intention of their authors, thereby positing a public sphere in which postcolonial nation-states discarded and overcame their own histories. James Morier wrote *The Adventures of Hajji Baba of Ispahan* as a horrid colonial ridiculing of anything he saw as Persian, yet Mirza Habib Isfahani's Persian translation of the very same text transformed it into a critical cornerstone of the Constitutional Revolution of 1906–1911.

In this book I have navigated the varied and continuous ways by which Persophilia traveled back to the conflicting and self-dialectical sites of accommodation or contestation with the imperial power that had occasioned it. The dialectic becomes conducive to a production of knowledge in multiple, varied, and unanticipated directions. The intellectual scene at these sites of accommodation or resistance is very much integral to the globalized condition of knowledge production—but the dynamics is not unidirectional, it is reciprocal. The knowledge that is produced in the metropolitan capitals reverberates back onto the colonial sites and, by accommodation or resistance, adaptation or rejection, generates a rich and diversified public sphere and posits a new world that is subsequently alienated from itself by being labeled with any number of terms such as "the third world," which thereby produces "third world literature" in a mythical space called "the East" or "the Orient," all narrated around the centrality of an even more mythical space called "the West," whether by contestation (Edward Said) or by acclamation (Raymond Schwab). The critical task ahead, toward which I have written this book, is to excavate the archeology of this public sphere and thereby de-alienate it from itself.

A central purpose of my book has been to override the East–West divide and thus dismantle the mystifying delusion of "the West" as the primal cause and the central referent of world history, replacing it with a closer understanding of the succession of empires and the moods and manners of knowledge production conductive to each. The only reason I have paid this close attention to Persophilia is neither to add to what Schwab had done in his reading of the Oriental Renaissance in Europe nor to augment Edward Said's critique of the European mode of colonial knowledge production. They were both highly effective in doing what they deemed necessary to be done. My interest, in fact, lies entirely in the opposite direction to theirs: namely, to undo their respective consolidations of "the West" as the focal point of global knowledge production. That mode of knowledge production, to me, was and remains transitory, one of many I have investigated in the easternmost parts of the Muslim empires. In *The World of Persian Literary Humanism* (2012) it was precisely this multivariate succession of knowledge production that informed my way of reading the long history of Persian literary outputs. That study taught me that there is nothing strange or unique about "the West" doing precisely the same in its own imperial demarcations. Persophilia is the ideological mechanism and conduit of the circulation of capital and labor and a fortiori ideas essential to "Western civilization" as the modus operandi of capitalist modernity. Predicated on that idea, my purpose has been to de-link and thereby de-alienate and disabuse the postcolonial site, the world at large, of playing second fiddle to this "West" without disregarding the imperial power of ideas that have been circulated from the heart of its self-centering proclivities.

This shift of perspective and the reverse angle, as it were, are necessary because the way in which European Orientalism has been critically read has in fact inadvertently consolidated the centrality and polarity of "the West" as the primal cause of knowledge production—a paradoxical cross-essentialism that has blinded us to the most definitive modes of both colonial accommodation and postcolonial resistance to that hegemony. In this book, instead, I have offered a dialectical mode of knowledge production in the context of an imperial setting and the sites of contestations it inevitably generates. By delegating that world to the mystical "East," or even the more mysterious "Orient," or perhaps most tellingly "the Rest," we have in effect corroborated the self-asserted centrality of the ideological formation that calls itself "the West." By proposing a circularity of knowledge production that in fact reflects the circularity of labor and capital that has produced the world in which we live, I have intended this book as a way of overcoming that supreme mode of alienation in which the overwhelming majority of the world is deprived of its varied modes of agential (let alone revolutionary) defiance, active and agential formation of subjectivity, and the dialectical disposition of postcolonial subject formation, and thus, above all, of the very worldliness that makes that agential formation possible.

The bourgeois public sphere that European capitalism had conditioned and its imperialism facilitated was at its very inception a global phenomenon.

That sphere was never categorically "European" except by an ideological claim that desired to center its capital formation and delegate the colonial to its periphery. The construction of public sphere in and around the European imaginary had variations on the same theme that manifested themselves variedly. Cultural movements—in art, literature, drama, opera, and so on—at the center were already pregnant with themes and representations from the periphery; and when through their imperial hegemony they went to the physical sites of those peripheries, they already felt familiar in their bourgeois public sphere.

The West–East binary was an effective but fictive border to facilitate the domination of the bourgeois class in both the center and its manufactured peripheries of the globe. That domination was not of "the West" over "the East," but of capital over labor, the bourgeois over the proletariat, and the bourgeois space was the sphere where this domination was facilitated. Persophilia was only one crucial aspect of this global phenomenon. So, contrary to Edward Said's assumption, the ruling class of "the East" was normatively invested in the Orientalism project; and, contrary to Raymond Schwab's assumption, Orientalism was not a merely European development, for by the power of the globalized capital this was already global.

The fundamental difference between the European public sphere and its extension into the colonized world was precisely the naked disposition of capital and labor, and thus the more immediate and exposed the presence of subaltern classes in colonial extensions of the public sphere became. The Iranian public sphere (like any other public sphere located on the margin of the myth of "the West") was not a replica of the European bourgeois sphere, nor was it even an extension or a reflection of it. My argument throughout this book has been to demonstrate in various registers how the European public sphere triggered the formation of the Iranian public sphere, reminded it of its own imperial age, resolved its cultural paradox, and created a new *public reason*. It is that public reason—formed under very specific historical circumstances of colonial domination and postcolonial defiance—that, in emulation of European capitalist modernity, Iranians and other postcolonial nations call "modernity"; while in *The World of Persian Literary Humanism* I have already laid out the theoretical foundation of a genealogical tracing that altogether abandons the anxiety of European modernity in the formation of the non-European postcolonial reason.

FROM SAID TO HABERMAS AND BEYOND

By breaking the false and falsifying binary of "the West" and "the Rest" via a particular genealogy of a public sphere that stands for a far more universal organicity, I have sought to argue the necessity for a mode of knowledge production beyond colonial or even postcolonial subjection. The presumption of the postcolonial was and remains contingent on the colonial and thus limited by it. To me, the defiant subjection is not formed on the ideologically manufactured site of East or West but on the syncretic site of the lived experiences and dialectical organicity of traveling ideas, institutions, and movements. Here the theme of "traveling" is not limited to Said's notion of "traveling theories." These traveling ideas become revolutionary or conservative from one origin or another to one destination or another. The point is Gadamer's and Said's notion of "worldliness" multiplied by historically varied, overlapping, and interpolated worlds that these ideas encounter and enable. The Persophilia that took form on the European stage eventually projected varied aspects of Persian culture in a global scene by virtue of the transnational bourgeois public sphere it had generated and sustained. Because the operation of capital and labor and the market it required were global, so was the transnational public sphere it had enabled.

Edward Said's *Orientalism* was perhaps the greatest insight of the twentieth century into the nature and function of colonial knowledge production; yet it was precisely the power of this insight that also blinded us to the structural continuity and tension between the expansive bourgeois public space of Europe and its vast imperial conquests. Said's concern was primarily, if not exclusively, with the mode of knowledge production at the disposal of that imperial project. Even when he was reading the masterpieces of European literature, such as the novels of Jane Austen, his attention was obviously and rightly drawn toward their implications for colonial knowledge and sentiment production, and thus toward the literary (ideological) constitution of the colonial subject. But precisely because of that systematic and pathbreaking insight into European cultural productions we have ignored their role in the literary formation of the public sphere, as best noted and theorized by Jürgen Habermas. However, Habermas's own project, too, was very much limited to the European scene and entirely oblivious to its colonial consequences. What would happen when non-Europeans read, translated, and reflected on that literature; who was making these translations and disseminations; and what would be the social and spatial implications of their activities all lay beyond Habermas's attention or interest. In this book I have tried to trace such a trajectory in one specific domain, in very specific terms, by way of adding an external, transmigratory force in the formation of one specific postcolonial *public space* and its corresponding *public reason* and perforce *subjectivity*.

Habermas's conceptualization of "public sphere" has been subject to legitimate criticism for the division that it posits between public and private space, a distinction that is integral to the subjugation of women. Scholars like Joan Landes, Nancy Fraser, and others have in fact argued that the European bourgeois public sphere—the way Habermas understood it as the constellation of free speech, a free press, and free assembly that gathered to mediate between state and society—was quite exclusive to powerful men who, in varied forms of voluntary associations, used it in a manner that would exclude other classes and strata. So it is critical here to reemphasize that I have extended the term to colonial sites in order to demarcate a space categorically distinct from the royal court and its subjects and from the clerical jurisdiction over the mosque and its precincts. I completely share the criticism that the nature of the bourgeois public sphere in its European vintage is such that it limits the democratic practice of justice. But I argue that on the colonial site the inner contradictions of the bourgeois public sphere more readily burst into the open and result either in the formation of parapublic spheres underground or in exilic communities or lead directly to revolutionary uprisings. Habermas shows how theories of literary public sphere had a catalytic effect on society at large but has had no reason for or interest in exploring the fact that, on the colonial site, the literary public sphere in fact leads to the articulation of a public reason, which in turn begins to modify and inform the revolutionary reason, as I have articulated them in detail in my book *Shi'ism: A Religion of Protest* (2010). In other words, the literary public sphere (carrying the stamp of the revolutionary reason) does not only sustain the bourgeois public sphere, it also challenges, potentially dismantles, and in any case enriches it.

My contention in this book, as a result, has been to demonstrate (1) how the postcolonial public sphere was triggered by the European bourgeois public sphere in formal and representational affiliations, the circulation of labor and capital, and the structural formation of transnational class formations that categorically crossed national boundaries, yet became a reality unto itself by the very logic of the capitalist mode of knowledge production and subjection; (2) that whatever implications they had for the colonial production of their Oriental subject, these representations (à la Orientalism or Persophilia) did not exhaust their literary implications for the formation of the bourgeois public sphere and had unanticipated consequences in the postcolonial sites; (3) that leading intellectuals, diplomats, merchants, journalists, and so on, from the extended domains of the European empires came to these European cosmopolitan cities, absorbed the implications of the representations—especially when they saw themselves reflected in those literatures—and translated and disseminated them in their homeland; and (4) that these transmutations eventually occasioned a conversation in the former imperial setting and generated a politically potent but categorically contrarian public domain from which eventually emerged a generation of self-alienated intellectuals contrapuntally corroborating the fictive centrality of the West—whether in defiance (such as Jalal Al-e Ahmad or Ali Shari'ati) or in compliance (such as Hassan Taqizadeh or Daryoush Ashuri).

To overcome that alienation, the task for the next generation of scholarship that lies ahead, in which direction this book is located, is geared toward a genealogy of the formation of the public and parapublic spheres in the postcolonial sites in dialectical interaction with the European bourgeois public sphere. This line of investigation will ultimately guide us toward the historic recognition of the dialectic of the *public* and *revolutionary* reasons. The nature and disposition of this dialectic define the (always) delayed defiance of the postcolonial subject. From inside the postcolonial nation-states like Iran the formation of that public space defined the contours of the *Vatan*/Homeland, while from outside that homeland that encounter accounts for the cosmopolitan worldliness of this very notion.

This book on Persophilia is the historic location of a third angle on the genealogical formation of that public sphere that I have navigated over the last few years. In my *Shi'ism: A Religion of Protest*, I put forward the proposition that, during the Safavid period in the sixteenth century, Shi'ism was thoroughly urbanized and turned into a cosmopolitan "civil religion," removed from both its historical battlefields and its feudal scholasticism, with its *revolutionary reason* urbanized into a *public reason*. I then suggested that, at the Dasht-e Moghan gathering, Nader Shah Afshar (1688–1747) had managed to dismantle not just the Safavid dynasty but along with it the civil societal possibilities it had made evident, and with that the syncretic

and cosmopolitan Shi'ism that it had enabled through a public reason—
so much so that, effectively, with the Safavids also ended the possibility of a
Shi'i state apparatus with a corresponding conception of a civil society. I
offered this argument predicated on the idea that the Safavids had in effect
internalized the revolutionary angst of Shi'ism, and in turn given space to a
nascent *public reason* that would have made a civil societal turn in Shi'i political culture not just possible but perhaps even inevitable. Economic pros-
perity, increased volumes in foreign trade, participation in regional rivalries
among the superpowers of the time, and a substantial increase in urbanization might be considered chief among the reasons and causes for such a significant transformation from revolutionary reason to public reason. After
Nader Shah put an end to that process, we effectively discontinued a sustained Shi'i theory of state and a corresponding conception of civil society.
Thus, in the post-Safavid era, from the Afsharids to the Zands to the Qajars,
what we in effect witnessed was a succession of tribal warlords and clannish
kinships, with an increasingly evident appeal to a pre-Islamic conception of
Persian kingship to camouflage that nomadic disposition.

Based on that argument, I then sought to identify and resolve a paradox
that has unfolded in Shi'ism over the last two centuries. As a result of its
own internal history of repeated failures at manufacturing a *public space* and
a contingent *public reason,* Shi'ism finally collapsed into a dead, clerical scholasticism and relinquished its creative imagination—settling deeply into
and troubled by a politics of despair. Accentuating that despair, in the making
of an alienated aesthetics of emancipation at once rich in its creative imagination but deprived of worldly relevance, the *revolutionary reason* of Shi'ism
finally bypassed its failed attempts at *public reason* and reached for an *aesthetic reason.* The *aesthetic reason* that dwelled in this alienated creativity was
the ultimate salvation of that resurrected *public reason,* though in hidden,
distanced, estranged, and introverted forms. It is only on the site of contemporary asymmetric warfare and the forced condition of a will to resist power
that Shi'ism is now being led back to face its alienated split identity and
come to terms with it. A final, full-bodied, recognition of its syncretic cosmopolitanism is now in the offing.

This was the direction of the excavation of the public sphere I had done
taking the *scholastic* route. But soon after that I began retracing the same
genealogy along a different path. In the *World of Persian Literary Humanism*
(2012) I retraced the formation of that public sphere from an entirely different

angle, the vantage point of literary humanism, to augment and expand the scholastic perspective of the *Shi'ism* book. In this second approach, I demonstrated how, to the Persian literati of the eighteenth century forward, Europe was an immaterial empire in whose cosmopolitan cities—London, Paris, or Madrid (in contrast to Isfahan, Herat, Delhi, or Istanbul)—these poets and prose stylists were not welcome, for Persian was no longer the lingua franca of the new imperial imagination. I termed this period *"Ashub/ Chaos,"* wherein Persian poets and literati exited their habitual courts but, because they did not find any welcome in European imperial court, and thus entered into what they now effectively created as a *public sphere* and called it *Vatan*/Homeland. This was an exceedingly exciting and prolific phase, because Persian literary humanism had to come to terms with alterities that were not of its own making. The central trope of Persian literary humanism, in turn, changed to adapt to the new environment and thus radically expanded not just its modes of operation but also its locus classicus from the royal court to the emerging public sphere. I subsequently traced these manifestations in film, drama, fiction, and poetry. But to come to this point I had guided my readers through a thematic periodization of Persian literature as it moved from *Nezhad/Ethnos* to *Sokhan/Logos* to *Hanjar/Ethos* and had now come to *Ashub/Chaos* as its defining trope. By doing so I proposed a decentered knowing subject at the heart of a multifaceted literary humanism that generation after generation of poets and prose stylists had internalized and moved forward. As such, my project was also geared to dismantle both the nativist and the Orientalist narratives, seeking to rescue Persian literary humanism from such constitutionally distorting modes of knowledge production and bringing it back to life ultimately as *a theory not of an alternative modernity* but in fact as *an alternative theory to modernity.*

So, while in *Shi'ism* I zeroed in on the formation and structural disposition of *public space* through a historical and doctrinal investigation of scholasticism, and in the *World of Persian Literary Humanism* did the same through literary humanism, both those complementary modalities were internal to the successive imperial settings in which Islam and Persian humanism had thrived. Now, here in this book, I have carried the same investigation through the extended consequences of European imperialism and the bourgeois public space that sustained and nourished it. Through these three complementary angles, I have thus narrowed my focus to the genealogy of the public sphere and the formation of the postcolonial subject in one specific—and specifically detailed—postcolonial site that might not be too dissimilar to other circumstances in other parts of the colonized world.

By performing a magnificent deconstructive surgery, Edward Said's epoch-making *Orientalism* gave primacy of agency to European modes of knowledge production and, by taking off from the European imperial force of representation, shifted an entire generation of scholarship to recenter the myth of "the West" as the focal point of history, thereby paradoxically helping to camouflage even further the multiple worlds he wanted to liberate from "Western" representation but in effect trapping them even more securely. To counter that thrust, the task in front of us is not to reverse the order and opt for "nativism"—a false binary suggested by the persistent centering of the myth of "the West" even by, or perhaps particularly by, the critique of "the West." We must begin with the world that European imperialism envisioned, enabled, and imposed upon the globe, but then crack open the interstices that separate the presumed center and the peripheralized sites of colonial domination, push them open, and from those cracks investigate alternative sites, not just of resistance to European imperialism but of the surfacing of the horizons that have been blinded by the power of the rising sun from "the West." The task, therefore, is no longer to make a mere critique of European representation, but to achieve a critical grasp of the modes and manners of "non-Western" subjection, to find agential historicity in worlding a map for the longest time glossed and covered over by the single myth of "the Western world," which, either through imperialism or through the critique of that imperialism, keeps inscribing itself not just on older maps but on the ones waiting to surface.

The critical distance between the Persophilia of the eighteenth and nineteenth centuries and the Iranophobia (a veritable version of Islamophobia) of the twentieth and twenty-first centuries—as perhaps best evident in the so-called Iranian nuclear issue—marks precisely the horizons of those emerging maps.[2] Here we might suggest that, as the bourgeois public sphere expanded exponentially by a succession of subaltern classes contesting it, it surely lost its yearning for non-European cultures and climes: Oriental Renaissance eventually yielded to Islamophobia, and Persophilia to Iranophobia. The fluidity of capital and labor eventually led to massive labor migrations far beyond the limits of European bourgeois expectations and liberal tolerance. They needed the cheap labor but not the colored laborer who came to perform it. Iranophobia, which picks up from Christian

Islamophobia and abandons the liberal bourgeois public reason, is perhaps the most accurate barometer of the habitually self-centered myth of "the West" losing its confidence in its ability to absorb and assimilate the world into its own allegories and no longer allowing its manufactured "others" to come and expose its shivering shadows. From Oriental Renaissance to Islamophobia, as from Persophilia to Iranophobia, "the West" has marked and demarcated its own panegyrics—from lyricism to eulogy.

ROMANCING PERSIA

From the fictional harem scenes in Montesquieu's *Persian Letters;* to Sir William Jones Persianizing his name as "Youns Oksfordi"; to Goethe's identification with Hafez that became a European fad giving rise to many other blond-haired, blue-eyed Hafezes roaming around in European salons, to his naming the collection of his own ghazals *West-östlicher Divan* as an homage to Hafez's *divan;* to Hegel's induction of the Persian into the Hall of History; to Ralph Waldo Emerson thinking himself a reincarnation of Sa'di; to Benjamin Franklin trying to pass off a story from Sa'di's *Golestan* as a lost passage from the Bible; to Edward FitzGerald's becoming a reincarnation of Omar Khayyám, which later led to Ezra Pound (1885–1972) naming his own son Omar; to the homoerotic narrative built around the character of Bagoas as Alexander the Great's lover in Mary Renault's *The Persian Boy* (1972); to the Cyrus Spitama character in Gore Vidal's *Creation* (1981/2002)— the European (and later American) romancing of Persia circled a wide and wondrous gyre. With FitzGerald's *Rubáiyát of Omar Khayyám* an enduring homoerotic element had been introduced into the very colorful fabric of European Persophilia. FitzGerald was a covert homosexual,[3] and these elements were quietly written into his translation of Omar Khayyám. Romancing Persia ran the gamut of European eroticism.

This romancing of Persia has had a long and illustrious history in European art. As the eponymous heroine of biblical stories, Esther was the Jewish queen of the Persian king Ahasuerus/Xerxes. The incident of how through her wit, grace, and beauty she managed to save Persian Jews from persecution has been invariably depicted in the course of European art history. From the iconic simplicity of the Azor masters' *Mordecai Is Led through the City by Haman* (c. 1430) to the austerity of Michelangelo's *Punishment of Haman*

(Sistine Chapel ceiling, 1511), we witness the sedate decorum with which the story has been depicted. The commotion and drama of Tintoretto's *Esther before Ahasuerus* (1547–1548) eventually yields to Hieronymous Francken II's *Feast of Esther,* in which we see a modicum of feminine sexuality introduced in the image of Esther. By the time we get to the dramatic composition of Rembrandt's *Haman Prepares to Honor Mordecai* (c. 1665) or the royal formality of his *Esther Is Introduced to Ahasuerus* (c. 1665), we are already on our way to the political and formal potency of Filippo Gherardi's (1643–1704) *Esther and Ahasuerus,* or the majestic solitude of Aert de Gelder's *Esther and Mordecai* (1685), before we finally reach the odalisque depiction of Esther by François-Léon Benouville in his *Esther* (1844) and the formal frivolity of Chagall's *Ahasuerus Sends Vashti Away* (1960). In the same vein, Roxana, a Persian princess and wife of Alexander the Great, was the subject of many similar renditions. Persian princesses provided European painters with varied forms and gradations of erotic asceticism or romanticism.

At a critical point the romancing of Persia reached a crescendo (though through a circuitous route) with Frederic Leighton's (1830–1896) *The Fisherman and the Syren: From a Ballad by Goethe, 1856–1858,*[4] based on a poem by the latter, which the German lyricist had composed on the model of a Hafez ghazal. Leighton had traveled extensively in "the East" and was strongly attracted to Islamic art, and this particular painting, perhaps his most celebrated work, brings a decidedly Orientalist aura to the visualization of European romanticism.[5] The corporeal attraction between the siren and the fisherman—a blonde white female figure and a colored male—becomes emblematic of the European fascination with the figment of its own imagination, a fatal attraction not just for the fisherman but for the siren too, for the seduction and the destruction are mutual and self-negating: the sea nymph and the mariner are blended into one upon the rock of their mutual desires. The attraction exposes not just the humanity of the siren but also the maritime habitat of the fisherman, thus, through the seductive lure bridging the difference between fact and fantasy, the earthly man and the fairy nymph.

Just like the siren's allure and seduction of the fisherman, the European romancing of Persia dissolved the colonial divide and thus perforce the postcolonial frontier fictions and allowed for an expansive, transgressive, overarching subjectivity to emerge. In making the Persian foreign familiar,

Persophilia also made the European familiar foreign, and thereby the homely un-homely, the canny uncanny, the *heimlich* un-*heimlich*. The presumed solidity and sovereignty of the bourgeois knowing subject was thus made innately suspect, compromised, and suspended by its irresistible attraction to its own undoing, to the uncanny, the un-*heimlich*, the foreign familiarity of the Persian.

Persophilia was in effect the undoing of Orientalism at large. As Orientalism sought to position and alienate the Oriental in order to posit the European as the self-centering *original* and the *authentic*, Persophilia was the sign too familiar to the foreign feigning of the European as self-sustained authenticity. Persophilia was the Achilles heel of the European, the home of the familiar foreigner who brought the Oriental home to "the West." As Orientalism sought the other, Persophilia exposed the manufacturing self, the exposed puppeteer who did not know there was no curtain between him and his audience. Persophilia became the undoing of "the West," of the normative underpinning of bourgeois liberalism as it sought historically to *authenticate* and universalize itself by *alienating* all its others. The devil of Orientalism is in the details of Persophilia—or in any other specific register of the European other, from China to India and beyond, upon which the double-edged sword of any metaphor "the West" concocts to authenticate itself turns around to dismantle it. Persophilia was a Trojan horse, picked up like a trophy yet with a bellyful of self-negating metaphors, dangerous liaisons, and subversive forces that the idea of Europe could not keep in check and repressed. The irresistible attraction was mutual. The Persians, as they were now thus designated, too, were attracted to "the West"—the very figment of the selfsame imagination. As Persians (thus Persianized) sought to be "westernized" in terms alien to their history but domestic to their colonial conditions, in Persophilia, Europe was not just attracted to an/other culture, for here it had fallen victim to the most prevalent poetic metaphor of Persian origin, like a moth drawn to the flame of a candle, to its own annihilation. Just like the siren and the fisherman drawn to their mutual demise, Persophilia was the undoing of "the West."

THE FISHERMAN (1778)

The waters rush'd, the waters rose,
A fisherman sat by,

While on his line in calm repose
He cast his patient eye.
And as he sat, and hearken'd there,
The flood was cleft in twain,
And, lo! a dripping mermaid fair
Sprang from the troubled main.

She sang to him, and spake the while
"Why lurest thou my brood,
With human wit and human guile
From out their native flood?
Oh, couldst thou know how gladly dart
The fish across the sea,
Thou wouldst descend, e'en as thou art,
And truly happy be!

Do not the sun and moon with grace
Their forms in ocean lave?
Shines not with twofold charms their face,
When rising from the wave?
The deep, deep heavens, then lure thee not,—
The moist yet radiant blue,—
Not thine own form,—to tempt thy lot
'Midst this eternal dew?"

The waters rush'd, the waters rose,
Wetting his naked feet;
As if his true love's words were those,
His heart with longing beat.
She sang to him, to him spake she,
His doom was fix'd, I ween;
Half drew she him, and half sank he,
And ne'er again was seen.[6]

Notes

INTRODUCTION

1. For a pioneering study of the European and American literati's and philosophers' interest in matters Persian, see John D. Yohannan, *Persian Poetry in England and America: A Two Hundred Year History* (Persian Studies Series) (Delmar, NY: Caravan Books, 1977).

2. See Raymond Schwab, *The Oriental Renaissance: Europe's Rediscovery of India and the East, 1680–1880* (Social Foundations of Aesthetic Forms) (New York: Columbia University Press, 1984).

3. See Edward Said, *Orientalism* (New York: Vintage, 1978).

4. For a preliminary comparison of Schwab's and Said's readings of Orientalism, see Geoffrey P. Nash, "New Orientalisms for Old: Articulations of the East in Raymond Schwab, Edward Said, and Two Nineteenth-Century French Orientalists," in Ian Netton, ed., *Orientalism Revisited* (London: Routledge, 2013): 87–97.

5. See Jürgen Habermas, *The Structural Transformation of the Public Sphere: An Inquiry into a Category of Bourgeois Society* (Cambridge, MA: MIT Press, 1991).

6. In some more recent scholarship, such as Patricia Springborg's *Western Republicanism and the Oriental Prince* (Cambridge: Polity Press, 1992), this Eurocentricism is seriously challenged, and a more organic link is investigated between aspects

of European political thought and institutions and their "Oriental origins." As Springborg rightly demonstrates, this radical bifurcation was posited and exploited in order to give "the West" its jargon of authenticity, authority, and power to dominate the world. But her concern is to argue, and rightly so, that there are non-European traits in the formation of European culture that European identity has violently suppressed. Hers is a necessary and critical project. But my project is of a different sort. Here I wish to investigate the formation of the European *public sphere* (with and without all its evident and repressed origins) that had extended colonial consequences in an organic and consequential way.

7. See Edward W. Said, *Culture and Imperialism* (New York: Vintage Books, 1994).

8. See George Jellinek, *History through the Opera Glass: The Rise of Caesar to the Fall of Napoleon* (London: Kahn and Averill, 1994), 6.

9. See Hamid Dabashi, *Post-Orientalism: Knowledge and Power in Time of Terror* (Piscataway, NJ: Transaction Publishers, 2008).

10. See Jellinek, *History through the Opera Glass*, 3.

11. See Hamid Dabashi, *The World of Persian Literary Humanism* (Cambridge: Cambridge University Press, 2012).

12. See Edward Said, *Culture and Imperialism* (New York: Vintage, 1994).

13. See Hamid Dabashi, *Post-Orientalism: Knowledge and Power in Time of Terror* (Piscataway, NJ: Transaction Publishers, 2008).

14. For further details see William Kremer, "Why did men stop wearing high heels?" Available on BBC website at: http://www.bbc.co.uk/news/magazine-21151350. Accessed on 28 March 2013.

15. By using the term "Enlightenment" in this generic way I do not discount the significant body of literature produced over the last couple of decades in which the term and the era have been seriously complicated. Karen O'Brien, in her *Narratives of Enlightenment: Cosmopolitan History from Voltaire to Gibbon* (Cambridge: Cambridge University Press, 1997), for example, has demonstrated how within Enlightenment thinking there was a strong cosmopolitan strand far beyond the formation of national cultures. Jonathan I. Israel, meanwhile, in his *Radical Enlightenment: Philosophy and the Making of Modernity 1650–1750* (Oxford: Oxford University Press, 2002) and *Democratic Enlightenment: Philosophy, Revolution, and Human Rights 1750–1790* (Oxford: Oxford University Press, 2013), has brought out the more repressed radical forces within Enlightenment thinking. But by far the most powerful argument among all these studies is the magnificent work of Walter D. Mignolo, *The Darker Side of Western Modernity: Global Futures, Decolonial Options* (Durham, NC: Duke University Press, 2011), in which he argues persuasively that the phenomenon of colonialism is the darker side of European Renaissance, Enlightenment, and a fortiori modernity. I am fully cognizant of all these critical reflections on the

Enlightenment—and it is precisely with that set of critical antennae that I here investigate the organic link connecting the European public sphere to its colonial borders.

16. For more details see Jellinek, *History through the Opera Glass*, 5.

17. See Immanuel Wallerstein, *The Modern World-System I: Capitalist Agriculture and the Origins of the European World-Economy in the Sixteenth Century* (Berkeley: University of California Press, 2011), and all the subsequent volumes.

18. See Niall Ferguson, *Civilization: The West and the Rest* (London: Penguin Books, 2012).

19. See Umberto Eco, *The Limits of Interpretation* (Bloomington: Indiana University Press, 1991).

20. For a translation, see Jalal Al-e Ahmad, *Occidentosis: A Plague from the West (Gharbzadegi)*, trans. R. Campbell (Berkeley, CA: Mizan Press, 1983).

21. See Mohammed Sharafuddin, *Islam and Romantic Orientalism: Literary Encounters with the Orient* (London: I. B. Tauris, 1994): 215–216.

22. I have detailed this point in *The World of Persian Literary Humanism*, passim.

23. See Montesquieu, *Persian Letters,* translated with an introduction and notes by C. J. Betts (London: Penguin Books, 1973), 17.

24. For more on Mirza Saleh Shirazi, see my *Iran: A People Interrupted* (New York: The New Press, 2007), chap. 2.

25. Montesquieu, *Persian Letters,* 17.

26. Ibid.

1. DISTANT MEMORIES OF THE BIBLICAL AND CLASSICAL HERITAGE

1. See "Cyrus Cylinder: How a Persian monarch inspired Jefferson" (BBC, 11 March 2013). Available at: http://www.bbc.co.uk/news/world-us-canada-21747567. Accessed on 25 May 2013.

2. Ibid.

3. Ibid.

4. See Angelina Perri Birney, "The Cyrus Cylinder, Eleanor Roosevelt and the Universal Declaration of Human Rights" (10 April 2013). Available at: http://perribirney .wordpress.com/2013/04/10/the-cyrus-cylinder-eleanor-roosevelt-the-universal -declaration-of-human-rights. Accessed on 25 May 2013.

5. Ibid.

6. Ibid.

7. See "Cyrus cylinder's ancient bill of rights 'is just propaganda'" (*The Telegraph,* 16 July 2008). Available at: http://www.telegraph.co.uk/news/worldnews/europe /germany/2420263/Cyrus-cylinders-ancient-bill-of-rights-is-just-propaganda.html. Accessed on 25 May 2013.

8. For my review of the film when it first appeared, see Hamid Dabashi, "The '300' stroke" (Al-Ahram, 2–8 August 2007). Available at: http://weekly.ahram.org .eg/2007/856/cu1.htm. Accessed on 28 June 2013.

9. See Tom Holland, *Persian Fire: The First World Empire and the Battle for the West* (New York: Anchor, 2005), xviii.

10. Ibid., xxi.

11. Ibid., xix.

12. Ibid.

13. Ibid., xxii.

14. See Christopher Nadon's *Xenophon's Prince: Republic and Empire in the Cyropædia* (Berkeley: University of California Press, 2001). Xenophon's *Cyropaedia* has also entered the American business world, in which there is an endless thirst for new and innovative "leadership" of corporations for making more profits. See, for example, this edition and abridgement of the book prepared by Larry Hedrick, *Xenophon's Cyrus the Great: The Arts of Leadership and War* (New York: Truman Tally Books, 2006).

15. Nadon's *Xenophon's Prince*, 4.

16. Ibid., 24.

17. See Xenophon, *The Persian Expedition,* trans. Rex Warner, with an introduction by George Cawkwell (London: Penguin, 1951). Arrian's account had succeeded Plutarch's *The Age of Alexander,* translated and annotated by Ian Scott-Kilvert, with an introduction by G. T. Griffith (London: Penguin, 1973).

18. See Arrian, *The Campaigns of Alexander,* trans. Aubrey Sélincourt; revised with a new introduction and notes by J. R. Hamilton (London: Penguin, 1958).

19. See T. E. Lawrence, *Seven Pillars of Wisdom* (Hertfordshire: Wordsworth Press, 1997).

20. See Plutarch's *Of the Malice of Herodotu.* Available at: http://www .bostonleadershipbuilders.com/plutarch/moralia/malice_of_herodotus.htm. Accessed on 9 July 2013. For Plutarch's own account, see *The Persian Wars,* trans. George Rawlinson, with an introduction by Francis R. B. Godolphin (New York: The Modern Library, 1942).

21. See Edith Hall, *Inventing the Barbarians: Greek Self-Definition through Tragedy* (Oxford: Clarendon Press, 1989).

22. Ibid., 54–55.

23. See S. Van Riet, "The Impact of Avicenna's Philosophical Works on the West," *Encyclopedia Iranica.* Available at: http://www.iranicaonline.org/articles/avicenna-xii.

24. See Edwin M. Yamauchi, *Persia and the Bible* (Grand Rapids, MI: Baker Books, 1990), 26.

25. Ibid.

26. Ibid.

27. See A. J. Arberry, *British Orientalists* (London: William Collins of London, 1943), 8. For a pioneering study of British Orientalism in Persia, see Abolqasem Taheri, *Seyr-e Farhang Iran dar Britannia: Tarikh-e Devist Saleh Motale'at-e Irani/The Course of Iranian Culture in the UK: The Two Hundred Year History of Iranian Studies* (Tehran: Anjoman-e Asar-e Melli, 1352/1973).

28. Ibid., 26–27.

29. See David Damrosch, *The Buried Book: The Loss and Rediscovery of the Great Epic of Gilgamesh* (Henry Holt and Company, 2006), 24.

30. For the long and fascinating history of how the cuneiform was deciphered, read the excellent essay of Irving L. Finkel, "The Decipherment of Achaemenid Cuneiform," in J. Curtis and Nigel Tallis, eds., *Forgotten Empire: The World of Ancient Persia* (London: British Museum, 2005), 25–29.

31. Damrosch, *The Buried Book,* 51–52 et passim.

32. These were later collected and digitized in one volume, George Rawlinson, *The Seven Great Monarchies of the Ancient Eastern World* (Amazon Digital Services: Kindle Edition, 2011).

33. See A. T. Olmstead, *History of the Persian Empire* (Chicago: University of Chicago Press, 1948), vii.

34. Ibid., xv. For more details of the history of archeological findings leading to the Achaemenid Empire, see Jean-Louis Huot, *Persia: From the Origins to the Achaemenid,* 2 vols. (London: Barrie and Jenkins, 1970). For a short and succinct essay, see John Curtis, *Ancient Persia* (London: British Museum, 1989). For a more detailed account, see John Curtis and St. John Simpson, *The World of Achaemenid Persia: The Diversity of Ancient Iran* (London: I. B. Tauris, 2010).

35. See Nancy Fraser, "Transnationalizing the Public Sphere: On the Legitimacy and Efficacy of Public Opinion in a Post-Westphalian World," *Theory, Culture & Society* 24.4 (2007) 7–30. Available at: http://eipcp.net/transversal/0605/fraser/en. Accessed on 10 June 2013.

36. Ibid.

37. Ibid.

38. Ibid.

39. Ibid.

40. For a comprehensive examination of the Cyrus Cylinder and its significance, see John Curtis, *Cyrus Cylinder and Ancient Persia: A New Beginning for the Middle East* (London: British Museum, 2013).

41. Beeta Baghoolizadeh did an excellent review of this tour and dismantled many of its myths. See her "Reconstructing a Persian Past: Contemporary Uses and Misuses of the Cyrus Cylinder in Iranian Nationalist Discourse" (6 June 2013). Available at: http://ajammc.com/2013/06/06/reconstructing-a-persian-past-contemporary-uses-and-misuses-of-the-cyrus-cylinder-in-iranian-nationalist-discourse.

2. MONTESQUIEU, THE BOURGEOIS PUBLIC SPHERE, AND THE RISE OF PERSIAN LIBERAL NATIONALISM

1. See Sarah Searight, *The British in the Middle East* (London and the Hague: East–West Publications, 1969/1979), 92.

2. Ibid., 91.

3. Ibid., 92.

4. Ibid.

5. As I have demonstrated in my *Iran: A People Interrupted* (New York: The New Press, 2007).

6. See John Davidson's introduction to his edition and translation of Montesquieu's *Persian Letters*, Montesquieu, *Persian Letters* (1721). Available at: http://rbsche .people.wm.edu/teaching/plp. Accessed on 10 July 2013.

7. See David Randall, "Ethos, Poetics, and the Literary Public Sphere," *Modern Language Quarterly* 69.2 (2008): 221–243. Available at: http://mlq.dukejournals.org /content/69/2/221.abstract.

8. See Montesquieu, *Persian Letters,* translated with an introduction by C. J. Betts (London: Penguin, 1973), 24.

9. See Montesquieu, *Persian Letters,* in *Complete Works of Montesquieu,* 4 vols. Available at: http://oll.libertyfund.org/?option=com_staticxt&staticfile=show .php%3Ftitle=1338&chapter=74623&layout=html&Itemid=27. Accessed on 10 July 2013.

10. John Davidson's introduction to his edition and translation of Montesquieu's *Persian Letters* (1721).

11. See ibid.

12. See Iradj Amini, *Napoleon and Persia: Franco-Persian Relations under the First Empire* (Washington, DC: Mage Publishers, 1999), 16.

13. For some speculations in this regard, see Mohamad Tavakoli-Targhi, "The Homeless Texts of Persianate Modernity," in Ramin Jahanbegloo, ed., *Iran between Tradition and Modernity* (New York: Lexington Books, 2004), 130. For later contacts, see Amini, *Napoleon and Persia;* for similar contacts with Great Britain, see Denis Wright, *The Persians amongst the English: Episodes in Anglo-Persian History* (London: I. B. Tauris, 1985).

14. Wright, *The Persians amongst the English.*

15. See Fereydun Adamiyat, *Andisheh-ha-ye Mirza Fath Ali Akhondzadeh/The Thoughts of Mirza Fath Ali Akhondzadeh* (Tehran: Khwarizmi Publications, 1349/1970), 108.

16. Edward Said, *Orientalism* (New York: Penguin, 178), 202–203.

17. Far more important than all these books was the study of Xiaomei Chen, *Occidentalism: A Theory of Counter-Discourse in Post-Mao China* (Oxford: Oxford University Press, 1995), in which the author describes the "favorable depiction of Western

culture and its negative characterization of Chinese culture." The contention is that this exposure to Occidentalism was in fact "liberating for the Chinese culture." Minus the false binary this study assumes with Edward Said's *Orientalism*, Xiaomei Chen's linking of the European and Chinese public spheres (effectively not theoretically) resonates with my study here.

18. See M. R. Ghanoonparvar, *In a Persian Mirror: Images of the West and Westerners in Iranian Fiction* (Austin: University of Texas Press, 1993).

19. See Mohamad Tavakoli-Targhi, *Refashioning Iran: Orientalism, Occidentalism and Historiography* (New York: Palgrave Macmillan, 2001), ix–x.

20. See S. N. Eisenstadt, "Multiple Modernities," *Daedalus* 129 (Winter 2000): 1–229. Available at: http://www.havenscenter.org/files/Eisenstadt2000 _MultipleModernities.pdf. Accessed on 15 July 2013.

21. Tavakoli-Targhi, *Refashioning Iran,* 23.

22. Ibid., 33.

23. See Hamid Dabashi, *Post-Orientalism: Knowledge and Power in Time of Terror* (Piscataway, NJ: Transaction Publishers, 2008); see the first chapter on Ignaz Goldziher.

24. See Joseph A. Massad, *Desiring Arabs* (Chicago: Chicago University Press, 2008), passim.

25. See Tavakoli-Targhi, "Homeless Texts of Persianate Modernity," 130.

26. German philosopher Gottfried Wilhelm Leibniz (1646–1716), for example, was known for being a great Sinophile, while Karl Wilhelm Friedrich Schlegel (1772–1829) was an Indophile.

27. For a detailed study of the satirical dimensions of Montesquieu's *Persian Letters,* see the excellent work of Stephen Werner, *The Comic Philosophers: Montesquieu, Voltaire, Diderot, Sade* (Birmingham, AL: Summa Publications, 2002), 7–32.

28. See Montesquieu, *Persian Letters,* 83.

29. See Dabashi, *Post-Orientalism,* chap. 1.

30. Werner, *Comic Philosophers,* 20.

3. SIR WILLIAM JONES, ORIENTALIST PHILOLOGY, AND PERSIAN LINGUISTIC NATIONALISM

1. A. J. Arberry, *British Orientalists,* 23–24.

2. Ibid., 24.

3. Ibid., 29–30.

4. Some scholars like Rajeev Kinra and Mohamad Tavakoli-Targhi have suggested the possible influence of Indian philologists like Saraj al-Din Khan Arzu (c. 1689–1756) on the development of Jones's idea of "Indo-European languages." See Mohamad Tavakoli-Targhi, "Orientalism's Genesis Amnesia," in Vasant Kaiwar and Sucheta Mazumdar, eds., *Antinomies of Modernity: Essays on Race, Orient, Nation*

(Durham, NC: Duke University Press, 2003), 100–125; and Rajeev Kinra, "This Noble Science: Indo-Persian Comparative Philology, ca. 1000–1800 CE," in Yigal Bronner, Whitney Cox, and Lawrence McCrea, eds., *South Asian Texts in History: Critical Engagements with Sheldon Pollock* (Ann Arbor, MI: Association for Asian Studies, 2011). However, more recent scholarship casts doubt on this possibility. See Arthur Dudney, "A Passion for Meaning: Khan-i Arzu's Philology and the Place of India in the Eighteenth-Century Persianate World" (PhD diss., Columbia University, 2013). It is not entirely improbable that Indian philologists like Arzu had an impact on the development of Jones's ideas, but, as we see, the tradition of this thinking in Europe itself is far longer and consistent. Scholars like Muzaffar Alam, in "The Pursuit of Persian: Language in Mughal Politics" (*Modern Asian Studies* 32.2 [1998]: 317–49), or Tavakoli-Targhi and Rajeev Kinra are of course correct in outlining the trajectory of Indo-Persian philology in the region itself; but the European path of the idea (as well as its horrid racial consequences) has a more deeply rooted European vintage. I am grateful to Dr. Dudney for kindly sharing the subject of his doctoral dissertation with me.

5. I am grateful to my Columbia colleague Sheldon Pollock, the Arvind Raghunathan Professor of South Asian Studies, for generously sharing his critical intimacy with this philological history with me.

6. Sir William Jones, "Third Anniversary Discourse: On the Hindus," *Asiatick Researches,* a lecture delivered on 2 February 1786 and published in 1798, as cited in William J. Poser and Lyle Campbell, "Indo-European Practice and Historical Methodology," *Proceedings of the Eighteenth Annual Meeting of the Berkeley Linguistics Society: General Session and Parasession on The Place of Morphology in a Grammar* (1992), 214–236. Available at: http://www.billposer.org/Papers/iephm.pdf. Accessed on 30 July 2013. Also quoted in A. J. Arberry, *British Orientalist,* 30.

7. Maurice Olender, *The Languages of Paradise: Race, Religion, and Philology in the Nineteenth Century* (Cambridge, MA: Harvard University Press, 1992), 36.

8. Ibid., 53.

9. Ibid., 84.

10. See Fereydun Adamiyat, *The Thoughts of Mirza Fath Ali Akhondzadeh,* 69.

11. Ibid., 71.

12. Ibid., 73.

13. Ibid., 75.

14. Ibid., 70.

15. Ibid., 76.

16. Ibid.

17. See Benedict Anderson, *Imagined Communities: Reflections on the Origin and Spread of Nationalism* (London: Verso, 2006).

18. See Mohammad Ali Foroughi, *Payam-e man beh Farhangestan/My Message to the Academy* (November 1936). Available at: http://issuu.com/shirazeh/docs/payam _be_farhangestan?e=2036644/4288910. Accessed on 3 August 2013.

19. See Hamid Dabashi, "Jonbesh-e Sabz Bazgasht-e Farhang Jahanshahri Mast/ The Green Movement Is the Return of Our Cosmopolitan Culture," *Jaras,* 8 Ordibehesht 1389/28 (April 2010). Available at: http://www.rahesabz.net/story/14504. See also Hamid Dabashi, "Tamamiyat-e Arzi Iran dar Geruv-e Farhang-e Iranshahri-ye Mast"/"Our National Integrity Is Contingent on Our Persopolitanism" (*Jaras,* 13 Tir, 1389/4 [July 2010]). Available at: http://www.rahesabz.net/story/18706.

4. GOETHE, HEGEL, HAFEZ, AND COMPANY

1. John D. Yohannan, "Persian Literature in Translation," in Ehsan Yarshater, ed., *Persian Literature* (Stony Brook: State University of New York Press, 1988), 479.

2. Ibid., 479.

3. Ibid.

4. Ibid., 480.

5. For further details see ibid., 480ff.

6. Ibid., 481.

7. Ibid., 482.

8. See Gauri Viswanathan, *Masks of Conquest: Literary Study and British Rule in India* (New York: Columbia University Press, 1989).

9. In my *Persian Literary Humanism* (Cambridge, MA: Harvard University Press, 2012) I have sought radically to alter that conception by placing the literary history of Mughal India squarely in the context of Persian literary history of the last fourteen hundred years and across multiple empires from the Ghaznavids to the Safavids.

10. Yohannan, "Persian Literature in Translation," 482.

11. Ibid., 482.

12. Ibid., 485.

13. For a critique of this colonial project and the restoration of Persian literary humanism to its historical context, see my *Persian Literary Humanism.*

14. Annemarie Schimmel, "The Genius of Shiraz," in Yarshater, *Persian Literature,* 221–222.

15. Ibid., 225.

16. He was of course wrong in this assessment. For a corrective reference see Peter Chelkowski's "Nezami: Master Dramatist," in Yarshater, *Persian Literature,* 179. While noting the presence of Ta'ziyeh drama in Iran, Chelkowski refers to Nezami's poetry as "closet drama." The term is ill-fitted and inappropriate. Not only Nezami and the Ta'ziyeh performances but also a host of other widely popular dramas have been extensively documented in Persian performing arts. See Jamshid Malakpour, *Adabiyat-e Namayesh dar Iran/Drama in Iran,* 2 vols. (Tehran: Tus, 1363/1984).

17. As quoted in Talat S. Halman, "Jalal al-Din Rumi: Passions of the Mystic Mind," in Yarshater, *Persian Literature,* 192.

18. Schimmel, "The Genius of Shiraz," 225.

19. Heshmat Moayyad, "Lyric Poetry," in Yarshater, *Persian Literature,* 40. Moayyad quotes Ernst Buetler in his introduction to *West-östlicher Divan,* who believes that "Er [i.e., *West-östlicher Divan]* ist nächst dem 'Faust' das bedeutendste und zugleich persönlichste Werk des Dichters."

20. Schimmel, "The Genius of Shiraz," 225.

21. Ibid., 216–217.

22. Martin Kitchen, *The Cambridge Illustrated History of Germany* (Cambridge: Cambridge University Press, 1996), 141.

23. Schimmel, "The Genius of Shiraz," 220.

24. Annemarie Schimmel, *Mystical Dimensions of Islam* (Chapel Hill: University of North Carolina Press, 1975), 70.

25. G. W. F. Hegel, *The Philosophy of History* (New York: Dover Publications, 1956), 173.

26. Ibid., 173. To be sure, Immanuel Kant (1724–1804) was also wont to compare all Orientals to their European similitudes: "If the Arabs are, so to speak, the Spaniards of the orient," he thought, "similarly the Persians are the French of Asia. They are good poets, courteous and of fairly fine taste. They are not such strict followers of Islam, and they permit to their pleasure-prone disposition a tolerably mild interpretation of the Koran. The Japanese could in a way be regarded as the Englishmen of this part of the world, but hardly in any other quality than their resoluteness—which degenerates into the utmost stubbornness—their valor, and disdain of death. For the rest, they display few signs of a finer feeling." See Immanuel Kant, *Observations on the Feeling of the Beautiful and the Sublime* (Berkeley: University of California Press, 1960), 109–110.

27. Hegel, *The Philosophy of History,* 174.

28. Ibid., 175. Hegel has equally high praise for Persian art and poetry during the Islamic period, which through an assessment of Hafez and Rumi's "pantheism" he considers in continuity with pre-Islamic Persia. For a more detailed discussion of the place of Persia in Hegel's thoughts, see the excellent essay in *Encyclopedia Iranica,* available here: http://www.iranicaonline.org/articles/hegel-georg-wilhelm-friedrich.

29. Yohannan, "Persian Literature in Translation," in Yarshater, *Persian Literature,* 484.

30. Ibid., 480.

31. G. W. F. Hegel, *On Art, Religion, Philosophy: Introductory Lectures to the Realm of Absolute Spirit,* edited with an introduction by Glenn Gray (New York: Harper Torchbooks, 1970), 301.

32. Ibid., 302.

33. Ibid., 299.

34. Ibid., 300.

35. Ibid., 302.

36. Ibid., 300.

37. Ibid., 300–301.

38. Yohannan, "Persian Literature in Translation," in Yarshater, *Persian Literature,* 483.

39. Schimmel, "The Genius of Shiraz," in Yarshater, *Persian Literature,* 219.

40. Kitchen, *The Cambridge Illustrated History of Germany,* 164.

41. For the intimate link between S. H. Nasr and Frithjof Schuon, see Seyyed Hossein Nasr, ed., *The Essential Frithjof Schuon* (Bloomington, IN: World Wisdom, Library of Perennial Philosophy, 2005).

42. For more on these and other ideologues of the Islamic revolution in Iran, see Hamid Dabashi, *Theology of Discontent: The Ideological Foundation of the Islamic Revolution in Iran* (New York: New York University Press, 1993).

5. FROM ROMANTICISM TO PAN-ISLAMISM TO TRANSCENDENTALISM

1. Here I have in mind the pioneering work of Fritz R. Stern, *The Politics of Cultural Despair: A Study in the Rise of the Germanic Ideology* (Berkeley: University of California Press, 1974).

2. See Morteza Motahhari, *Erfan-e Hafez (Tamasha-gah-e Raz)* (Tehran: Sadra, 1368/1989).

3. See, for example, Mohammad Sharafuddin's *Islam and Romantic Orientalism* (London: I. B. Tauris, 1994), and John M. MacKenzie's *Orientalism: History, Theory, and Arts* (Manchester: Manchester University Press, 1995) as two examples of what their authors believe to be correctives to Said's reading of Orientalism.

4. Annemarie Schimmel, "Persian Poetry in the Indo-Pakistani Subcontinent," in Ehsan Yarshater, *Persian Literature,* 424–425.

5. For a short essay on the impact of the Persian translation of this book, see Hamid Dabashi, "Found in Translation," *New York Times,* 28 July 2013. Available at: http://opinionator.blogs.nytimes.com/2013/07/28/found-in-translation/?_r=0.

6. Annemarie Schimmel, "Iqbal's Persian Poetry," in Ehsan Yarshater, ed., *Persian Literature* (Stony Brook: State University of New York Press, 1988), 423.

7. For the details of this historic meeting, see Ronald Hayman, *Nietzsche: A Critical Life* (Oxford: Oxford University Press, 1980), 97.

8. Ibid., 423.

9. John D. Yohannan, "Persian Literature in Translation," in Yarshater, *Persian Literature,* 485.

10. Ibid., 484.

11. Wilhelm Halbfass, *India and Europe: An Essay in Philosophical Understanding* (Delhi: Motilal Banarsidass Publishers, 1990), 124. I am grateful to Theodore Riccardi Jr., who brought this and other material related to Brockhaus's relation to Wagner to my attention.

12. Cosima Wagner, *Diaries*, vol. 2: *1878–1883*, edited and annotated by Martin Gregor-Dellin and Dietrich Mack, translated and with introduction, postscript, and additional notes by Geoffrey Skelton (New York: Harcourt Brace Jovanovich, 1977), 461.

13. Friedrich Nietzsche, *The Gay Science: With a Prelude in Rhymes and an Appendix of Songs*, trans. Walter Kaufmann (New York: Vintage, 1974), 330.

14. For more on this link, see Peter Viereck, *Metapolitics: From Wagner and the German Romantics to Hitler* (Piscataway, NJ: Transaction Publishers, 2003), and for an even more critical reading of the link between pre-Nazi German thoughts and the rise of the Third Reich, see Fritz R. Stern, *The Politics of Cultural Despair: A Study in the Rise of the Germanic Ideology* (Berkeley: University of California Press, 1974).

15. For more on the relationship between American transcendentalism and Persian poetry, see Arthur Christy, *The Orient in American Transcendentalism* (New York: Columbia University Press, 1932). For more on the relationship between Emerson and Goethe, see Frederick B. Wahr, *Emerson and Goethe* (Hartford, CT: Transcendental Books, 1971), and John D. Yohannan, "Emerson's Translations of Persian Poetry from German Sources," *American Literature* 14.4 (1943): 407–420.

16. Yohannan, "Persian Literature in Translation," 484.

17. Ibid., 484.

18. Ibid.

19. For more on the relationship between Emerson and Persian poetry, see Frederic Ives Carpenter, *Emerson and Asia* (New York: Haskell House, 1930), and John D. Yohannan, "Ralph Waldo Emerson," *Encyclopedia Iranica*. Available at: http://www.iranicaonline.org/articles/emerson. See also John D. Yohannan, "The Influence of Persian Poetry upon Emerson's Work," *American Literature,* 15.1 (1943): 25–41. See also Mansur Ekhtiar, *Emerson and Persia: Emerson's Developing Interest in Persian Mysticism* (Tehran: Tehran University Press, 1976). Atefeh Akbari Shahmirzadi has also written an excellent MA thesis, "From Shiraz to Concord: Ralph Waldo Emerson's Renderings of Hafez" (Columbia University, 2013).

20. Schimmel, "The Genius of Shiraz," 219.

21. This according to Yohannan, "Persian Literature in Translation," 490.

22. Ibid., 490.

23. Ibid., 481.

24. As quoted in ibid., 490.

25. Ibid., 485.

26. See Arthur Versluis, *American Transcendentalism and Asian Religions* (Oxford: Oxford University Press, 1993), 266.

27. Henry David Thoreau, *The Writings of Henry David Thoreau: Journal,* ed. B. Torrey (Boston and New York: Houghton Mifflin Company, 1906), 290.

28. Available at: http://mlk-kpp01.stanford.edu/primarydocuments/Vol5/July1959_MyTriptotheLandofGandhi.pdf. Accessed on 27 October 2013.

29. See Afshin Marashi, "Imagining Hafez: Rabindranath Tagore in Iran, 1932," *Journal of Persianate Studies,* vol. 3, issue 1 (2010): 46–77. Available at: http://booksandjournals.brillonline.com/content/10.1163/187471610x505951.

30. See Hamid Dabashi, *Islamic Liberation Theology: Resisting the Empire* (London and New York: Routledge, 2008).

31. See Hamid Dabashi, *Theology of Discontent: The Ideological Foundation of the Islamic Revolution in Iran* (New York: New York University Press, 1993).

32. See Mehrzad Boroujerdi, *Iranian Intellectuals and the West: The Tormented Triumph of Nativism* (Syracuse, NY: Syracuse University Press, 1996); and Ali Mirsepassi, *Political Islam, Iran, and the Enlightenment* (Cambridge: Cambridge University Press, 2010).

33. See Dabashi, *Theology of Discontent,* the chapter on Ayatollah Khomeini (chapter 8).

34. After a detailed and persuasive argument in a recent doctoral dissertation, Ajay Chaudhary takes such assumptions critically to task, demonstrates how Al-e Ahmad's ideas had scarcely anything to do with those German thinkers, and suggests "an alternative intellectual genealogy that brings Al-e Ahmad's Marxist influence more clearly into view . . . [and] "how Al-e Ahmad departs from Marx, on both strategic and philosophical grounds, only to converge with the (also Marxian) approach of Walter Benjamin." See Ajay Singh Chaudhary, "Religions of Doubt: Religion, Critique, and Modernity in Jalal Al-e Ahmad and Walter Benjamin" (PhD diss., Columbia University, 2013).

6. NIETZSCHE, HAFEZ, MOZART, ZARATHUSTRA, AND THE MAKING OF A PERSIAN DIONYSUS

1. The Persian translation of *Thus Spoke Zarathustra* was made by Daryoush Ashuri between 1970 and 1976 and published by Agah Publishing in Tehran. Oddly enough, the translator became a fanatical advocate of "Western modernity" as if nothing of Nietzsche's antimetaphysical thinking had slipped through his Persian. Thus the very translator of this seminal text became the epitome of the contradictory function of the text in its Persian environment.

2. Friedrich Nietzsche, *The Gay Science,* trans. Walter Kaufmann (New York: Vantage Books, 1974), 327.

3. Ibid.

4. Ibid., 327–328.

5. For more details of Bismarck's imperialist projects, see Shelly Baranowski, *Nazi Empire: German Colonialism and Imperialism from Bismarck to Hitler* (Cambridge: Cambridge University Press, 2010), 9–67.

6. Nietzsche, *The Gay Science,* 328.

7. Ibid.

8. Ibid., 329.

9. Ibid.

10. Ibid., 329–330.

11. Ibid., 331, n.126 by Walter Kaufmann.

12. Ibid., 330.

13. For a comprehensive study of the significance of Persia for Nietzsche, see "Nietzsche and Persia," *Encyclopedia Iranica*. Available at: http://www.iranicaonline .org/articles/nietzsche-and-persia.

14. Ibid.

15. Cited in ibid.

16. Cited in ibid.

17. For attempts at appropriating Nietzsche's Zarathustra toward racist Aryanism, see ibid.

18. Ibid.

19. Ibid.

20. See Jenny Rose, *The Image of Zoroaster: The Persian Mage through European Eyes* (New York: Bibliotheca Persica Press, 2000), 189.

21. Ibid., 3.

22. Ibid., 4.

23. Ibid.

24. Ibid., 78.

25. Ibid., 111.

26. Ibid., 141.

27. Ibid., 166–167.

28. See Kathleen Marie Higgins, *Nietzsche's Zarathustra* (Philadelphia: Temple University Press, 1987), 239.

29. Ibid.

30. Ibid.

31. Ibid., 241.

32. Friedrich Nietzsche, *Thus Spoke Zarathustra: A Book for All and None,* ed. Adrian del Caro and Obert B. Pippin, trans. Adrian del Caro (Cambridge: Cambridge University Press, 2006), 5.

33. Ahmad Shamlou, "*Sorud Ibrahim dar Atash*/The Ballad of Abraham in Fire," in *Ibrahim dar Atash/Abraham in Fire* (Tehran: 1352/1973), 13–15.

7. EDWARD FITZGERALD AND THE REDISCOVERY OF OMAR KHAYYÁM FOR PERSIAN NIHILISM

1. See Garrett Wallace Brown and David Held, *The Cosmopolitan Reader* (Malden, MA: Polity Press, 2010).

2. Ibid., 4.

3. John D. Yohannan, "Persian Literature in Translation," in Ehsan Yarshater, ed., *Persian Literature* (Stony Brook: State University of New York, 1988), 486.

4. As quoted in ibid., 487.

5. Ibid., 485.

6. Ibid., 487.

7. See A. J. Arberry, *FitzGerald's Salaman and Absal* (Cambridge: Cambridge University Press, 1956), 5.

8. Ibid., 7.

9. Ibid., 14.

10. Ibid., 29.

11. Ibid., 30.

12. Ibid., 31.

13. Ibid., 35.

14. Concerning FitzGerald's homosexuality, see H. Montgomery Hyde, *The Love That Dared Not Speak Its Name: A Candid History of Homosexuality in Britain* (Boston: Little, Brown and Company, 1970). See also James Blyth, Edward FitzGerald, and "Posh": "Herring Merchants" (1908). Available at: http://www.gutenberg.org/files /20543/20543-h/20543-h.htm.

15. For a general introduction to Sadegh Hedayat's life and literature, see Homa Katouzian, *Sadeq Hedayat: The Life and Literature of an Iranian Writer* (New York: Palgrave Macmillan, 1992).

16. For an excellent example of this genre, see Porochista Khakpour, "This Book Will End Your Life: The Greatest Modern Persian Novel Ever Written," as the introduction to a new edition of Sadegh Hedayat, *The Blind Owl*, trans. D. P. Costello (New York: Grove Press, 2010). Available at: http://therumpus.net/2010/10/why-i -love-sadegh-hedayats-the-blind-owl.

17. For a pioneering study of this masterpiece, see Michael Beard, *Hedayat's Blind Owl as a Western Novel* (Princeton, NJ: Princeton University Press, 1990).

18. See Jürgen Habermas, *On Society and Politics: A Reader,* ed. Steven Seidman (Boston: Beacon Press, 1989), 231.

19. Ibid.

8. MATTHEW ARNOLD, PHILOSOPHICAL PESSIMISM, AND THE RISE OF IRANIAN EPIC NATIONALISM

1. For a comprehensive examination of these translations, see Hourieh Yektat-alab and Amin Karimnia, "Translations of Shahnameh of Firdausi in the West," *Khazar Journal of Humanities and Social Sciences,* n.d., 36–52. Available at: http://www .academia.edu/4612436/Translations_of_Shahnameh_of_Firdausi_in_the_West.

2. See Justus Collins Castleman, *Matthew Arnold's Sohrab and Rustum and Other Poems* (New York: The Macmillan Company, 1905), xix.

3. Ibid., xxv.

4. Ibid., 10.

5. On the influence of one on the other, see J. Warshaw, "Sainte-Beuve's Influence on Matthew Arnold," *Modern Language Notes* 25 (March 1910): 77–78.

6. James Walter Caufield, *Overcoming Matthew Arnold: Ethics in Culture and Criticism* (Surrey, Eng.: Ashgate, 2012), 6.

7. Ibid., 200.

8. Ibid., 15.

9. See "Ferdowsi, Abu'l-Qāsem iv. Millenary Celebration," in *Encyclopedia Iranica;* available online at: http://www.iranicaonline.org/articles/ferdowsi-iv.

10. Ibid.

11. My graduate student at Columbia University, Ali Ahmadi Motlagh, wrote an excellent thesis detailing all these developments, "Ferdowsi in the Twentieth Century" (MA thesis, Columbia University, 2008).

12. The full text of Kasra'i's poem and a learned essay on the origin of the story of Arash the Archer is available at: http://www.parand.se/t-kasraei-arash.htm. Accessed on 29 December 2013.

13. For an English translation of the novel, see Simin Daneshvar, *Savushun: A Novel about Modern Iran* (Washington, DC: Mage Publishers, 1991).

14. See Mostafa Rahimi, *Tragedy-ye Qudrat dar Shahnameh/The Tragedy of Power in Shahnameh* (Tehran: Nilufar Publications, 1990).

15. See Hamid Dabashi, *Iran, The Green Movement and the USA: The Fox and the Paradox* (London: Zed, 2010), 205.

9. JAMES MORIER, *HAJJI BABA OF ISPAHAN,* AND THE RISE OF A PROXY PUBLIC SPHERE

1. See Aijaz Ahmad, "Orientalism and After: Ambivalence and Cosmopolitan Location in the Work of Edward Said," *Economic and Political Weekly* 27.30 (25 July 1992): 98–116. The essay was subsequently published in Aijaz Ahmad's *In Theory: Nations, Classes, Literatures* (London: Verso, 2008).

2. "Orientalism and After," 108.

3. See Aijaz Ahmad's "Jameson's Rhetoric of Otherness and the 'National Allegory,'" *Social Text,* no. 17 (Autumn 1987): 3–25.

4. Ahmad, "Orientalism and After," 108.

5. Consider, for example, the fact that an Iranian merchant named Mirza Ali Mohammad Kashani, living and working in Calcutta, in 1926 paid for the publishing costs of a book on a leading revolutionary activist like Seyyed Jamal al-Din al-Afghani to be published in Berlin. The journal *Iranshahr,* which was the vehicle for this publication, thanked this merchant in its 23 May 1926 issue (see *Iranshahr,* 23 May 1926).

6. I have had another occasion to discuss Mirza Habib Isfahani and his translation of Morier's book in my *Iran: A People Interrupted* (New York: The New Press, 2008), from which account I have borrowed and expanded in this section of this chapter. For another account of Mirza Habib Isfahani, see the entry under his name in *Encyclopedia Iranica,* available at: http://www.iranicaonline.org/articles/habib -esfahani. Accessed on 6 January 2014.

7. For a thorough discussion of these controversies, see Ja'far Modarres Sadeqi's introduction to his critical edition of Mirza Habib Isfahani's translation of James Morier's original, *Sargozasht-e Hajji Baba-ye Isfahani* (Tehran: Nashr-e Markaz, 1379/2000).

8. For more on James Morier and his brothers, see Henry McKenzie Johnston, *Ottoman and Persian Odysseys: James Morier, Creator of Hajji Baba of Isfahan, and His Brothers* (London and New York: British Academic Press, 1998). Reading this account of Morier and his brothers one is struck by the similarity of Morier's own diplomatic career and that of his "Hajji Baba" character—he was projecting too obviously.

9. See Umberto Eco, *Limits of Interpretation* (Bloomington: Indiana University Press, 1990), 33.

10. The same holds true for Morier's European or American readers. Just because he wrote *Hajji Baba* in a malicious Orientalist tone does not mean everyone read it that way. Much of the popularity of the novel in Europe or the United States might in fact have been entirely independent of what Morier intended by it. We know, for example, that Nathaniel Hawthorne also read Morier's *Hajji Baba* by way of trying to have a better understanding of Persia. See Luther S. Luedtke, *Nathaniel Hawthorne and the Romance of the Orient* (Bloomington and Indianapolis: Indiana University Press, 1989), 51.

10. PICTURING PERSIA IN THE VISUAL AND PERFORMING ARTS

1. For an excellent collection of essays addressing this issue, see Jonathan Bellman, ed., *The Exotic in Western Music* (Boston: Northeastern University Press, 1998). The collection has an excellent essay by Ralph P. Locke on "Cutthroats and Casbah Dancers, Muezzins and Timeless Sands: Musical Images of the Middle East" (104–136), though it pays no particular attention to Persian elements.

2. For further details, see Wolfgang Mommsen, *Theories of Imperialism* (Chicago: University of Chicago Press, 1982), 29–58.

3. See Jellinek, *History through the Opera Glass,* 3–4.

4. See Peter Chelkowski, "Aya Opera-ye Turandot-e Puccini bar Asas-e Kushk-e Sorkh-e Haft Peykar-e Nezami Ast?/Is Puccini's 'Turandot' based on the Red Pavilion of Nezami's *Haft Peykar?*" *Iranshenasi* (Zemestan 1370/Winter 1991): 715–721.

5. See Jellinek, *History through the Opera Glass,* 6–8.

6. Fereshteh Daftari, *The Influence of Persian Art on Gauguin, Matisse, and Kandinsky* (New York: Garland Publishing, 1991), 20.

7. Ibid., 21.

8. Ibid., 161.

9. Ibid., 39–40.

10. Ibid., 41.

11. Ibid., 43.

12. Ibid.

13. Ibid., 45.

14. Ibid., 46.

15. Ibid., 62–63.

16. Ibid., 159.

17. Ibid., 165.

18. Ibid., 166.

19. Ibid., 217.

20. Ibid., 253.

21. Ibid., 255.

22. Ibid., 256–257.

23. Ibid., 257.

24. Timothy Mitchell, *Colonising Egypt* (Cambridge: Cambridge University Press, 1988), 13.

25. For a short account of the early history of cinema in Iran, see Hamid Dabashi, *Close Up: Past, Present, Future* (London: Verso, 2001); for a more comprehensive account, see Hamid Naficy, *A Social History of Iranian Cinema*, 4 vols. (Durham, NC: Duke University Press, 2011).

26. For more details on the history of photography in Iran, see Iraj Afshar, *Ganjineh Aks-ha ye Iran: Hamrah Tarikhcheh-ye Vorud-e Akkasi beh Iran/A Treasury of Photographs in Iran: Plus a Short History of Photography in Iran* (Tehran: Tahuri Publications, 1368/1989).

27. See Hossein Mohammad Zadeh Sediq, *Namayesh-Nameh ha-ye Mirza Aqa Tabrizi/The Plays of Mirza Aqa Tabrizi* (Tehran: Tahuri Publications, 1354/1975).

11. E. G. BROWNE, PERSIAN LITERATURE, AND THE MAKING OF A TRANSNATIONAL LITERARY PUBLIC SPHERE

1. From the Constitutional Revolution forward, the subject of Iranian nationalism—for which Browne had established a solid literary foundation—has been extensively studied. Richard W. Cottam's *Nationalism in Iran* (1964) is among the earliest sources, while Kamran Scot Aghai and Afshin Marashi's edited volume, *Rethinking Iranian Nationalism and Modernity* (2014) is the most recent. Equally important are Rasmus Christian Elling's *Minorities in Iran: Nationalism and Ethnicity*

after Khomeini (2013) and Ali M. Ansari's *The Politics of Nationalism in Modern Iran* (2012). James A. Bill's *Musaddiq, Iranian Nationalism and Oil* (1988) examine the issue in a critical anticolonial period, while Majid Sharifi's *Imagining Iran: The Tragedy of Subaltern Nationalism* (2013) is a solid critique of all dominant notions of nationalism. Publication of Firoozeh Kashani-Sabet's groundbreaking *Frontier Fictions: Shaping the Iranian Nation, 1804–1946* (Princeton, NJ: Princeton University Press, 2011) is a threshold in conceptualizing our understanding of Iranian nationalism in its seminal stage. My concern in this chapter, however, is entirely different and is primarily engaged with the impact of a transnational literary public sphere on the nationalization of an imperial literary history that was later put at the service of a nation-building project.

2. In a recent essay, Mahmoud Omidsalar has challenged the idea that leading Iranian scholars like Mohammad Qazvini were influenced by European scholars in their methodologies. (See Mahmoud Omidsalar, "Allamah Qazvini va Shiveh-ye Gharbi Tahghigh/Allamah Qazvini and Methodology of Western Scholarship," *Ayeneh Miras* 12.33 [1393/2014]). Omidsalar argues that Qazvini already had a solid command of and had thus been exposed to European scholarship while he was still in Iran; this knowledge was subsequently expanded when he went to Europe. In Europe, he was both conversant with and critical of such leading Orientalist scholars as Anthony Ashley Bevan (1859–1933), Alexander George Ellis (1851–1942), Henry Frederick Amedroz (1854–1917), Hartwig Derenbourg (1844–1908), Antoine Meillet (1866–1936), Clément Huart (1854–1926), Paul Casanova (1861–1926), Gabriel Ferrand (1864–1935), Louis Massignon (1883–1962), Henri Massé (1886–1969), Edgard Blochet (1870–1937), Paul Pelliot (1878–1945), Sebastian Beck (1878–1951), Edward Sachau (1845–1930), Oskar Mann (1867–1917), Bernhard Moritz (1859–1939), Eugen Mittwoch (1876–1942), Martin Hartmann (1851–1918), Anhalter Bahnhof, and perhaps most important, Edward Granville Browne (1862–1926). This critical position does not compromise the fact of the transnational public literary space that I articulate in this chapter. Whether Qazvini was aware and conscious of European scholarship about Persian literature before, during, or after his extensive European sojourns makes little difference to the fact that in the production of the transnational literary public sphere both he and his European counterparts were at work simultaneously.

3. For a critical assessment of the concept of *public sphere* from a non-European perspective, see the excellent essay by Boaventura de Sousa Santos, "Public Sphere and Epistemologies of the South," in *Africa Development* 37.1 (2012): 43–67. As is evident in this book, my critical encounter with the concept of *(literary) public sphere* is rather different than that of Boaventura de Sousa Santos, for I take the global implications of capitalist modernity through the formation of a transnational public sphere, to which I then add the site-specific notion of *parapublic sphere,* or *proxy public sphere,* which come together to result in a different dynamic of their consequences on

the colonial sites. Nevertheless, Boaventura de Sousa Santos's and my critical stances commence from similar concerns.

4. See Ehsan Yarshater, ed., *Persian Literature*.

5. There is an excellent study of these aspects of Persian literature by John D. Yohannan, *Persian Poetry in England and America: A 200-Year History* (Delmar, NY: Caravan Books, 1977).

6. For the first volume of this history, see J. T. P. de Bruijn, ed. (Ehsan Yarshater, general editor), *A History of Persian Literature. Volume One: General Introduction to Persian Literature* (London: I. B. Tauris, 2008). Yarshater has already provided a sample of the sort of historiography operative in this massive project in his shorter volume, Ehsan Yarshater, ed., *Persian Literature* (New York: State University of New York Press, 1988).

12. *PERSICA SPIRITUALIS:* NICHOLSON, SCHIMMEL, CORBIN, AND THEIR CONSEQUENCES

1. Pierre Bourdieu, *The Political Ontology of Martin Heidegger* (Stanford, CA: Stanford University Press, 1991), 8.

2. Ibid., 10. Bourdieu further refers to Siegfried Krakauer's *From Caligari to Hitler: A Psychological History of German Cinema* (Princeton, NJ: Princeton University Press, 1947) as singularly expressive of the phenomenon. For a more detailed examination of German cinema of the period, see Anton Kaes, *From Hitler to Heimat: The Return of History as Film* (Cambridge, MA: Harvard University Press, 1989).

3. Oswald Spengler, *Man and Technics* (London: Allen and Unwin, 1932).

4. Ibid., 97, in Bourdieu, *Political Ontology of Martin Heidegger,* 11–12. Notice also the origin of German Orientalism in Spengler's reading of postwar Germany. It is crucial to note here that German Orientalism was rooted in a mystical flight from technological modernity rather than a colonial construct of the Oriental "other."

5. Bourdieu, *Political Ontology of Martin Heidegger,* 25–26.

6. Ibid. Equally crucial to understanding both the ideological and the social premises of Heidegger's critique of technological modernity and its location in European nihilism is Karl Löwith's *Martin Heidegger and European Nihilism,* ed. Richard Wolin (New York: Columbia University Press, 1995).

7. Bourdieu, *Political Ontology of Martin Heidegger,* 26.

8. See Max Horkheimer and Theodore W. Adorno, *Dialectic of Enlightenment* (New York: Continuum, 1994). The original version of this classic critique of the Enlightenment project, *Dialectik der Aufklärung,* was published in 1944.

9. See Luc Ferry and Alain Renaut, *Heidegger and Modernity,* trans. Franklin Philip (Chicago: Chicago University Press, 1990).

10. In addition to Bourdieu's book see Hans Sluga, *Heidegger's Crisis: Philosophy and Politics in Nazi Germany* (Cambridge, MA: Harvard University Press, 1993).

While Sluga's equally sociological examination seeks to place Heidegger in the political predicaments of his time, Richard Wolin, in *The Politics of Being: The Political Thought of Martin Heidegger* (New York: Columbia University Press, 1990), traces the origin of Heidegger's attraction to Nazism right back to his *Being and Time* (1927). In all these cases, without exception, the alternately vindictive or apologetic tone of the account prevents the simple recognition that Heidegger's attraction to Nazism makes his critique of modernity more, not less, legitimate.

11. William V. Spanos, *Heidegger and Criticism: Retrieving the Cultural Politics of Destruction,* foreword by Donald E. Pease (Minneapolis: University of Minnesota Press, 1993), 3.

12. See Victor Farías, *Heidegger and Nazism,* trans. Paul Burrell and Gabriel Ricci (Philadelphia: Temple University Press, 1989). The original was published in France in 1987.

13. I have developed this idea in some detail in Hamid Dabashi, *Close Up: Iranian Cinema, Past, Present, Future* (London and New York: Verso, 2001).

14. Bourdieu, *Political Ontology of Martin Heidegger,* 26.

15. Ibid., 8.

16. Martin Heidegger, *The Question of Being,* translated with an introduction by William Kluback and Jean T. Wilde (London: Vision Press Limited, 1959), 45. For a full discussion of the similarity of Heidegger's conception of technology to that of Jünger, see Bourdieu, *Political Ontology of Martin Heidegger,* 29–40. Even more extensive is Richard Wolin's discussion of Heidegger's indebtedness to Jünger in *The Politics of Being,* 88–92 and 140–141.

17. See Bourdieu, *Political Ontology of Martin Heidegger,* 29–40.

18. Ibid., 32.

19. Jalal Al-e Ahmad, *Gharbzadegi/West-Strickenness* (Tehran: Ravaq Publishers, 1341/1962), 15–16. My translation.

20. For further discussion of Al-e Ahmad's role in the construction of the Islamic ideology, see my *Theology of Discontent: The Ideological Foundations of the Islamic Revolution in Iran* (New York: New York University Press, 1993), 39–101.

21. See Hans Sluga, *Heidegger's Crisis,* 29–52, for a discussion of this active appropriation of a diverse number of thinkers into a triumphant narrative of German nationalism.

22. Sluga, *Heidegger's Crisis,* 44.

23. Ali Shari'ati, *Tashayyu'-e 'Alavi va Tashayyu'-e Safavi/The Safavid Shi'ism and the Alavid Shi'ism* (Tehran: Hosseiniyyeh Ershad Publications, 1350/1971), 110. For a reliable history of Shi'ism in its social and historical context, see Said Amir Arjomand, *The Shadow of God and the Hidden Imam: Religion, Political Order, and Societal Change in Shi'ite Iran from the Beginning to 1890* (Chicago: University of Chicago Press, 2010). See also Hamid Dabashi, *Shi'ism: A Religion of Protest* (Cambridge, MA: Harvard University Press, 2011).

24. Shari'ati, *The Safavid Shi'ism and the Alavid Shi'ism*.

25. For this by now standard reading of Al-e Ahmad and Shari'ati, see Mehrzad Boroujerdi, *Iranian Intellectuals and the West: The Tormented Triumph of Nativism* (Syracuse, NY: Syracuse University Press, 1996); Ali Mirsepassi, *Intellectual Discourse and the Politics of Modernization: Negotiating Modernity in Iran* (Cambridge and New York: Cambridge University Press, 2000); Ali Mirsepassi, *Political Islam, Iran, and the Enlightenment: Philosophies of Hope and Despair* (Cambridge: Cambridge University Press, 2011); Farzin Vahdat, "Return to Which Self?: Jalal Al-e Ahmad and the Discourse of Modernity," *Journal of Iranian Research and Analysis* 16.2 (November 2000); and Farzin Vahdat, *God and Juggernaut: Iran's Intellectual Encounter with Modernity* (Syracuse, NY: Syracuse University Press, 2002).

26. In a recent doctoral dissertation, Ajay Singh Chaudhary, in "Religions of Doubt: Religion, Critique, and Modernity in Jahal Al-e Ahmad and Walter Benjamin" (PhD diss., Columbia University, 2013), 97, has radically challenged these ideas and proposed "an alternate intellectual genealogy that brings Al-e Ahmad's Marxist influence more clearly into view. Finally, I will examine how Al-e Ahmad departs from Marx, on both strategic and philosophical grounds, only to converge with the (also Marxian) approach of Walter Benjamin."

27. Sluga, *Heidegger's Crisis*, 45.

28. Ibid., 47.

29. Ibid.

30. See Joseph Massad, *Islam in Liberalism* (Chicago: University of Chicago Press, 2015).

CONCLUSION

1. See Kojin Karatani, *The Structure of World History: From Modes of Production to Modes of Exchange* (Durham, NC: Duke University Press, 2014), 41.

2. There is an excellent study of Iranophobia by Haggai Ram, *Iranophobia: The Logic of an Israeli Obsession* (Stanford, CA: Stanford University Press, 2006). Though limited to the Israeli scene, this study does point to the larger context of the phenomenon.

3. For more on FitzGerald's homosexuality, see H. Montgomery Hyde, *The Love That Dared Not Speak Its Name: A Candid History of Homosexuality in Britain* (New York: Little, Brown and Company, 1970), and James Blyth, *Edward FitzGerald and Posh* (London: J. Long, 1908).

4. I am grateful to Kajette Solomon of Bridgeman Art Library in New York for her kind assistance in procuring permission for the use of this work on the jacket of my book. The painting can be seen online at http://www.bbc.co.uk/arts/yourpaintings/paintings/the-fisherman-and-the-syren-188740.

5. For more on the sensuality of this work, see Lynda Nead, "Frederic Leighton's *The Fisherman and the Syren*," *Women: A Cultural Review* 13.1 (2002). Available at: http://www.tandfonline.com/doi/abs/10.1080/09574040210122986?journalCode =rwcr20#.U0E4tF4dIy4. Accessed on 6 April 2014. For more information about Leighton's travels and his interest in Islamic art, see this very useful website: http://www.rbkc.gov.uk/leightonarabhall/virtual_tour_home.html. Accessed on 7 April 2014.

6. Kuno Francke, *The German Classics of the Nineteenth and Twentieth Centuries,* vol. 1: *Masterpieces of German Literature,* translated into English (FQ Books, 2010). For the original German, see Johann Wolfgang von Goethe, *Goethe's Minor Poems,* selected, annotated, and rearranged by Albert Maximilian Selss (London: Truebner and Co. Ludgate Hill, 1875), 4.

Acknowledgments

Like my previous books published by Harvard University Press, this book too has been graciously shepherded with the kind and capable care of its executive editor-at-large, Sharmila Sen. Words fail me to express my gratitude to her for the generosity of her visionary intellect. These books are what they are and do what they aspire to do for the posterity of scholarship in their fields entirely enabled by and indebted to Sharmila Sen's empowering vision. The editorial assistance of Heather Hughes has as always been critical in seeing my books through production in a timely and professional manner. Two anonymous peer reviewers have graciously taken time from their own work to read my manuscript and have given me the benefit of their generous and gracious comments. Deborah Grahame-Smith, the production editor, has been punctual and impeccable in seeing my book through to publication.

A book of this historical magnitude and range would be impossible to research and write without benefiting from a magnificent body of scholarship produced on its related themes. All these great scholars are noted and acknowledged in the notes that accompany every chapter.

The chairman of my department, Timothy Mitchell, as well as my other distinguished colleagues provide me with a generous and hospitable environment at Columbia from the security and serenity of which I can write. This book is still very much in the shadow of my other great Columbia colleague, the late Edward Said. If at times I have seen things slightly differently than he did I am still entirely indebted to his visionary scholarship. In the course of writing this book I have had occasions to solicit the generous advice of and benefit from the scholarship of my friends and colleagues Sheldon Pollock and Touraj Daryaee.

My wife, Golbarg Bashi, and my children, Kaveh, Pardis, Chelgis, and Golchin, have warmed my heart and sustained my hopes in the course of writing this, as all my other works. My good friend Farhad Arshad has been a solid comrade through the thick and thin of much of my life. My doctoral students are a constant source of joy and confidence as I write and as I see them through their own scholarship. My research assistant, Hawa Ansary, has taught me new meanings to the words competence, diligence, and unwavering and caring assistance.

I dedicate this book to two dear old friends, Teresa and Mahmoud Omidsalar, as a token of my gratitude for their having graced my life for so many years.

Index

www.ingramcontent.com/pod-product-compliance
Lightning Source LLC
Chambersburg PA
CBHW021829090426
42811CB00032B/2091/J